For Those Who Have Faced the Fire Monster Close Up, It Is Alive— Something Malevolent—A Destroyer without Conscience. . . .

There were no more human sounds now. Just the dreadful cracking of bones, the roar of the fire winds, the popping of resin exploding in trees, the rumble of loosened boulders rolling downhill. Erickson couldn't make himself say what he thought. It was too terrible for words. He and Haugh merely stood looking at each other. Then they turned slowly and started walking. . . . They thought they were the only survivors. They thought it so intensely that when the charred figure appeared out of the brush it was almost a physical shock. The apparition moved like a zombie with awful blackened hands thrust out in front of him. . . . His pack had been burned off, leaving marks where nylon straps branded raw imprints across his shoulders. Erickson finally discovered his voice. He murmured disbelievingly, "Eric?" Hipke's eyes stared straight ahead, unblinking. . . .

THE BRAVE MEN AND WOMEN

Brent "Big" Johnson—Soft-spoken and introspective, he was in great physical shape. His body looked as though it had been carved out of Sawtooth granite. At six-foot plus, he was the classic Westerner with a chiseled jaw and unbridled confidence—always ready to prove he had what it takes to go head-to-head with a raging inferno. . . .

Kent Hamilton—He could think of nothing worse than being burned alive, and he had come close enough to worry. Burn scars crept out of his shirt collar and his right shirt sleeve. Kent was married to fellow firefighter April Hamilton. Their relationship was unique—most smokejumpers were either single or divorced. The job was often death for relationships. . . .

George Steele—At forty-six, he had over twenty years' experience flying into smoke, with 285 jumps. A terse and wiry jumper with a heavy mustache, Steele was one of the oldest smokejumpers around. In '85 he jumped a fire and broke his leg, his arm, and his jaw, and knocked out a bunch of teeth, but that didn't deter him. . . .

PRAISE FOR CHARLES W. SASSER'S
ONE SHOT—ONE KILL

"Shocking and brutal. . . . The reality of sniping is achieved superbly by personal accounts. . . . Each account is remarkable, detailing vivid memories of combat action."

—*Marine Corps Gazette*

Don Mackey—If this reckless, young Burt Reynolds look-alike had forseen the future the afternoon of July 5, when he stepped from CASA jump plane 117BH at Walker Field, he may have taken one look at the streamers of smoke rising from the mountains and climbed right back into the airplane. . . .

Sarah Doehring—One of the few women capable of enduring the rigorous physical training required to join one of the most elite bands in the world, her levelheaded finesse helped keep the men's macho pride in check— and everyone out of unnecessary danger. . . .

Andy Wilson—Twenty-six years old, clean-cut, and darkly handsome, the young pilot preferred bombing fires from the air, even though he believed it was an honor to let Mother Nature take your life. . . .

PRAISE FOR CHARLES W. SASSER'S
HOMICIDE!

"Authentic . . . gives us a personal look at the triumphs and frustrations of those we pay to face those horrors every working day."

—Publishers Weekly

"Brings to life the ugly realities, black humor, and battle-scarred idealism of a veteran cop's world."

—Action Digest

Books by Charles W. Sasser

Smokejumpers
Last American Heroes
   (with Michael W. Sasser)
Shoot to Kill
Always a Warrior
Homicide!
The 100th Kill
One Shot—One Kill
   (with Craig Roberts)
The Walking Dead
   (with Craig Roberts)

Published by POCKET BOOKS

Smoke
AMERICA'S ELITE AIRBORNE FIREFIGHTERS
Jumpers

CHARLES W. SASSER

POCKET BOOKS
New York   London   Toronto   Sydney   Tokyo   Singapore

An *Original* Publication of POCKET BOOKS

POCKET BOOKS, a division of Simon & Schuster Inc.
1230 Avenue of the Americas, New York, NY 10020

ISBN: 0-671-52713-4

First Pocket Books printing April 1996

10 9 8 7 6 5 4 3 2 1

POCKET and colophon are registered trademarks of Simon & Schuster Inc.

Front cover photo courtesy of National Interagency Fire Center

Printed in the U.S.A.

This book is dedicated to the valiant firefighters who fought on Storm King Mountain—and to those who lost their lives there

Acknowledgments

The author wishes to thank the many people who made this book possible. Their help in the monumental tasks of researching and writing made a difficult project less grueling.

While the people to whom I owe gratitude are too numerous to list completely, I should like to give special thanks to:

Kathy Voth, Bureau of Land Management, who steered me onto my course;

Dave Curry, Roger Stilipec, Paul Hefner and Shawn Lawler of the Western Slope Fire Coordination Center, who willingly gave of their time to news media to explain wildfire fighting organization and concepts;

Reporters David Frey, Casey A. Cass and Nan Johnson of the *Glenwood Post,* whose "insider" coverage of the Storm King fire provided valuable insight;

Firefighters Kent and April Hamilton, Western Slope air coordinators, who opened the door to understanding the dangerous world of wildland firefighters;

Tanker pilots Andy Wilson, Earl Dahl and Gary Towle, who shared their world with me;

Smokejumpers George Steele, John "J.C." Curd, Brent Johnson, Tim Pettitt, Rod Dow, Tim Eldridge, Ken Franz and Steve Nemore, who helped mold my perspective;

ACKNOWLEDGMENTS

And, of course, special thanks to the survivors of the Storm King fire and to numerous other smokejumpers, hotshots, tanker pilots, helicopter pilots, helitacks and firefighters, who took an active role in one form or another in the creation of this book.

This book belongs not to the author as much as to the brave men and women who combat wildfires in the American West.

Preface

The information in this book is based on a variety of
sources—taped personal interviews, observations, witness
statements, official reports and other published accounts.
Actual names are used throughout except in those rare
instances in which correspondents could not recall names
or in which public identification would serve no useful
purpose and might cause embarrassment. While the forest
fire at Glenwood Springs was called a variety of names in
the press, it will for clarity be referred to as the Storm King
Mountain fire in this book.

In various instances, dialogue and scenes have by necessi-
ty been re-created. Where this occurs, I strived to match
personalities with the situation and the action while main-
taining factual content. The recounting of some events may
not correspond precisely with the memories of all involved.
I must be forgiven for any such errors. Hundreds of people
were involved; time has a tendency to erode memory in
some areas and selectively enhance it in others.

In addition, the material has been filtered through the
author, who must apologize to anyone omitted, neglected or
somehow slighted in the preparation of this book. While I
am certain to have made some interpretational mistakes,

PREFACE

I am just as certain that the content of this book is accurate to the spirit, and reality of the U.S. Forest Service, U.S. Bureau of Land Management and other state and local agencies charged with the hazardous job of fighting wildfire. My objective was to present a true account of the selfless and heroic service of smokejumpers, hotshots, tanker pilots, helitacks and others who combat forest fire in the American West. To that end, I am confident not to have neglected anyone.

Introduction

EACH YEAR WHEN THE SNOWS MELT AND DRY winds from the south blow away the spring rains, young gladiators from across the nation receive the call to combat man's ancient enemy—wildfire. Wildfire rampages through the mountains and deserts and forests of the American West from about April to October, when the rains return. Wildland firefighters, gladiators in yellow Nomex fire gear and helmets, form a brave thin line to protect lives and property from nature run amuck.

Statistically, fire fighting is the most hazardous occupation in the United States. The danger is multiplied for forest firefighters. Many are injured each fire season. A number die. Western fire fighting lore blazes with tales of blowups and conflagrations. Firefighters can list almost in order the fatal fires in the American West, including their dates and the names of the victims. Tales of killer fires pass along from generation to generation of firefighters who study and discuss them at length. What went wrong? How could *I* have cheated Fate were *I* caught in the same situation?

The record for the largest number of lives taken by a single fire occurred in August 1910. Wildfire swept across western Montana and the Idaho panhandle, burning three million acres and killing seventy-eight firefighters.

Wildfire blowup killed twenty-five firefighters in Griffith Park, California, in 1935.

In August 1937, seventeen firefighters died battling the Blackwater Creek fire near Yellowstone National Park in Wyoming.

1

Fire at Hauser Creek, California, claimed eleven fire-fighter lives in 1943.

On August 5, 1949, fifteen smokejumpers parachuted onto a blaze in the Montana wilderness. All but three of them died in the Mann Gulch fire. A forest ranger also perished in the blaze.

Sudden wind changes reversed a fire's direction in the Mendocino National Forest in northern California in 1953, trapping and burning to death fifteen smoke eaters.

In 1966 a blaze in the Angeles National Forest near Los Angeles overran and annihilated thirteen firefighters.

In July 1976 sudden high winds caused a blowup at a wildfire near Parachute, Colorado. Flames one hundred feet tall fanned up the side of a ridge to trap and kill three ground firefighters. A tanker pilot crashed his plane and also died while dropping a load of retardant on the fire.

A blowup jumped a fireline in central Arizona in June 1990 and took the lives of six fighters.

As recently as August 20, 1993, two firefighters perished fighting a fast-moving one hundred-acre brushfire near the Los Angeles suburb of Altodena.

In 1957 a task force studying ways to prevent wildland fire fatalities learned that most fire deaths could be attributed to firefighters ignoring or otherwise violating ten basic common sense rules. The task force devised a "Ten Commandments" for firefighters. The "10 Standard Fire Orders," as the commandments were called, along with "18 Watch Out Situations," became the firefighter's bible. Firefighters studied them as diligently as any catechism student pored over scripture.

10 Standard Fire Orders

1. Fight fire aggressively but provide for safety first.
2. Initiate all action in response to current and expected fire behavior.
3. Recognize current weather conditions and obtain forecast.
4. Ensure that instructions are given and understood.
5. Obtain current information on fire status.

6. Remain in communication with crew members, your supervisor and adjoining forces.
7. Determine safety zones and escape routes.
8. Establish lookouts in potentially hazardous situations.
9. Retain control at all times.
10. Stay alert, keep calm, think clearly, act decisively.

18 Watch Out Situations

1. Fire not scouted and sized up
2. Country not seen during the daylight
3. Safety zones and escape routes not identified
4. Unfamiliar with local weather and local factors influencing fire behavior
5. Uninformed on strategy, tactics and hazards
6. Instructions and assignments not clear
7. No communications link with crew members and supervisors
8. Constructing fireline without a safe anchor point
9. Building fireline downhill with fire below
10. Attempting frontal assault on fire
11. Unburned fuel between you and the fire
12. Cannot see main fire and are not in contact with anyone who can
13. You are on a hillside where rolling material can ignite fuel below
14. Weather is getting hotter and dryer
15. Wind increases or changes direction
16. Spot fires frequently cross line
17. Terrain and fuels make escape to safety zones difficult
18. Taking a nap near the fireline

As Moses warned his people of the consequences of violating God's Ten Commandments, the people who fought wildfire were likewise warned of the consequences of violating their commandments and failing to recognize a Watch Out Situation. Violating Standard Fire Orders, as every fighter had drilled into him, might quickly turn a situation into a tragedy.

The year 1994 was the U.S. Forest Service's most disastrous fire year since 1910. More than seven thousand firefighters manned firelines in ten western states. The Colorado Rockies were the most hard hit. Lightning started thirty-eight new blazes over the Fourth of July holiday weekend in western Colorado. Fires burned unchecked over thousands of acres on Colorado's western slopes. Governor Roy Romer called for four hundred extra firefighters.

Smokejumpers, ground-pounding infantry "hotshots," fire engines and air tanker bombers massed like combat invasion troops in the Grand Junction district of the Bureau of Land Management. Troops attacked the enemy from both the land and the air as fire threatened to engulf whole forests and cities.

Smokejumpers, the elite Special Forces of the fire service, led the assaults since many forest fires begin high on remote lightning-struck ridges or deep in virgin forest where conventional fire forces cannot easily reach. Again and again, smokejumpers spearheaded desperate sorties and raids against an enemy intent on turning the Rockies and all that lived there to ashes. They arrived on wings, parachuting out of the sky to land in tiny glades or clearings near the blaze. Self-sustaining, the jumpers brought with them all the supplies and equipment they needed in combat. They liked to boast they could drop out of the sky, land in treetops and gulleys or on ridgetops or the sides of cliffs and stop any fire before 10 A.M. the next morning.

On July 2, 1994, lightning struck a tree snag high on a ridge leading off a mountain called Storm King near Glenwood Springs, Colorado. All an ordinary-looking blaze needed to become a killer was the right temperature, wind, humidity and fuel. The fire on Storm King Mountain proved to be the smokejumpers' ultimate challenge, testing to the limits their training, skills, courage and will. In the burning hell that became Storm King Mountain, fate made its selections from among the wildland firefighters. Some never returned from the fire on the mountain. For those who returned, their lives were changed forever.

1

WISPS OF SMOKE CLAWED AT THE BRIGHT WINGS of the twin-engined Otter. George Steele hunkered, tense and waiting, among seven other smokejumpers jammed into the airplane's tubular belly. Air furnacing up from the inferno fifteen hundred feet below on Sunshine Mesa rattled the jumpers in the aircraft like pebbles in a tin can. Their colorful helmets and wire face masks banged together. Hard pads in their drab earthen-brown jumpsuits clacked.

"Okay, gang," the spotter shouted from up front with the pilot. He scanned the rugged terrain below searching for an opening clear of the fire into which to drop his "stick" of eight parachutists. "I think I've found a jump spot. George?"

Steele quickly adjusted the reserve parachute on his chest. He checked the D rings where his red PG (personal gear) bag rode below the reserve. He drew in a deep breath and duck-waddled to the open door to take a look. Slipstream howled past. The airplane banked, circling the mesa. Steele snapped his static line to the cable and gripped either side of the door, riding out the windstorm generated by the forest fire.

Blue sky above trailed tendrils of gray smoke. Below lay steep long spines of mesas and hogbacks covered with curly green forest, mostly PJ (pinyon juniper). They formed the northern rim of Colorado's fertile North Fork Valley. The valley cradled the tiny town of Paonia between the high Rockies on the east and the North Fork of the Gunnison

5

River that flowed west on the northern outskirts of town and flanked Colorado Highway 133. Green and narrow near the mountains, the valley widened and browned out in the west as it opened onto the desert.

On the valley's northern rim, among mesas called Sunshine, Stucker, Wakefield and Fry, red-and-orange flames flickered angrily out of the green around the edges of a growing protoplasmic cancer of black char. Smoke belched skyward. Highway 133 and the North Fork River fortressed Paonia against the fire, but the mesas and ridges and mountainsides and arroyos along the valley wall were studded with expensive ranch-style homes, Spanish-like adobes and yellow-and-red pine contemporaries.

People dashed frantically about in their yards. Some stood on their roofs to watch the approaching flames. Others broke out hoses and started watering down their buildings. A handful of firefighters from Paonia and several other nearby towns already labored to build firelines around houses. A man standing on top of his barn waved joyously at the flying Otter.

The fire monster was bent on driving out the intruders and claiming the wilderness.

One hell of a blaze. Dubbed the Wake fire from the prominence of Wakefield Mesa, the fire started on a Sunday morning, the day before Independence Day 1994. Dry lightning storms rattled over the western steppes of the Colorado Rockies, reaching down with spiteful electric fingers to touch flame to dry lodgepole pine or dead clumps of pinyon clinging to high windy pinnacles. Colorado was experiencing its worst drought in two decades. Storms that produced lightning without moisture had crashed and banged in the mountains for the last two weeks. They sounded like God bowling. Lightning had already ignited nearly forty fires in the Colorado Rockies during the first four days of July.

In response to the many fires, the Bureau of Land Management (BLM) and the U.S. Forest Service had mobilized for war. In Grand Junction, the Walker Field airport headquarters of BLM's Western Slope Fire Coordination Center resembled Ike Eisenhower's command post preparing for the Normandy invasion. The scene included: tanker bombers loaded with retardant; ground-pounding hotshots, the infantry of fire fighters, massing for attack; helitacks buzzing around in helicopters; command airships coordinating retreats, raids, assaults and counterattacks; smokejumpers donning wire-masked helmets and heavy fire-retardant suits and parachutes in Pavlov-like response to the ringing of fire alarms.

On Sunday, the infant Wake fire smoldered in the trunk and branches of a drought-stricken spruce. It smoldered all day and all night. Then on Monday, July 4, it turned into a gobbler racing through the PJ and cheatgrass, whipped by an afternoon's westerly wind. Squirrels and magpies fled ahead of the flames. Unless stopped, fire would soon race into the boughs that tapped against the windowpanes of refugees from Los Angeles and other big cities who, seeking solitude, liked to sit in their foyers and watch squirrels play in pine boughs.

From the air, the fire resembled a giant black devil's footprint inscribed in about thirty acres of flames. Steele saw one large house directly in the devil's path.

Smokejumpers were the shock troops of the U.S. Forest Service and the BLM. Only four hundred strong nationally, they composed the elite Special Forces of forest firefighters. They were the first line of offense and defense against the fire monster. When lives and property were endangered, fire management officers turned to the smokejumpers—the immediate reaction force trained to parachute into the fires of hell to wage battle. Smokejumpers held the line until the infantry arrived.

George Steele sighted along the skin of the aircraft. Slipstream tugged at his jowls.

"See the jump spot?" the spotter yelled from the cockpit. "It's as big as a football field."

He grinned.

Steele found it. A patch of cheatgrass in the forest upwind

of the fire. The pilot flew over it for a closer look. Steele had never seen a football field that small. It was more the size of two average bedrooms combined. Sharp-pointed spruce surrounded it. They caught drifts of smoke like a comb drawn through wool. A boulder loomed menacingly at the clearing's western edge.

"It'll do," Steele said.

"What?"

"Go for it," Steele said.

On the next pass, he dropped a purple wind streamer to check the winds. Then he sat in the door with his boots outside in the slipstream. The flaming earth below moved slowly between them. The Otter climbed to normal jump altitude at three thousand feet. The "wind dummy" always went first to make sure of the winds and the jump spot. The others followed two at a time from each pass until the entire stick of eight was on the ground. Then the spotter dumped the cargo chutes with the team's fire fighting equipment.

Smokejumpers, military paratroopers and sky divers all shared a touch of the Icarus complex, wanting to appear on the earth from the sky. But, still, no matter how many jumps he made, a parachutist never quite felt comfortable in that time just before hurling himself out the open door of the airplane. At forty-six years old, after over twenty years flying into smoke and 285 fire jumps, Steele felt the dryness in his throat. There was something *unnatural* about leaping into space from a perfectly good aircraft. Out that door into the terrible wind of the slipstream, consigning one's fate to a square of colored cloth not much larger than a queen-size bedspread. At least the U.S. Government no longer contracted the lowest bidder to manufacture parachutes, as it had in the early days of smoke jumping.

For the smokejumper, every jump was a combat jump. Fire fighting was hazardous in itself. Parachuting onto a fire compounded the danger. Flying out of the sky to land in rocky, wooded, rough terrain took its toll. Most jumpers bore the scars of their trade. As "jumper-in-charge" and therefore first out, Steele sighted along the aircraft's skin, judging its speed and drift as the ship converged on the jump spot below in the trees. Unsteady air threatened to jolt him out of the plane before he was ready.

"Ready!" cried the spotter, who had worked his way back to jump master the passes.

Steele's white helmet bobbed up and down. He tensed.

Sometimes he thought he was too old for this shit. Most jumpers tended to be young and reckless. Too young to feel their own mortality. Steele knew only a few jumpers as old or older than he. Jack Seagraves was 51, Rod Dow was pushing 50 while Tim Pettitt was a mere 43 and James Thrash 44. Maybe there were a few other troglodytes, but Steele couldn't name them offhand. This business, if you did it very long, had a way of pressing upon you an awareness of your mortality the middle-aged seldom liked to face.

"Why do you keep doing this?" some of the younger jumpers asked him occasionally.

He thought about it each time, ruminating over it like it was something he had chewed over before without finding an answer.

"I like it," he would answer and shrug.

Terse answers were typical coming from the wiry jumper with the heavy mustache, unless he had had a beer or two to loosen him up some. Most people described Steele in one word—*laconic*. For him, three or four words were a sentence; three sentences strung together became a speech. When he laughed—only occasionally—it was like the short bark of a squirrel. His teeth would be pressed together as though it hurt him to pull them apart to let the laughter out.

Maybe it did hurt him. In 1985 he jumped a fire near Elko, Nevada, and broke his leg, his arm, his jaw and knocked out a bunch of his teeth. His jaw had been wired together for almost six months; he took his meals through a straw. He still flinched at the sight of a straw.

The spotter slapped Steele hard on the shoulder to make sure he had the jumper's attention. Steele felt his heart pounding. He had leaped into the flames for over two decades, but no matter, a part of him was always afraid each time.

"Go!"

Steele sprang from his airborne perch. His static line attached to the aircraft ripped out the drogue chute. The drogue was round and about three feet in diameter. Its only function was to stabilize the jumper in air to keep him from tumbling or going into back lock before he pulled his main parachute.

Five seconds later, flying toward the smoking forest below, Steele pulled his main. The positive jerk of the main canopy opening snapped his feet up and forward.

Then he was floating. Flying. His heart beat normal again. The tiny clearing below grew larger. Smoke rose in a fierce thick column on his left flank. Above, a Navy-surplus P2V Neptune patrol plane, now a tanker fire bomber, sailed over the mesa scouting a target upon which to release its load. Even as Steele toggled into position on an upwind track for landing, crews of ground-pounding hotshots were being trucked to the fire.

Troops were massing. Like military forces in combat. The fire monster, that demon of hellfire and brimstone, had launched an offensive against the high ground overlooking Paonia.

But perhaps it wasn't the *main* offensive. Perhaps the Wake fire was only a probe, a diversion such as Allied forces used to distract Hitler before D day at Normandy. Because while troops massed at Paonia, a fire was gaining a toehold northeast of Paonia near a mountain called Storm King rising seven thousand feet above I-70 between Denver and Grand Junction. The fire had started in a single tree on Saturday. A thin flame, high above Canyon Creek Estates on the west and West Glenwood Springs on the east, glowed little brighter than a match struck in a dark stadium.

It would grow.

2

THE RIDGE UPON WHICH THE SINGLE TREE smoldered on Saturday and Saturday night swept off the southwestern ramparts of Storm King Mountain. It hogbacked southerly for less than a mile, gradually losing altitude, until it fell abruptly toward I-70 and the Colorado River that paralleled the interstate through the valley. Motorists speeding east and west between the mountains that closed in from either side like a tunnel paid little attention to the smoking tree. Few even noticed it.

It burned in a year that was fast becoming one of the nation's deadliest years for forest fires, a year in which Smokey the Bear, the U.S. Forest Service's most famous wildfire symbol, was celebrating his fiftieth birthday.

It had been a dry winter in the West—and now an even drier spring and summer. From Colorado to California, from Washington to New Mexico, across the entire moisture-starved western states, millions of acres of dried-out timber and deadwood needed only a spark to set it roaring. No significant rain had fallen on western Colorado since April 9. Kiln-treated lumber at a lumberyard generally retained about 12 percent moisture content by weight; some forests in the Rocky Mountains contained only about 10 or 11 percent moisture.

For two days over the weekend approaching Monday's Fourth of July holiday, the Lightning Detection System (LDS) operated by the BLM triangulated some nine thousand dry-weather lightning strikes along the western slopes of the Rockies. The lightning lit up patches of gambel oak and PJ in the forests that furred steep mountain slopes, high hidden valleys and remote drainages where clusters of new homes had mushroomed in recent years. Solitude-seekers fleeing the cities never seemed to learn from the blackened

11

devil's footprints stamped all over the mountains. They came and claimed their pieces of the wilderness and resented others who came after them. They also resented the fires—but the fire came anyhow with the same relentless pressure as more solitude-seekers.

Of the thirty-eight new lightning-induced blazes erupting in western Colorado on Saturday and Sunday, firefighters battled only the largest and most threatening. The Buninger and Long Canyon fires northwest of Grand Junction had together burned more than 2,200 acres. The fire at Bitter Creek torched 3,820 acres. By Monday, new fires like the Wake fire at Paonia would claim even more resources.

Commanders at the Western Slope Fire Coordination Center (WSFCC) in Grand Junction grew exasperated trying to explain why crews hadn't been dispatched to at least thirteen fires left unchecked. They were all fires that, so far, had consumed less than five acres each and appeared to pose no immediate menace to residences.

"There is a shortage of resources right now," explained Mike Brown, a Western Slope resources coordinator. "I'm talking about helicopters, fire engines, air tankers, hotshots and smokejumpers. We just have more fires than we have resources."

The burning tree on Storm King Mountain was a tiny spark of light against the mountain stars on Saturday night. On Sunday morning, reporter Nan Johnson of the Glenwood *Post* noticed the fire. She slowed her car as she crossed the overpass above I-70 that linked the two sections of Glenwood Springs. A thin wafting of smoke, almost like a heat devil, climbed into the mountain air.

The fire was almost seven miles away and on top of a mountain. The reporter assumed someone was taking care of it. It was, after all, not much larger than a campfire.

Glenwood Springs was the burial place of Doc Holliday and the home of curative hot springs where Buffalo Bill Cody had once bathed. A resort town in the summer whose hot spring spas attracted thousands of tourists, its population dropped to a steady six thousand or so in the off-season winter months. The town had grown up on both sides of

I-70 and the Colorado River. The river valley opened up to the south of the interstate where Glenwood sprawled out leisurely along Route 82 toward Carbondale. To the north, the rest of the town looked cramped, stuffed between the steep rise of the mountains of the White River National Forest and the band formed by I-70 and the river. Squeezed in its growth here between mountains and river, the town sprouted motels and strip malls in a thin line along the north edge of I-70 and a service road that connected Glenwood Springs proper to West Glenwood Springs kneeling at the eastern foot of Storm King Mountain.

The service road continued west alongside I-70 to connect West Glenwood to the Canyon Creek Estates around to the western foot of Storm King. Canyon Creek Estates was a development of two-hundred-thousand-dollar houses scattered on large forested plots. Smaller communities, campgrounds and mobile home parks had sprouted up along Mitchell Creek, South Canyon and other drainages and valleys between the mountains.

Forest grew off Storm King and its ridges down into both West Glenwood and the Canyon Creek Estates. Forest fire was therefore a constant threat. While motorists buzzing past on I-70 might not have noticed the burning tree, residents living at the foot of Storm King spotted it immediately and cast up wary eyes. Garfield County Sheriff Levy Burris received calls about the fire as early as Saturday afternoon.

"We could beat it out with a shovel—if we could get up there," one caller explained.

Sheriff Burris dutifully reported the blaze to the BLM's Grand Junction District Dispatch Center. He was told the fire was being monitored, along with several dozen other lightning-strike fires.

Anxious residents continued to call in. At 11:00 A.M. on Sunday, Burris personally scouted out the fire. It burned high on a nearly inaccessible ridge, one of the fingers off Storm King. The sheriff pulled his car off to the side of I-70, got out and glassed the flame with binoculars.

"From down here," he radioed Grand Junction Dispatch,

"it looks like two trees torching. There are a lot of houses scattered up South Canyon and Mitchell Creek."

"We're fully committed," Dispatch responded, "but we'll try to get you an air attack if you feel it's needed."

Burris squinted into his binoculars against the high sun. At first, he judged the fire to be on state or private property along the edge of BLM land. If it *were* on private land, that meant he would have to take personal responsibility for approving air support.

"I'll keep an eye on the fire," he said, "and keep you advised."

"Roger that. We're stretched thin—but we'll do what we can."

Three hours later Sheriff Burris again stood on the shoulder of I-70. He gazed up the east drainage toward the high ridge upon which the fire burned. PJ, stands of gambel oak brush, rock scree and boulders choked the steep drainage. A narrow round chimney of white smoke climbed lazily off the spine of the ridge, smudging the looming presence of Storm King beyond.

The fire was growing.

"It's about a half acre now and it looks pretty active," the sheriff radioed Grand Junction Dispatch. "If you can get us some aircraft, I'll approve it."

Dispatch telephoned Paul Hefner, manager of the Western Slope Fire Coordination Center at Walker Field. WSFCC coordinated all resources for the district. Dispatch asked for one load of smokejumpers, an air tanker and a lead command plane.

"I don't know where the hell we'll get them from," Hefner said.

Wildfire raged throughout the western states. Additional firefighters had been summoned from as far east as Arkansas and Louisiana. Hefner had requested jumpers and hotshots be diverted from other regions of the West to help with Colorado's overload. Colorado simply had more fires burning than it had fighters to combat them.

District Fire Control Officer Winslow Robertson was inspecting blazes near Rifle, about twenty-five miles from

Storm King Mountain. He volunteered to drive over for a look at the Storm King fire.

In the meantime, Clay Fowler, BLM Engine-611 foreman in Glenwood Springs, joined Sheriff Burris on I-70. The two men studied the fire.

"I can see the canopies of two trees burning, that's about all," Fowler advised Dispatch. "It's inaccessible by road. Looks like a low rate of spread. I recommend we observe it for a while."

Walker Field sent its twin-engine Air Commander to take a look. The air support command-and-control officer—generally called Air Attack—studied the blaze as the Commander circled it. Then the aircraft set a course back to Grand Junction.

"Lead-64?" the air support officer radioed.

"Lead-64, go ahead."

"The fire involves about an acre to an acre-and-a-half. It's burning on a steep ridgetop, spreading slowly downhill. There are no structures in danger at this time."

When Winslow Robertson arrived, he concurred with both Clay Fowler and the air command officer. The Storm King fire merited no direct action at this time; it was still low priority.

The decision fell heavily upon residents at the foot of the mountain. After all, soldiers in combat say the only war that concerns them is the war within the vicinity of their own foxholes. Same thing with wildfire; the fire that threatens *you* is the most important fire.

"I think it ought to be put out immediately," groused Don Shrull, who owned a hunting camp in the area. "Two men could have put it out at the start, or a half-dozen men. They say they're shorthanded, but they had two men to come out and watch it."

Generals at Grand Junction Dispatch and WSFCC had to ignore the complaints and concentrate upon the *Big Picture*. After all, they reasoned, they couldn't be bothered with an enemy patrol or probe when they needed all available troops to repel major assaults elsewhere. The Wake fire at Paonia had jumped to a higher priority than the small one at Storm King. Paonia demanded protection. Its fire was becoming a gobbler. The fire monster had escaped.

"It's coming toward us!" shrieked residents on Sunshine Mesa. *"It's coming fast!"*

The resolution to monitor the Storm King blaze seemed both logical and practical. After all, the fire was a slow one inching downhill.

But nature could be both whimsical and deadly. The behavior of wildfire depended upon a thousand variables, few of which man's limited understanding of nature could predict.

3

WHAT DETERMINES WHETHER A WILDFIRE WILL creep along the forest floor or explode into the treetops? Why does fire spare one canyon, only to fill the next with a firestorm of flames thirty stories tall? Imagine striking a match to a crumpled sheet of paper and predicting which fold or ridge will burn next. Now enlarge and transfer that miniature landscape to the forested side of a mountain or a vast hidden valley. Mix in changing winds, humidity, temperatures and abundant fuels.

The fire monster becomes a living thing. Unpredictable and lurking. He crawls. He walks. He lies down at night, only to awaken by day to rampage through the woods.

Disaster fires, like most forest fires, start as very ordinary-looking ground fires. Contrary to Smokey the Bear's exhortation that "Only *you* can prevent forest fires," lightning starts the majority of wildland blazes. Lightning that ignited Storm King on Saturday and the Wake fire at Paonia on Sunday struck where lightning usually gets its first chance to strike—high up on a ridge but lower to one side in the first snag of dead trees.

For a fire to burn, it requires oxygen, high temperature

and fuel—the so-called fire triangle. Fire may smolder in dead trees for hours, even days, while it showers the ground below with live ashes. Lightning fire becomes a ground fire once ashes flare and begin gnawing at the scattering of dead leaves, needles and clumps of grass below the trees.

Fire basically moves in an oval, pushed from behind by the wind. It always moves faster *uphill* than downhill. It may move slowly at first underneath the trees as it consumes available ground fuels. While it moves, it slowly heats the air around it to the point of ignition. It dries out higher fuels in the tree branches.

Should the wind suddenly change or pick up and infuse the fire with a fresh load of oxygen, the fire triangle leaps into the lower branches of the trees. The blaze "crowns." It takes to the treetops in a "blowup" that sounds like a 747 taking off. It begins to make its own weather.

As the hot, lighter air from the flames rises, cold, heavier air rushes in to replace it. The fresh air is then heated and belched out, only to again be replaced in a circular "convection effect" that can produce tremendous winds. Soon a great "firestorm" fills the sky with burning branches, leaves and pinecones. They shower ahead of the main fire, causing "spot" fires that may trap life between them and the main fire attacking from behind. Above the howling of the fire winds, the flames sound as though they are cracking bones.

"What would you do to control a crown fire?" was the big question on an exam early in the history of the U.S. Forest Service. One young ranger answered it by saying, "Get out of the way and pray like hell for rain."

As the Wake fire exploded on the mesas above Paonia on July 4, black unburned smoke defined itself into columns and took off like an old steam engine coming out of a tunnel as it chased fuel down arroyos and canyons. Unburned smoke boiled high until it reached oxygen, then exploded into bright flames among the smoke clouds. The flames popped like lightning.

A tornado of flame sucked up an entire tree. Fire-generated winds turned a fire tornado onto its side where it performed barrel rolls across the treetops. Fire bands leaped from tree to tree, in an aerial highway display of brilliant orange.

An early pioneer in the science of fire behavior, Harry T. Gisborne, witnessed the blowup of the ninety-thousand-acre Half Moon fire in Montana in 1929. The fire blackened two square miles in less than two minutes. Flames traveled so fast that Gisborne claimed to have later found the body of a grouse killed "still alertly erect in fear and wonder."

Nearby, he said, lay the body of a squirrel stretched out full-length.

"The burned-off sticks of his little hands," he said, "were reaching out as far ahead as possible, the back legs were extended to the full in one final, hopeless push, trying, like any human, to crawl just one painful inch farther to escape this unnecessary death."

Disaster fires such as the 1949 Mann Gulf fire that claimed thirteen lives or the 1910 Idaho blaze that took seventy-two are caused by a combination of adverse conditions—dry weather and winds, a lot of fuels, lack of manpower and suppression equipment. All these conditions were present on the western slopes of the Colorado Rocky Mountains during that first week of July 1994.

Fighting such fires is combat on a major scale. Comparing fire forces to military combat forces is inescapable, the organization is so similar.

The National Interagency Fire Center—the Pentagon as it were—coordinates wildfire fighting throughout the nation from Boise, Idaho. Down the chain of command fall the various regional coordination centers such as the Great Basin Coordination Center in Salt Lake City and the Rocky Mountain Coordination Center in Denver. They are like army regions of influence.

On the western slopes of the Colorado Rockies, like a theater of war, operational control under Denver is assumed by the Grand Junction District of the Bureau of Land Management. District has its own fire forces, like a company or a battalion. If these forces prove inadequate to handle fires in the district, District may request reinforcements through the coordination center in Denver, which may in turn appeal to the Fire Center in Boise.

Once a fire grows to "project size," beyond District's ability to handle alone, it becomes an "expanded dispatch." District fire fighting agencies combine with local, BLM and Forest Service firefighters, some of whom may be drawn in from other states and regions, in a kind of task force. "Overhead," as the brass is called, becomes an Interagency Fire Management Team commanded by a "fire management officer."

The senior fire management officer—the "general"—establishes a base command center near the action, normally in a National Guard armory, fire station, school or other available public building. The fire management officer has his colonels and captains—"operations officers" and "fire incident commanders"—who actually lead troops in combat.

A Coordination Center, such as the Western Slope Fire Coordination Center at Grand Junction's Walker Field airport, is the hub for the acquisition and deployment of fire fighting resources within the district. It establishes priorities for resources, receives and disseminates fire intelligence, calls for and prepositions smokejumpers and hotshots, and manages helicopters, helitack crews and air tanker bases.

The similarity to military organization continues down the chain of command to the troops in the field. Like many elite special operations forces in the military, smokejumpers are less rigid in their structure than hotshots or conventional district firefighters. The smokejumpers' basic operational unit is a "stick," a contingent of eight jumpers. It is commanded by a "jumper-in-charge," who, since smokejumpers are most often the first firefighters committed to battle, is the fire incident commander unless the blaze grows beyond his operational control.

The basic hotshot team is a twenty-person "platoon." It is commanded by a superintendent and a foreman. The platoon is further broken down into two squads, each led by a squad boss. It may be further partitioned into specialty "fire teams." For example, the "lead sawyer" takes charge of the chain saw team.

While smokejumpers are shock troops, immediate reaction forces dispatched first to try to stop a blaze before it gets out of control, hotshots—the "ground pounders," the fire fighting infantry—provide most of the labor for extended combat. Like the majority of forest firefighters, hotshots and smokejumpers work seasonally during a fire year which runs roughly from April to October. Many are college students on summer jobs while others are young professionals in other businesses attracted by a summer's adventure. Stationed at various locations throughout the West, they are always "tooled up" and ready to fly or bus to wherever they may be needed.

During the 1994 summer of blazes, Oregon, Idaho, Montana, Minnesota, Oklahoma, New Mexico and other states had committed troops to fires raging in the West. About seven thousand firefighters, 175 fire engines, 38 helicopters and 32 air tankers manned firelines in Colorado and nine other western states. As lightning-induced flames blackened the Rockies, Colorado Governor Roy Romer urgently requested four hundred firefighter reinforcements from other states. The year was rapidly becoming the Forest Service's most disastrous fire year since 1910.

Fighting fire is a mixture of science, common sense and luck, not always mixed in even proportions. All suppression methods are designed to break the fire triangle of oxygen, fuel and temperature at its most vulnerable point. Firelines built around a blaze deprive it of fuel. Water, wetting agents, fire-retarding chemicals and even dirt are used to cool the fire monster below ignition temperature or smother him by denying him oxygen.

Ground fires can be murderous, but mostly they are just hard work. Caught early enough they can be stomped out or beat down with axes, saws and shovels. Two or three hours may make the difference between containment and a firestorm that sweeps wild to destroy thousands of acres of timberland along with houses, livestock and even humans.

The job of attacking a fire begins with establishing an "anchor point" from which to begin digging and scraping a fireline to deprive the fire of fuel. A fireline is a shallow trench dug down to mineral soil. The width depends upon the size of the fire. It can be anywhere from a few inches wide to the width of a bulldozer. Nothing flammable such as tree branches or fallen trees can be left across it to provide a pathway for the fire to escape. The anchor point should be located in relatively fuel-free terrain near an escape route firefighters can use in case the fire monster counterattacks successfully.

An attack can either go direct or indirect. In an indirect attack, firefighters squeeze in on the head of the fire by flanking the fire on either side with firelines. The objective is to force the head into an open meadow or rocky outcropping where it can be direct-attacked and extinguished. Using Pulaskis (a double-bitted ax with one of the bits made into a hoe), shovels, chain saws, McLeod's (a shovel bent at the neck), hoes and other tools, firefighters find more labor than glamour in routine fire fighting.

Direct attack on a fire is more dangerous. Firefighters go straight for the monster's head, for the jugular. Against a large fire, direct attacks are desperate measures to protect life or property in the fire's path and are often made in coordination with helicopters and air tankers. Direct attack on a crown fire in which flames have used ladder fuels to climb into tree branches is especially hazardous. Sawyers work desperately to cut firebreaks and deprive the charging fire of fuel while ground pounders cut line. Converted Navy patrol P2Vs, former B-25 bombers, cargo DC-4s and P-3 patrollers bomb the flames with loads of heavy water-soluble retardants; Ranger helicopters with 250-gallon-capacity buckets dangling from long lines or the heavier war-surplus Chinooks with their one-thousand-gallon buckets dump water on the blaze.

Fire itself may be used as a weapon. Firefighters carry fusees in their packs for setting their own fires. Confronted with high, fast-moving flames, troops may pull their firelines back to a safe distance and use a "burnout" or "burnback" to widen the line against the approaching flames.

A "backfire" is different from a burnout. It is a last measure to stop a holocaust from overtaking dwellings or other structures. The idea is to set a second fire in advance of the main fire and then depend upon "convection effect" to draw the backfire into the main fire. Theoretically, the two fires meet each other, collide and then die for lack of fuel.

Theoretically.

It doesn't always work that way. Anyone messing with backfire is literally playing with fire. What occasionally happens is that the backfire gives the main fire a fatal jump on firefighters.

No technical advance influenced the Forest Service's methods of spotting and fighting wildfire as much as the airplane and later the helicopter. Airplanes arrived at about the same time the Forest Service was organized. By 1925 the Forest Service was using planes to spot forest fires, by 1929 airplanes were dropping supplies to firefighters on the ground. In 1940 Earl Cooley was one of two parachutists to jump on a forest fire, opening the way for the organization of the smokejumpers a year later. Both air tankers and helicopters came into wide use fighting wildland fires during the 1960s.

With the ability to quickly spot fires from the air, put smokejumpers on them before blazes turn into "gobblers," and, if needed, bomb fire from the sky with a flood of water and retardant, the BLM and the Forest Service went modern. They built an "Air Force" and a "paratrooper battalion" to support ground troops. The bold and brash smokejumpers go farther than any other firefighting services in challenging three of the four elements of the universe—air, earth and fire. They like to boast that they can drop out of the sky and land *anywhere*—in treetops, gulleys, on ridgetops or on the sides of cliffs—and still scrape a line around any fire and stop it before 10:00 A.M. the next morning.

"They can't send us to hell," smokejumpers like to say, "because we'd put it out."

Normally, if a fire grows to a stage where it cannot readily be extinguished by the elite ready reaction force from the sky, the smokejumpers withdraw to get ready for the next alarm. However, on Monday, July 4, the Wake fire became a major campaign into which generals hurled all available troops, even if it meant neglecting smaller fires like the one at Storm King Mountain. As George Steele and his stick of jumpers parachuted into battle, command-and-control aircraft circling the fire called for additional ground attacks and air assaults. Dwellings were being threatened. Even smokejumpers remained in combat, committed as ground pounders until the fire monster's attack could be halted.

Hotshots, volunteer firefighters, smokejumpers and local fire personnel scraped line on the fire's flanks, ignited burnbacks and watered down houses in the flame's path. Airtack in his twin-engine Commander flew high above to direct the action on the ground as well as in the air where tankers flew bombing runs and helicopters darted back and forth from the river with their big dangling buckets.

On Monday afternoon, after the blowup interrupted the Fourth of July parade in Paonia, Colorado Governor Roy Romer's caravan made its way slowly down Grand Avenue. It eased past the Ben Franklin drugstore and the Cave Cafe with its blue Western-motif false front. It halted momentarily on Third Street near the Paonia fire department for the governor to take a look at the fire on the mesas across the river and beyond State 133. No one was present at the fire department; the fire chief and his volunteers were up on the mesas.

The local press made much of the fact that Romer did little grandstanding. He made no attempt to pose as a firefighter or tactical advisor. After all, noted one reporter, what the governor knew about fires could be inserted into his eye and still have room for a buzz saw. What he did was simply observe. Dressed in khaki trousers and an open-necked work shirt, the governor resembled some paunchy, white-haired local out on a holiday afternoon to rubberneck the fire. He could have been any of the spectators lining the street. Observers had gathered like that during the Civil War to watch the battles from a safe distance.

Romer shaded his eyes against the bright sun. Afternoon westerly winds had whipped the fire into a frenzy. Smoke billowed hundreds of feet into the sky. It leaned toward the east, riding the winds. Airplanes and helicopters buzzed the fire like wasps stirred up out of a hayloft.

The governor's driver ferried him up 035 Drive to the end of the road, within a mile or so of the flames. He got out of the car and squinted some more. A red-and-white P2V tanker roared low overhead on a final approach to bomb the enemy.

"All hell is breaking loose," the governor exclaimed. "If we didn't have the slurry bombers, we might lose fifty homes."

4

NEWSROOMS CALLED MONDAY, JULY 4, A "HOT news day." Fire stories weren't the only news burning the wires. A crowded boat capsized off the west coast of Haiti and drowned 150 Haitians trying to get to America. Flooding in Georgia would eventually kill thirty people. A fifty-one-year-old woman died in Denver following multiple amputations in an attempt to save her life from the flesh-eating bacteria called Strep A. Another woman in Los Angeles found a bloodstained knife near O. J. Simpson's house. On a lighter side, U.S. Marines and Army soldiers battled each other with *cream puffs* in the annual Grand Junction Fourth of July parade.

But headlines in Paonia and Glenwood Springs and in other western towns threatened by fire took second place to more immediate concerns. At a Mitchell Creek mobile home park in the afternoon shadows of Storm King Mountain, neighbors gathered in their patchy front yards to gaze uneasily at the thin spiral of slow smoke oozing from the mountain ridgeline.

One man lighted a cigarette. He stared at the smoking weed. He stomped it out.

"All we need is a cold front with wind to come through," he said, "and we could be roasting Fourth of July hot dogs in our own backyards by midnight."

"We could always do a rain dance," his neighbor suggested.

"Pray for rain," someone else conceded. "Pray for rain."

At Paonia, residents among the PJ on the mesas north of town didn't have to turn on their television sets to pick up the latest fire intelligence. All they had to do to double the beat of their hearts and dry up their saliva glands was step outside their front doors and take a look. Whipped by winds funneled down North Fork Valley from the western flats of Colorado, the fire made its run off Sunshine Mesa where it started. It spread to Stucker Mesa and up the face of Wakefield Mesa, on its way to devouring some three thousand acres of pinyon, juniper, pine and cheatgrass. By midafternoon the fire stretched more than a mile wide across Wakefield Mesa; it was more than eight miles long. Some twelve hundred firefighters were being committed to the campaign.

On a distant corner of Wakefield Mesa, Karla Tschoepe stood on the lawn next to her log-and-stone red-roofed ranch house. Karla was a tough old homesteader who had ranched in the area for twenty-five years. She had survived drought, hard times, fire, immigrating Californians and men. She got up before dawn to take care of her livestock and eye the smoke southwest of her ranch.

Flames burst into view shortly after lunch. She watched them race up from behind a forested ridge a half-mile behind her house and then flow down its near face toward the first of her outbuildings, the goat barn. A second probe of flames sped along an unburned finger toward her house.

A convoy of volunteer firefighters from Paonia, Redlands Mesa and Hotchkiss drove up in pumpers, engines and several pickups and flatbed trucks. The fighters jumped out with whoops of excitement and started running hose from Karla's water lines. Some of them lit backfires beyond the goat barn. By 5:00 P.M. the battle at the ranch was fully joined. Hotshots from as far away as North Carolina joined volunteers on the fireline.

"Maybe you'd better think of evacuating," suggested BLM firefighter Jerry Hagen.

"Maybe," she replied. Her weathered face set into hard, deep lines. "But I'm not finished yet."

Flames licked from the tree crowns beyond her goat barn, boiling smoke hundreds of feet into the air. The dauntless old woman strapped a forty-year-old Ruger pistol to her blue-jeaned hip, jerked low the brim of her straw Western hat and prepared to fight.

Cattle lowed nervously from a pasture where she had already herded them as far away from the forest as possible. Karla released her goats from their pens and trotted them out into the middle of the mowed hay meadow to wait out the fire. Then she emptied her chicken coops of 450 chicks, loaded them into the back of a pickup truck along with a guitar, some record albums and other personal belongings. She looked around. She looked at the house, the approaching fire. She shrugged philosophically and joined her goats in the middle of the hay meadow.

"Isn't it something?" she mused rhetorically. "I can't think of anything in that house that I'd risk my life for. A person spends a whole life gathering up junk—and it's gone in an instant. I guess you have to say the fun is in gathering up the junk.

"You see all these disasters on TV—the floods, the fires. We're all in the same boat. But I guess as long as you've got your life . . ."

She paused to smile wistfully.

"As long as you've got your life . . ."

Smoke and flying ash poured over the roof of the house. She had seen fire before, but nothing like this. She hooked her thumbs into the loops of her jeans.

"The house—it's gone," she murmured.

Fifty firefighters manned the final perimeter around the house and outbuildings. They clawed desperately at the earth with shovels and Pulaskis to widen the fireline. Hose crews sprayed water into the very maw of flames leaping one hundred feet into the sky. Flames the height of a ten-story building!

Their eyes smarted from bitter ash and smoke. Sweat drenched their bodies underneath heavy yellow fire coats and Nomex trousers. They shouted and sweated and fought, unwilling to concede defeat. Some of them collapsed from the heat and lack of oxygen. Commanders carried or dragged them from the battle's front line and poured water over them to cool them down. Then they charged back into the fight.

"Goddamn you!" a fighter cursed the fire monster.

The fire monster screamed back at him. For those who have faced the fire monster close up, he is something *alive.* Something malevolent, a destroyer without conscience.

Miraculously, the embattled line held. By 6:00 P.M. the fire, if not in retreat, was at least diverted. It swept around the flanks of the ranch core, seeking more vulnerable targets. Everything in a circle around the ranch lay charred black and smoldering.

"We've got a few angels up there flapping their wings," Karla whispered from her hay meadow, which had also survived for lack of fuels to burn.

Lines of worry suddenly further eroded the tired old face.

"My neighbors! What about my neighbors?"

Three firefighters in a pickup truck roared up to a ranch-style house in the juniper on Stucker Mesa where Felix and Pauline Belmont, a retired couple from New York, were packing for evacuation. The fire's edge was still a half-mile away.

The firefighters pounded on the door. Their faces were black with soot.

"Get the hell out of here! Now!" they shouted before speeding off down narrow 035 Drive to warn other residents.

Belmont and his wife grabbed some photographs, personal papers and a few final items. They drove off minutes before flames engulfed their house. The fire left nothing standing except a stone fireplace. Broken glass, ashes and rubble lay in a pile. An unburned garden hose remained stretched along the front of the house. It was still connected to the irrigation pump, but the pump stopped when the electricity went off. Belmont had tried to save his house.

Farther along Stucker Mesa, Karen Mills and her daughter had only about twenty minutes to decide what to save. She opted to take the clothing and jewelry she wore as a professional singer and performer.

"I took things that caught my eye, but no socks," she explained later. "We were thinking we were packing for just a little while."

Her house burned.

Less than a half-mile away, elk rancher Steve Wolcott sent his children to friends' homes in Paonia, but he remained behind. Having seen the devastation following other wildfires, he had built his house with cement roof tiles. The fire scorched his house in passing, but left it intact. His elk huddled in the middle of their field to survive.

As smokejumper George Steele hung in his parachute harness drifting toward the tiny jump spot in the smoking forest, the three-story house he saw with flames converging on it belonged to Chuck Behrensmeyer and his wife, Jane McGarry. They had built it together year by year over a period of sixteen years.

When the fire monster broke his leash, Jane was in Paonia with some of her neighbors watching the Fourth of July parade. Smoke from the young fire had caught her eye that morning. She hesitated leaving her home unprotected, but then decided it was a small fire. Besides, her husband assured her, firefighters had it under control. He volunteered to help fight the flames while Jane eased into Paonia.

Suddenly, a huge plume of smoke engulfed the northern sky as the Shriners' tiny cars cut wheelies on Grand Avenue in Paonia and the high school marching band drummed past the Cave Cafe. Small crowds of people ran to the end of the block to get a better view. The parade made its way on through town, but many of the participants abandoned it. The blowup on the mesas attracted the majority of spectators.

"My home! My husband's up there!" Jane cried.

She and a friend climbed into her car and raced out of town, over the river and across the highway and up 035. Behrensmeyer ran home through the woods and met them. His round face looked flushed. The whites of his eyes showed the dread and fear he could not hide.

Jane cast a horrified glance at the terrible flames flickering angrily beyond in the forest. Smokejumpers' parachutes blossomed in the distant sky.

"What can we—?" she started.

"Nothing!" Behrensmeyer shouted. "There's not time."

"We *can't* go. We . . . we'll lose *everything.*"

"You gotta get outa here," yelled a firefighter, "or you'll lose your life too."

An approaching wall of red terror eighty feet high drove them from their home. They escaped with their pets and two vehicles—nothing else. Intense flames ran at the house and swept over it. Firefighters either had to cut and run or go up with the house. Nothing remained of the home except some twisted tin and some aluminum that melted and ran in a stream from the garage.

Safe in Paonia, Behrensmeyer cast a sorrowful look in the direction where home had once been.

"It's pretty hard to imagine living there again," he said. "The forest is gone. It's going to be years . . ."

The firestorm charged on. The home belonging to the W. P. Bishop family on the front ridge of Wakefield Mesa survived with only its front deck scarred and scorched. Acres of blackened tree stumps surrounded it. A homeowner on 3750 Road lost some outbuildings. Public radio station KVNF in Paonia went off the air when its broadcast antenna on the mesas burned. Bulldozers fought to build a fireline around the Fire Mountain Estates on Pitkin Mesa. Flames threatened a huge pile of coal at the Cypress Orchard Valley Mine.

The Wake fire destroyed three homes within an hour or so

after the blowup. It moved faster than any other fire in Colorado with the exception of a smaller sagebrush fire out on the desert.

"It's a miracle no one's died yet," firefighter Jerry Hagen pointed out. "There's only one road in and out of those homes up there."

Volunteers patrolled 035 to keep it open and aid refugees.

Incident Commander Steve Hart worried. He sniffed the wind. He studied the drift of smoke. It still bent toward the east. So far, the fire had not swept into the bulk of the housing tracts which lay farther north.

"But if we get a cold front and the wind shifts and blows from the south . . ."

He left it unfinished. He didn't want to say what he thought—that if the wind shifted and picked up there was no way in hell firefighters could stop the blaze before it engulfed ten times three houses or one hundred times three houses. The fire wouldn't stop running until it reached I-70. And it might even leap the interstate.

The Wake fire went on "expanded dispatch." The fire management team made the unusual decision to airdrop retardant directly on homes in an effort to save them.

"It has become that critical," Hart said.

5

TANKER PILOTS EARL DAHL AND ANDY WILSON landed their red-and-beige Navy P2V patrol plane at Walker Field and taxied to the cluster of tanks and pumps in front of WSFCC headquarters. The main command center was a typical government structure two drab stories high. Next to it, dwarfed by the main building, was the rough-pine garage affair that headquartered smokejumpers and the one-room porched cottage pilots used as their ready room.

The center appeared deserted; everyone was out fighting fires.

A man wearing jeans and a work shirt ducked out of a little trailer office next to the tanks. He sliced a palm across his throat and Wilson cut both engines. The man uncoiled thick black hose and ran the nozzle end up through a hatch in the belly of the P2V. It would take a few minutes to fill the airplane's retardant tanks with 2,450 gallons of the thick pink glop called "Fugitive."

Dahl in the left seat slipped the seat harness from his ample girth. He stretched and yawned. The stocky pilot looked all of his fifty-six years today with his tired face and his baggy khaki pants and T-shirt.

"Gonna grab a whiz and a sandwich," he said as his crewcut vanished down the exit hatch behind the cockpit. "Want me to bring you one, kid?" he called from the tarmac below.

"A whiz or a sandwich?"

"Whatever fits between bread."

"I'm afraid of the answer. I'll come in for myself. In a minute."

"A minute's all we got."

Wildfire on the western slopes kept the BLM's seven tankers presently assigned to WSFCC in the air from first light to twilight. Air Ops had backlogged so many requests for services during the past week that pilots flew ten-minute turnarounds—just enough ground time to take a quick piss and grab a sandwich while the "Fugitive" tanks were filled. Then back into the sky for another bombing run on the Wake fire or Hourglass or Spud Patch or Elk Springs or . . .

There were so goddamned many fires. Overtime. Wilson was going to sock away some money in overtime this year.

A twin-engine DC-4 taxied up in line behind the P2V as Wilson dropped through the hatch onto the tarmac. Wilson recognized Gary Towle at the controls. Towle was about fifty with a bald head and a full gray beard. He thrust them out the open side window of his airplane. He grinned and yelled something down at Dahl as Dahl shambled clear of the wing on his way to the command center. Dahl looked so earthy, almost common, like he could be just as much at home in a potato farmer's beat-up old Ford pickup as at the controls of a powerful airplane flying fires on a wing and a prayer.

Towle yelled down something about, "Hey, that old crate of yours has got pine needles in the intakes. Can't you get any lower?"

Dahl shot him a good-natured finger and didn't bother trying to respond over the DC-4's throbbing engines. Towle probably had cheatgrass or ants in his intakes. He flew his heavy DC-4 like most pilots flew Cessnas or Pipers. A story circulated about how he had crashed his tanker into a tree several years before. During the FAA accident investigation, one of the feds asked him, "Gary, what do you think happened?"

"Well," Towle drawled, "I guess I just got too fucking low."

Most of the tanker pilots flew "too fucking low" at least some of the time. They were the spiritual descendants of a fly-by-the-seat-of-your-pants breed which in the early days of aviation wired old Fokkers together and buzzed crowds. They would have been barnstormers and wing walkers, WWI aces and WWII bomber pilots. Now, they bombed fires.

They flew an assortment of bombers, patrol and cargo planes declared surplus in the years after WWII and Vietnam. Private companies bought up the airplanes, fitted them out with huge tanks to hold liquid retardant and then contracted them and their pilots out to the BLM and the U.S. Forest Service to fight fires. At twenty-six, Andy Wilson was virtually a kid in the outfit. In contrast to the crusty character-actor look of most bomber pilots, say the Chill Wills type, Wilson was athletic-looking, clean-cut and darkly handsome. He looked dashing in a baby-faced sort of way, like a young Indiana Jones.

That didn't mean he lacked flight experience; most of the B-17 bomber pilots in WWII were younger than he. He didn't add up to Dahl, who had flown tankers since 1976, but he *had* strapped a bomber regularly to his backside for over four years. Before that, he flew air passengers in New Guinea and Indonesia.

He preferred bombing the fire monster from the air over confronting him on the ground.

"Forest fires scare me shitless," he admitted in bull sessions with jumper friends or his helitack buddy Rich Tyler. "Even when I go camping, I get to thinking, 'What if a fire comes now? Where'd I go? What'd I do?' *I'll* stay in my airplane, thank you; *you* go into the fire."

He strolled away from the P2V as it was being filled, into the morning sunlight. Towle's DC-4 idled, rumbling, waiting to move into the slot for its gorge of Fugitive. In the distance, sixty miles to the southeast, smoke from the Wake fire smeared the sky. It resembled pencil smudge on teal wallpaper.

Colorado had been lucky so far. All these fires and no one killed yet. But it was just a matter of time.

"This valley," Wilson sometimes observed, "is northern California all over again, what with all the people moving in. Civilization spreading out. They're coming down here and asking to get burnt up. If you fly this country, you can see generations of old burns all over the mountains. Right in the middle of all these burns you see all these houses."

In recent years, environmentalists had adopted a new philosophy. Forest fires were natural, forest fires were *good.* They were nature's way of cleansing and renewing herself. Let nature take care of herself and let people get out of her way.

Wilson had met a woman one night in a bar. She turned out to be an environmental wacko who ran around eating bark, trying to kiss Bambi's ass and getting tomato farmers arrested for killing rats.

"You put out forest fires?" she asked, eyebrows arching. "You're fucking with nature. The government shouldn't allow people to build houses in the woods anyhow. If they get burned, it serves them right."

You couldn't just let people's houses burn. You *couldn't.* Wilson tried to explain that another reason for controlling forest fires was to keep down erosion. Where flames denuded cover and ground growth, entire hillsides washed down into rivers and killed fish. Landslides clogged drainages and blocked small streams. Mud slides destroyed homes and tore up roads.

"Mother Nature doesn't need any help from us," the wacko countered. "The damage done to this planet has been done by man, not by nature."

"What would you suggest?" Wilson asked, growing irritated. She probably didn't shave underneath her arms and her legs likely resembled a growth of PJ. "Kill off all the people so the kangaroo rats and the spotted owls can move into the suburbs?"

"Man'll kill himself off, given enough time. It's the best thing that can happen to planet Earth."

The more man isolated himself from nature, the more he idealized it. Most Americans lived in the cities and suburbs. Environmental wackos won battles because ordinary people who lived in the cities were ignorant about nature and man's place in the scheme of things. Maybe they would be ecstatic if man enclosed himself in concrete away from nature so trees and kangaroo rats and snail darters could thrive unmolested. Ridiculous. Wilson recalled reading once that wildernesses survived only because man found them useful as wilderness. Otherwise they became cornfields and parking lots. Man must learn to tread more gently upon his environment, but tread he would. He had no other choice except to bring himself to extinction.

"Give me three more minutes and she's full," the pumper man called out.

Wilson strolled over to him, stretching his legs. Some of the pinkish Fugitive globbed onto the ramp. Fugitive was another battle the environmental wackos had won.

Most pilots preferred the old "LC slurry." Like Fugitive, LC had a phosphate base, except it had no gum mixed with it. Slurry was a lot more effective against wood fires because, when dropped in trees, it misted to absorb heat instead of glopping like too-liquid Silly Putty. It cooled off flames and actually extinguished them.

Problem was that LC offended the refined aesthetic sensibilities of environmentalists. It left a red stain on the trees that took a few weeks to dissipate. Never mind that a red stain might be far preferable to a black char that took *years* to disappear. The slurry simply didn't look good to the wackos. It didn't *"look good."*

So, the government replaced effective LC with much-less-effective Fugitive, so-called because it left no stain on trees. When dropped, it hit like pink tomato soup. Engineers designed it to be heavy with gum with the idea that it would be used as a kind of liquid fireline rather than as a direct attack agency to actually put out flames. Theoretically, it coated fuels ahead of the flames and stopped the fire. The pink color went away almost as soon as it struck the ground.

That caused a second problem for pilots. After they made a run and circled around to loose a second load, they couldn't *see* the first load in order to tie into it.

"Every time you go around and miss," Wilson and the other pilots complained, "you double your danger. It's increasing our exposure to some really shitty situations."

But appearance won out over substance and common sense. The wackos tied a fighter's hand behind his back and then urged him to get in there and win one-handed.

Just the day before, Sunday, Dahl and Wilson bombarded the Pyramid Rock fire with Fugitive. They pounded the blaze with it until the ground actually glistened. Flames taunted them by continuing to play over and through the retardant.

Leave it to the wackos to force the exchange of something that worked for something less effective simply because it *looked* better.

Earl Dahl came rolling back across the ramp with his hurried short-legged gait, a half-eaten sandwich clasped in one hand. He waved at Towle in the DC-4 and shouted at Wilson.

"Hit it. Hit it! You'd better take a piss quick—or tie a rubber band around it. The Wake fire's making more runs at houses. They're begging for us. They want us to drop gunk right on the rooftops if we have to."

6

DAHL FLEW THE PILOTS' LEFT SEAT AS THE P2V Neptune hammered toward Paonia. Wilson sat relaxed in the right seat, hands in his lap. Flying second pilot meant he had little to do until they began their fire runs.

Past Orchard City, the desert flats began to narrow between mountain walls into the fertile North Fork Valley. The Neptune drummed hard and low and heavy with suppressant. It had window squares that wrapped themselves around the cockpit, opening up a 180-degree view of the world below. Wilson idly noted the sun-washed sparkle of the North Fork River as it cut through wheat fields and peach orchards.

"Freq?" Dahl asked through the intercom headset.

Wilson checked. He switched from the tower frequency to Wake Air Attack radio. Air Attack played traffic cop over the fire, directing choppers and tankers to keep them clear of each other and providing intel to the incident commander on the ground. Helicopters with slung buckets buzzed the smoke like mosquitos around a campfire. Wilson pulled himself forward in his harness and squinted through the windscreen to pick out the Bell Ranger crewed by his helitack friend Rich Tyler.

Tyler cheated Fate nine years ago when his chopper crashed. The crash had done something to him, made him more introspective. It had opened up deep water and he had seen his own mortality.

Close calls did things like that to you. Wilson had had his own close ones. Maybe not like Rich or like Towle flying into the tree, but any time a pilot flew low and fast into smoke and wind shears and down air he tempted bony Fate. If something went wrong—a sudden wind, an engine coughed and died . . .

You lived with it. Like smokejumpers said, "You look ol' Fate in the eyeballs every time you go up—and you laugh at the bastard and you give him the finger. But you know deep down that ol' Fate always has the last laugh."

Wilson made a mental note to get with Tyler as soon as they had some downtime. Maybe have dinner with him and Patty and little one-year-old Andy. The baby had probably grown so much he wouldn't even know him. There had been so damned much fire activity this year.

Ahead of the aircraft nose loomed a gigantic plume of gray-black smoke tethered to the valley's north rim. It hovered over Paonia like a predator prepared to strike. Little crowds of people knotted up on Grand and on Third to watch the battle being waged on the mesas.

On a bearing 20 degrees north of the Wake fire and beyond it hung a second, much-smaller plume of smoke attached to Storm King Mountain.

"That's our next one," Dahl's voice said through the headset.

"Job security," Wilson said back. He grinned.

Then it was down to business. Air Attack intruded through the headset with abrupt formality: "Air Tanker-14, this is Lead-64 . . ."

Dahl pressed his mike button and acknowledged. "This is 14 . . ."

"Tanker-14, is that you on a nine-zero heading north of Hotchkiss?"

Dahl said it was.

"Turn to a heading of three-six-zero. Circle to the north of the fire front. Winds are out of two-seven-zero. Make your approach from the east. Concentrate on the houses. Do you read? Concentrate on the houses."

"Roger that—concentrate on the houses," Dahl repeated. "Does that still mean to dump on the roofs?"

"Tanker-14, use best judgment."

Dahl glanced at Wilson as he dropped the Neptune's left wing and flowed into a turn. The air filled with smoke and flying ashes and radio traffic. The airplane bounced from unstable air pockets. Wilson tightened his harness. Below, the red living outline of fire inscribed itself in a huge uneven oval across the rise and fall of several parallel mesas. The center of the circle was a black steaming hole. Several houses huddled intact in the black, but others were charred rubble. A fire engine and several pickup loads of yellow-suited firefighters left a trail of dust along a road as they sped toward the raging head of the fire. The head moved easterly with the west wind pushing it. Other firefighters fought to save houses.

Air Attack cleared air space for the tanker to make its run on the fire monster's head. A Bell Ranger emptied its 250-gallon bucket of water on a hot spot. Flames hissed and steamed, but quickly recovered. The blue-and-white chopper bounced away and set a beeline for the river to refill its bucket.

Constant radio chatter in Wilson's ear. Air Attack chatting up choppers, shooting advice to ground commanders.

The P2V turned onto downwind north of the flames, banked onto crosswind and then settled on upwind for its bombing run. Dahl pointed.

"Target?" he asked.

Two miles ahead a nice house, a *really* nice house with a red roof and redwood decks, seemed to shudder with fear and dread where it perched on the edge of a forested ridge. Flames one hundred feet tall threw smoke ahead of them as they raced up the ridge through the trees and closed in on the house. Hot ash feathered the air.

"Go for it," Wilson agreed. His face felt tight. His heart beat from the adrenaline push. He reached for the selector switches that controlled the amount of Fugitive to be dropped on a run.

"Dump it all?" he asked.

"Dump it all. It's our only chance."

Dahl put the airplane down to 150 feet above ground

level. So low that firefighters on the line recognized the pilots' faces and hunched their backs against the wind blast of the plane's passing. Gigantic waves of flame along the bombing run flapped and hissed at the Neptune as it sailed past.

Bullets of sweat peppered Dahl's round face; sweat stung Wilson's eyes. The stench of tension filled the cramped cockpit. This kind of low flying required concentration. Most flyers had no concept of just how rough the air around a fire could be. It was like flying into a small hurricane. Flying that would curdle the blood of bus drivers in their big, safe jetliners thirty thousand feet above a crash landing.

Once committed to the run, Wilson felt his heart slow to normal. Whatever was dry and rough in his throat vanished. It was always like that with him—nervous before the battle but calm when it started. The ability to confront danger in perfect control of one's emotions made a good combat leader or a good tanker bomber pilot.

Little conversation passed between the pilots. Ill-matched though they seemed from first appearances, they worked together so perfectly coordinated they might have been reading each other's minds. Things got damned busy in the cockpit as the target rapidly approached.

"Flaps!" Dahl barked.

Wilson reached overhead and worked in full flaps while Dahl increased power to compensate for the drag. The ship's snout lowered against the increased drag and power until the pilots stared almost straight down into a kaleidoscopic passage of flame and smoke. The stall horn bleated intermittently, nerve-wrackingly, as rough hot air caused rapid airspeed changes. The airspeed indicator hand romped back and forth from 120 knots to 180 knots. Down air threatened to slam the aircraft into the fire. Only their harnesses saved the pilots from banging their heads or being hurled from their seats.

It was the wildest of roller coaster rides. Wilson fingered the "pickle" on his yoke, the "bombs away" button.

He sensed the frenzied tongues of the flames literally

licking at the cockpit. Heat scorched the right side of his face. He fixed his eyes on the red-roofed house; it lay in the smoke less than a half-mile ahead.

If anything went wrong at this speed, at this low altitude, the plane was history, along with its pilots. It wouldn't take much—a sudden wind shear, an explosive downdraft, *hell, a dust devil.* There wouldn't be enough of the bodies left to bury.

Quarter-mile ahead.

Wilson saw the reflections of flames in the house windows. His thumb hovered against the pickle.

Two hundred yards.

Firemen on the ground were running away for their lives. They had given up trying to save the house.

Suddenly, some change in the wind, a gust or something, hurled clouds of smoke at the house and covered it like a blanket. There were old pilots and there were bold pilots, but pilots who regularly flew directly into smoke seldom became old, bold pilots. The smoke was black too. Black smoke contained the turbulence of a micro thunderstorm. Little tornadoes of fire sometimes ripped through it, igniting anything they touched.

"Pull out!" Wilson barked. "We can't get to it!"

Dahl slapped in full power. He grimaced. Snakes of smoke squirmed around the windscreen. "Come on, baby."

Under full power, the airplane seemed to lift like an elevator. It slashed through the upper chimney of smoke. The cockpit darkened.

Then the plane soared out and high, climbing above the black smoke cloud. Wilson bled off the flaps; Dahl settled down the power and trimmed the plane to climb. Wilson shot a glance back and down, looking for the house in the smoke.

"I can't see it," he said. "It's in the fire."

He took a deep breath, his first full one since before they started their bombing approach.

"Try another target," he suggested.

"Wait."

Dahl dropped a wing and circled to take another look.

"The smoke's cleared," he said.

Sure enough, the house's red roof gleamed in the after-noon sun. It resembled spilled blood. Smoke briefly twisted away from it.

"You game for one more run?" Dahl asked. Asked it as though he half wanted his copilot to talk him out of it.

But what the hell?

"Is a pig's ass pork?" Wilson quipped with a shallow grin.

Someone needed them.

The P2V circled across the blackland the fire monster had already consumed. It quickly maneuvered onto another final approach. It dropped altitude. Once again flames flapped from its swift, low passage. Unburned trees ahead of the flames rattled and trembled in the slipstream. Shook like they were frightened.

Wilson stared. He exchanged quick, astonished looks with Dahl.

"Well, I'll be damned . . ." Dahl murmured. He wiped sweat off his forehead with the back of one hairy arm.

Ahead, the fire rushing up the slope had hurled a giant question mark of smoke and flame at the house. The question mark slanted toward the house so that it created a kind of tunnel above the structure, a cave of clear air between the red roof and a black rolling ceiling of smoke.

The P2V with engines thrumming headed directly for the tunnel.

"Jesus Holy Mother of God . . ." Dahl murmured, something like that.

His knuckles on the yoke turned sickly white to match the pallor of his face.

"One last run," Wilson said, unaware that he said it.

Then the pilots became too busy flying to think about the hazards. Flying at 150 miles per hour and one hundred feet above certain death presented little time for thinking. The partners reacted mechanically, as much a part of the machine as its wings and engines and vertical stabilizer. Flaps. Power. Nose pushed down. Wilson's thumb steady and true on the pickle, ready.

41

Ready.

Flames and smoke hissed angrily at the intruder. Flying ashes smashed themselves to death against the windscreen like suicidal insects. Burning branches filled the sky with meteors.

The airplane roared bravely into the low tunnel where red greedy eyes leered from the smoke. The sun disappeared; night fell. A night so low and unsettled it took on substance. A night so filled with tension that, while it lasted only a moment, seemed interminable.

"Bombs away!"

Wilson pressed the button. A wide pink smudge splashed across a canvas dominated by reds and blacks. Dahl lay a line so close between the house and the attacking flames that splashing retardant coated the redwood decks.

The fire monster howled. A gang of hotshots two football field lengths away turned and cheered.

The sudden dumping of a ton of liquid from the aircraft's belly radically altered the plane's trim. It yawed violently; the lightened tail seemed to want to overtake the nose. Dahl leaned on the throttle. Wilson began bleeding off the flaps. Both fought their yokes to keep the Neptune under control.

The airplane punched through the tunnel—into the brilliant sunlight beyond. Blackened by soot and ash, the red-and-beige ship soared out over the valley and Paonia. Behind, the tunnel through which it had just flown filled with black smoke. The house disappeared.

"We lost it anyhow," Wilson moaned.

Dahl said nothing. Grimly, he set a course down the valley back toward Walker Field.

Maybe next time.

"Air Tanker-14? This is Lead-64 . . ."

Wilson sighed. "Go ahead, 64."

"One-Four, that was some spectacular flying. You guys saved that house."

"What?"

They had to see for themselves. Dahl banked back toward the fire. Sure enough, there it sat. The *really* nice house with a red roof and redwood decks. A wasteland of black char surrounded it, but it still stood.

The two pilots exchanged startled looks. Then Dahl nodded. Hey, that was the way it was supposed to happen.

7

THE WAKE FIRE WAS UNDER HEAVY ATTACK FROM both ground and air. WSFCC Director Paul Hefner studied the colored markers on his fire map—one color for fires actively under attack, another for "hold over" blazes like the one at Storm King Mountain. Firefighters all along the western slopes were driving themselves to exhaustion.

Because forest fire fighting was largely a seasonal occupation, firefighters depended upon overtime to make wages stretch into their off-times. Lanky Rich Tyler, BLM's helitack foreman out of WSFCC, had got his share of overtime for the past several weeks. Whenever he had time to catch a few minutes with his wife and one-year-old son, he was generally so damned whipped from making bucket drops and ferrying firefighters and equipment that he fell asleep almost the moment he sank into his easy chair in front of the TV.

"Honey," he said to Patty on Monday night, "I've never seen this many fires in the nearly ten years I've been with the BLM. They're burning up the mountains."

He told her what he witnessed with Andy Wilson and Earl Dahl flying underneath the curl of smoke and flames to save the house on Wakefield Mesa. The Bell Ranger he crewed hovered to one flank of the fire as the P2V Neptune skimmed above treetops and the line of fire on its bombing run. The fire loomed ahead like a fluid red wall as it closed in on the house with the redwood decks.

The bucketful of river water dangling below the helicopter caused the bird to jerk and sway. The pilot hovered the craft, himself mesmerized by the daredevil feat of the fools in the tanker. Tyler bounced in the open crew door. He leaned out against the tether of his safety line and thrust his helmeted head out toward the display to make sure he caught the full run.

Pink Fugitive belched from the tanker like afterbirth. The airplane punched on through the smoke cave and screamed out over North Fork Valley. Tyler was sometimes a marathon runner, built long-muscled for it, but he had seldom felt such exhilaration in winning a race as he felt when Andy triumphantly busted through the smoke to safety. He threw a defiant fist at the sky. *Yes!*

"Underneath the smoke," Tyler explained to Patty. *"Underneath,* for Pete's sake. I sure thought ol' Andy was a goner. I've really ignored Andy this season. Patty, we need to have him out to the house."

"How about this weekend?"

Patty was pretty and small and she understood the camaraderie and loyalty wildland firefighters shared. It was a brotherhood. Rich had been a firefighter when she fell in love with him and married him. Her husband shared a special affinity with the tanker bomber pilot Andy Wilson. Not only were they both flyers and firefighters, they were also both from Minnesota. Tyler had studied forestry at the University of Minnesota and worked Forest Service fire engine crews during the season. In 1985 when he was twenty-three years old, he landed a job with a BLM helitack crew based out of Grand Junction, Colorado.

He had been flying on fires ever since. It was something in his blood. Other firefighters said you could always depend on Rich Tyler. He was devoted to his job. It was what he did best, loved most outside his family. Paul Hefner sometimes teased the helitack with one of his favorite anecdotes.

"We had this fire a year ago," he said. "We had to drag ol' Rich in when his son was born. . . . That guy is dedicated. He'll go the extra mile for nothing, for no pay."

In March, just before the fire season exploded in flames, Tyler granted an interview to the Grand Junction *Daily Sentinel.* Patty sometimes thought her husband expressed in it his subconscious dread of the future he seldom admitted otherwise. It made her understand how the incident nearly ten years ago might have affected him.

"There are hazards to the job," he conceded in the interview—and who should know them better? "You've just got to be cautious, keep your head up."

Fire fighting was hard on personal lives, he said. "With all the different little things—being on the road, away from your family for long stretches of time, not eating the best foods, long hours, physical exertion making you cranky, the hazards of the job—you need to make sure that trust exists. . . . Faith and friendship between the members of a crew is essential."

Other helitacks said Tyler seemed driven by his long-ago escape from Fate's bony hand. As foreman, he was a stickler for safety. It was like he wanted to minimize the risks for everyone around him.

"Sometimes it's like Rich thinks he should have died back then with his friends," the helitacks said. "Like he feels guilty because he lived and they died. It's almost like he feels he's living on borrowed time."

On August 5, 1985, shortly after Tyler enlisted with the helitacks, his chopper crew answered an alarm. Just before takeoff, Tyler rotated off the helicopter to the "chase truck" to accommodate one of the other crew members. Chopper pilot Jim Daugherty and three firefighters lifted off Walker Field. They were buzzing toward a fire near the Gunnison Gorge when their low-flying bird struck an unmarked power line and flipped. All four died.

Tyler, driving the chase truck, was one of the first to arrive at the crash site. He stared at the bloodied bodies twisted into the mangled wreckage. One of the corpses should have been his, *would* have been his except for . . . except for *what?* Fortune? Coincidence? One of those inexplicable crossroads in life where a simple decision, one elementary choice, altered the rest of your life?

"Rich lives with that day," a friend said. "He lives knowing he should be dead."

Firefighters always attributed Fate with a grim sense of

humor. You could cheat the bastard once. Rarely could you cheat him twice.

"Andy will like coming over Saturday night," Tyler said to his wife.

He had no way of knowing that Storm King Mountain lay between Monday and Saturday.

8

Five new fires start on July 4, two of which are one hundred acres or larger. Thirty-one existing fires remain uncontrolled. Local initial attack is spread thin. Radio communications is inadequate for the fire load and is a safety concern. Fire danger is very high to extreme with more lightning forecast for July 5. A red flag warning has been issued.

BLM assessment

NAMES OF THE LARGER FIRES BURNING IN COLO-rado reflected the state's unique geography. The Spud Patch fire sounded like a smoldering garden. Actually, it was a fast-moving fire that had already blackened 500 acres in San Miguel County. The Elk Springs fire would grow from a 200-acre fire to 1,200 acres overnight Tuesday. The 600-acre Little Horsethief III fire near De Beque threatened one of the state's main electric transmission lines. Wildfire caused electric brownouts in Denver and Colorado Springs. Son-Of-A-Gun on the west rim of the Gunnison Gorge, Renegade Point, Wake fire, Oil Springs Mountain, Rabbit Mountain—all fires vowing devastation unless stopped. Anxious residents from around Glenwood Springs had been calling since Sunday to complain about Storm King Mountain.

Fire danger indices for July were the highest recorded in

twenty-one years. As of the first week of July, the number of fires in the West was twice the annual average. Incident management teams had responded to five times the number of fires in a normal year. At a time in which the federal government had cut assistance by 80 percent to local fire fighting efforts, the West had burst into flame and deficit spending. Fighting the 3,000-acre Wake fire and the 1,200-acre Hourglass fire near Fort Collins would each cost one million dollars.

It sometimes irritated Doug Caldwell of the National Park Service the way immigrants kept moving to the West. Colorado was one of the nation's fastest-growing regions. Newcomers came and built their high-altitude dream homes in the middle of drought-dead trees, *inflammable* pines and pinyon and juniper, combustible cheatgrass and bunch grass and dry gambel oak thickets merely awaiting a spark.

"This is where I want to live," they said. "I want those beautiful trees draped over my roof. They're lovely. I moved here to surround myself with nature."

The 170-mile strip of Colorado cities starting at Fort Collins in the north and ending south of Pueblo was nestled against a huge repository of fuels that had been accumulating for a century.

"Where has common sense gone?" Caldwell asked rhetorically. "Do we need to bottle it and give it to people in those areas?"

Paul Hefner paced to a second-floor window at WSFCC. He gazed intently out over the runway. The desert sun sucked heat devils out of the concrete as a DC-4 tanker took off behind an Aero Commander and a commercial jetliner. A chopper flared and set down on the tarmac in front of smokejumper headquarters. Fire-blackened jumpers emerged, trotting wearily to clear the whistling blades. Before they did anything else, before eating or taking a piss or plugging the Coke machine, they gathered in the shade of the trees that masked the front of their garagelike building and prepared chutes and equipment for the next alarm.

It shouldn't be long in coming. Not *this* year.

All the fire activity, plus cutbacks in fire fighting funds, had exacerbated the conflict between the Western Slope Fire Coordination Center and BLM's Grand Junction Fire District. Hefner sighed and ran a hand through his hair. Sometimes he considered bouncing to some other less-stressful position in the fire fighting service. All the bullshit—the politicking, the backbiting—was starting to give him ulcers.

Most of the discord between WSFCC and Grand Junction Dispatch centered on the allocation of resources. WSFCC which Hefner directed held no responsibility for initial attack fire operations. District handled the fires, WSFCC dispensed "beans and bullets." The Center merely obtained resources and set priorities for their utilization based on what bureaucrats called "values at risk," a euphemism meaning life and property threatened by flames.

Grand Junction District accused WSFCC of being less than aggressive in supporting initial attack actions. WSFCC resources specialists retaliated by expressing contempt for the capabilities of BLM fire managers to use resources properly once they acquired them. Reorganization of Colorado BLM offices and funding cutbacks had eliminated the position of deputy of operations and combined that position with the Division of Administration. *Administrators* assumed command over fire operations. Branch Chief Ron Cole, Deputy Over Fire Gil Lucero and even Don Lotvedt, the state fire management officer, the equivalent of a combat division general in the army, all had limited experience fighting fires.

"In some cases," admitted Bob Moore, Colorado State Director of the BLM, "employees are placed in positions where they do not have the technical expertise in the programs they are charged to manage."

Rank-and-file firefighters cared less about the jockeying and feuding in the palaces of power. All a jumper or a hotshot wanted and needed to do his job were transportation to the front lines, beans, weapons and a place to lay his weary head afterward. Damn who acquired them for him or how they were acquired.

Hefner, who had fought his share of fires over the years, identified more with the scorched and tired troops manning the lines than with the "overhead," the bosses and upper management. He sympathized with the straightforward way the troops had of calling a spade a spade. Not a spade—a "goddamned shovel." Nothing delicate about their assessments when the overhead fucked up on supplies or tactics.

"Some of our so-called leaders," firefighters were heard grumbling, "wouldn't know a ground fire from an inflamed hemorrhoid."

A temp who had hired on for the summer to augment the three permanent positions at WSFCC came up behind Hefner.

"Boss?" he said.

Hefner turned. The temp was a smokejumper who had broken a bone and had to grind out the season behind a dreaded desk.

"Boss, you look tired."

"Those poor people up there in the mountains . . ." Hefner muttered.

The fire monster was gobbling their homes, their farms, their livelihoods. Hefner needed more hotshots, more jumpers, more of *everything*. Lives were going to be lost up there due to lack of resources.

"These people move to the Rockies," the temp said, "and they have no idea what fire can do to them."

A big fire had to be seen to be believed. Many of the survivors of the Wake fire would be moving out of the mountains afterward, even if their property came through unscathed. It happened after every fire. People met the fire monster head-on, witnessed his awesome power, and then decided to get out before the monster recuperated and returned.

Reporter Fred Malo of the Glenwood *Post,* a city boy, went out to experience a forest fire for himself. He drove with Silt Police Officer Frank Rupp to the Divide Creek fire where flames had vaulted County Road 311. They encountered a lone firefighter with a shovel trudging up the road to cut a fireline. They refused to leave him there alone.

The nearest flames danced some fifty yards off the road. Even at that distance, the heat the blaze generated reddened Malo's face and drove him back. A small fir standing twenty yards from the fire suddenly torched. Malo was a portly man with a scraggly beard. He thought his beard might combust spontaneously.

"Don't let the fire get behind you," he had been warned.

He pirouetted nervously on the road. Fire leaped behind him, in front of him and on both sides. It played leapfrog by throwing red blossoms ahead of it. Spot fires bloomed. Trees exploded from the heat of their own resin.

"Let's get out of here," Malo exclaimed. "Grab that firefighter and go!"

The fire monster dramatically reminded Malo that this wasn't the suburbs. These were the mountains—and the mountains could still be a dangerous place to live.

9

AS OF NOON ON THE FOURTH OF JULY, FIRE EATing slowly downhill from the ridge off Storm King Mountain had consumed less than ten acres. Still a ground fire, it gnawed at cheatgrass and fallen needles and whatever other fuels it found within its reach. Residents of the small communities along I-70 and the Colorado River, on both sides of the mountain, paused frequently during the holiday. They took long assessments of the growing fire while they grilled steaks or ate ice cream.

BLM District, the Sopris Ranger District and Sheriff Levy Burris all received nervous telephone calls as the holiday wore on. Rumors about the loss of houses in the Wake fire increased anxiety among those within reach of the Storm King fire. Demands for action grew more strident.

"That fire's growing!" one caller complained. "It's starting to come down toward West Glenwood. When are you going to do something about it?"

"If my trailer goes, somebody's going to pay for it," pledged another, who occupied a mobile home in the Mitchell Creek trailer park. *Somebody* had to be legally responsible.

At this early stage of its growth, the fire resembled a cancerous red blossom devouring the healthy flesh around it. A lazy plume of smoke towered off the ridge. It hung etched against the clear mountain sky as both a warning and a reminder that man in these mountains remained subservient to nature.

Finally, District responded to the deluge of complaints. Its overtaxed fire fighting machinery cranked over. Sam Shroeder of the Sopris Ranger District loaded up his engine crew of three and drove out to take a look. District then raised Butch Blanco. Blanco commanded troops fighting the Copper Spur fire. It was almost out.

"We're putting you in charge of the Storm King fire," Blanco was informed. "You're incident commander. Residents say the fire's growing. We don't want to upset the taxpayers."

At fifty years old, Butch Blanco wore the craggy hard lines of the natural outdoorsman. Born and raised in Glenwood Springs, he knew the western slopes of the Rockies better than any other firefighter in either the Forest Service or the BLM. As a kid he had hiked and hunted the White River and Gunnison National Forests, fished clear Crystal Creek that paralleled State 133 toward McClure Pass and rafted the Colorado. Forest firefighters had been his heroes in high school. As a young man, he worked as a plumber in Glenwood Springs while volunteering much of his spare time to the Glenwood Springs fire department.

At age forty-five, when many men thought of retirement, Blanco started a new career. He satisfied his long-standing dream by hiring on full-time as a firefighter with the Federal Bureau of Land Management. He soon rose in rank to become multiresource incident commander for the Glenwood Springs Resource Area. That meant he had the experience and authority to direct ground crews, engines and aircraft for fires in the Glenwood region.

Mike Mottice, BLM Resource Area Manager for Glenwood Springs, always spoke highly of Blanco, as did most everyone else in the fire fighting service who knew him.

"Butch," said Mottice, "has a deep, personal attachment to these mountains. He's competent and professional. Quite frankly, there couldn't be a better man placed in the position."

The Storm King Mountain fire was going to change Blanco's life. The unexpected was about to occur on his watch.

Of course, he knew none of that, had not even a premonition of it, on Monday afternoon when he left Glenwood Springs with firefighter Brad Haugh. To him, as he drove the seven miles on I-70 from Glenwood to Storm King, the fire was simply one of many he had confronted over the years. Even so, he sometimes cautioned rookie troops, you couldn't let fire fighting become routine. When you got careless was when the fire monster struck.

Haugh let his eyes follow the plume of smoke stuck to the Storm King ridge.

"What do you think?" he asked. "Can we have it out by this time tomorrow, Wednesday at the latest?"

Blanco never predicted a fire's death. He had seen one smoldering tree take out six hundred acres overnight. "Maybe," he said, noncommittal.

Several blue-jeaned firefighters loitered around the Sopris Ranger District fire engine parked on the service road at the foot of the steep dropoff that anchored the Storm King ridge to the highway. From busy I-70, the fire lay about a mile north, but the way to it was steep and rugged. The service road was as near as a ground vehicle could get to the smoke. Drainages to either side of the ridge—the east drainage and the west drainage—carried rainwater off Storm King, whenever there *was* rainfall, and dumped it underneath I-70 into the Colorado River. Walls of each drainage formed a steep V. PJ, pine and gambel oak furred the Vs. In some places trees grew so thick among the rock scree and boulders that a man had difficulty working his way through them.

"Where's Sam?" Blanco asked the firefighters as he got out of his car. He whiffed the peculiar pungent odor of burning juniper.

The firefighters pointed into the tree-and-boulder-choked throat of the west drainage. "He's scouting a way to get to the fire."

Blanco and Haugh waited with the Rangers, chatting about the weather, mostly about the lack of rain, and about how busy the fire season had been so far.

"Busier than a one-legged man at an ass kicking," a ranger said.

They didn't have to wait long. Sam Shroeder hailed them from the west drainage. Loose rock sliding ahead of him kicked up dust as dry and fine as old ashes. Gravity pulled the engineman to the service road. He rode in on a miniature landslide. Sweat caked dust in streaks of mud on his lean face. He wore dusty jeans, old fire-blackened boots and a faded work shirt.

"The ridge is too steep and rough to get to the fire from this direction," he panted. "Hell, you'd have to be a mountain goat."

The firefighters moved east on the road to the Canyon Creek exit to check out the east drainage. It appeared more accessible. BLM fire squad boss Michelle Ryerson and her crew of six met the incident commander there. They were all the firefighters District could spare. Blanco intended to hike in this afternoon for an initial assault. He needed to kick ass on this fire quickly; other more threatening fires demanded his attention.

He studied smoke coiling off the high ridge nearly a mile away. He glanced thoughtfully at his watch. After 5:00 P.M. The white summer sun hung as though caught on the jagged tops of the mountains to the west. It wouldn't be long though before it freed itself and dropped. Darkness came like lights out after that.

"There's maybe two or three hours more of light before nightfall," Blanco calculated.

"I'm here to tell you that's some rough country in there," Shroeder said, still wiping mud and perspiration from his face. "It'll take longer than two hours to reach the fire. By that time we'll be stumbling around up there in the dark. Somebody'll get hurt."

The discussion went around the circle.

"It's not like it's the Wake fire," one of Ryerson's firefighters pointed out. "It's already been creeping around up there for three days. It won't go anywhere until morning."

That settled it. It was common sense.

"Okay, we'll hit it right after dawn," Blanco said. "Sam, can we count on you?"

Shroeder nodded.

"Michelle, keep your crew in Glenwood Springs for the night and have it ready to go."

Blanco and Haugh along with Ryerson's firefighters and Shroeder's engine crew returned to Glenwood Springs to prepare for the attack. Blanco drove straight to the BLM offices where he consumed most of the evening on the phone trying to wheedle resources from District and the Western Slope Fire Coordination Center.

"Do you know how many times this week," complained a bedraggled Paul Hefner, "I've heard how the western slopes of the Rockies are burning down to rock and mineral?"

"Paul, this thing's gonna get out of hand if we don't stop it soon," Blanco argued.

Fire Management Officer Pete Blume joined in the long-distance discussion.

"Folks are getting scared over here in Glenwood," he said. "We really need to get something on that fire."

Hefner looked as though he needed a shave and a good night's sleep. He rose slowly from his desk on the second floor and paced with the phone. He stared out the window across the lighted runway of Walker Field. Tankers and helitacks did not fly night operations. Too hazardous. The few jumpers not already out on fires had retired to their motel rooms on Horizon Drive, which ran toward Grand Junction from the airport. Hefner was trying to do the best he could with what he had until Denver and Boise sent him more reinforcements.

"We've already lost three houses at Paonia," Hefner said. "Butch, we only have so much to go around. Priority right now has to be the Wake fire. Can you make out with Ryerson and Shroeder and their crews?"

He would have to.

At 8:00 P.M. a West Glenwood homeowner called in to say the Storm King fire had picked up speed downhill. Ten minutes later an aerial observer from the White River National Forest flew over the blaze to update reports on the monster's progress.

"The fire is on steep and inaccessible terrain," he relayed. Everyone already knew that. "It is actively burning in all directions, but primarily it is burning to the northeast on the ridge. Helicopters with buckets could be very effective. The area is too steep for crews and has few if any escape routes."

Steep or not, escape routes or not, Blanco had to go in. A good commander didn't hesitate attacking the enemy just because he offered a tough fight. A good commander never waited until the enemy reached the portals before ordering a charge.

Finally, Paul Hefner promised Blanco to do what he could in assigning resources to Storm King Mountain. "I'll do what I can," he said again. Maybe he could free a load of smokejumpers for Tuesday. He already planned on tanker bombers.

Blanco pushed back from his desk. He had done everything possible. It was 11:20 P.M. The phone rang. It was District Dispatch.

"Sam Shroeder wants you to know he and two Forest Service crews have been assigned to the Mamm Creek fire,"

Dispatch said. "He's not going to be able to help you in the morning after all. He'll try to get you some firefighters later in the day if he doesn't need them all."

Great. Even those resources Blanco scrounged himself were being seized. He hung up the phone and walked outside. He rubbed his face wearily with both hands. Like Hefner, he needed sleep. Every firefighter on the western slopes needed sleep.

Stars filled the warm black sky. To the southwest beyond McClure Pass, a thin reddish glow stained the horizon. The Wake fire. Northwest by just a few miles, the Storm King fire inscribed a red flickering arc against the black backdrop of Storm King Mountain. The ridge next to the one being chewed on by flames was called Hellsgate Ridge.

Hellsgate Ridge.

Maybe that should be the fire's name—the Hellsgate fire. For just an instant, Blanco envisioned flames on the ridge rocking back and forth like a broad jumper waiting for the gates of hell to open.

10

TROOPS CONTINUED MASSING AT WALKER FIELD while Butch Blanco checked out the Storm King fire on July 4, devising strategy for attacking it and trying to muster resources. Governor Romer had requested an additional four hundred firefighters from Boise to help Colorado gain control of the wildfires on the western slopes. During a fire season, the nation's seventeen thousand wildland firefighters could find themselves on firelines anywhere from Alaska to Arizona. Colorado was one of the hot spots this year. As many as five hundred hotshots and seventy smokejumpers plus hundreds of local Forest Service and BLM fighters would be deployed in the Colorado Rockies during July.

Reinforcements found themselves hurled into battle almost as soon as they deplaned on the flats at Grand Junction. They re-planed for a fire jump at Oil Springs or Rabbit Mountain; loaded up in buses or trucks to be hauled to Little Horsethief III or Wake or any of the other blazes currently heating up the western slopes.

From Grand Junction, only the bare fingers of the Rockies were visible rising out of the desert to the east. Yet, distant though the fires might be, a haze of smoke hung over the little city. It was thick enough at times to cause spontaneous coughing on Horizon Drive. The summer desert winds weren't strong enough or frequent enough to keep the smoke and ash blown away.

"It's very similar to a typical winter day in which particulates are trapped by an inversion," Perry Buda said in explaining the haze to the *Daily Sentinel*. Buda was an air pollution specialist for the Mesa County Department of Health.

Smokejumper Tony Petrelli coughed and rubbed his eyes when he reported to the jumpers shack at Walker Field for duty on July 4. Yesterday, he had fought fire in Springerville, Arizona. Today, Colorado. Tomorrow? Who knew? During the season, firefighters were a gypsy bunch; many of them remained gypsies even after the season ended.

The first thing a firefighter wanted to know upon arrival at a new station was, "How's the overtime?" Time-and-a-half and double time pay made the unemployed winters survivable. The standard greeting among firefighters started with, "How much overtime you got?"

"Colorado is overtime city," the other jumpers told Petrelli. "We have enough holdover fires waiting to last until Christmas."

That suited Petrelli. A wide grin flashed across his swarthy face. He was tanned and lean and walked with a swagger. He looked about 30, but could have been 25 or even 35. Latins, he said, hid their ages well.

He tabbed in his name at the bottom of the rotating jump list kept on the bulletin board in the smokejumpers shack. Jumpers often observed, with a kind of dark fatalism held in common with combat soldiers, that you put your name on The List and Fate selected from it.

Petrelli rotated and made his first Colorado fire jump that same day. Maybe it was Fate that put him and twelve other newly arriving Arizona jumpers onto the Oil Springs fire, twenty acres of flames rolling through PJ. They fought fire throughout Monday night, taking out only an hour or so after 3:00 A.M. to roll up in their blankets for catnaps.

They demobilized from the beaten blaze late Tuesday, just in time for Petrelli's name to go back on the jump list and rotate up for one of the sticks being formed to jump on Wednesday. He might rotate to Rabbit Mountain or Gunnison or Storm King or any of the blazes. Fate made the selection.

He checked off-duty at midnight Tuesday, stumbled wearily to his motel room on Horizon Drive where he listened to the Weather Channel before turning in. The forecast for Wednesday called for a dry cold front to move through with winds.

"Winds," the jumper muttered. "Winds."

He curled up in bed alone. Most smokejumpers were either single or divorced. The job played death with relationships. What woman wanted to wait faithfully at home while her man traveled around with a pack of gypsies six to eight months of the year?

That took away some of the glamour of the job. That and the fact that once you landed out of the sky the work was mostly backbreaking labor. Assholes and elbows. All the glamour of ditch digging.

But Petrelli would exchange it for no other job. Not yet. Smokejumping was the romantic's last refuge in a skyscraper, cybertronics world. The loneliness of the daredevil, smoke jumping, wildland firefighter was part of the myth and the attraction. It was up to this reckless and elite breed to carry over into the modern age the character and tradition of the lonesome cowboy of the Old West.

Petrelli couldn't stop thinking about the weather forecast. He got out of bed and padded to the window. Stars shown down on Horizon Drive. There was almost no traffic this time of night.

He went back to bed.

Winds were the smokejumper's nemesis, the fire monster's ally.

11

"YOU WOULDN'T DARE JUMP—IF YOU KNEW there was no God."

Lanky Tim Pettitt wrote the phrase down one time and memorized it. Jumping *made* you believe in God. There were no atheists in foxholes.

Some of the other jumpers said Pettitt was what the younger smokejumpers had to look forward to in their old age—if they lived long enough. Pettitt was not old, not at forty-three, but he and George Steele and Jack Seagraves and a few others like them were grandpaws in the business. Pettitt attended the U.S. Forest Service parachute school at McCall, Idaho, in 1975, nearly twenty years and 350 jumps ago.

His red hair and scraggly beard seemed perpetually stained with the soot and ash of the hundreds of fires he had fought. The craggy face behind the beard displayed the harsh lines of a maverick and often lonely profession. They were lines of time and of a sadness borne stoically like secrets hinted at but rarely expressed.

Pettitt had never married. He once conducted an informal survey which found that the divorce rate among jumpers was 80 percent on a first marriage, 60 percent on a second and maybe only about 30 percent or so on third and subsequent marriages. He told every woman he met right up front what he did for a living. He told them he owned a new house in Red Bluff, California, but he only lived there about four months out of the year. The other eight months found him on the road jumping forest fires. He didn't own a dog or any other pet because he was never home enough to take care of it. He never had a wife for the same reason.

"Tim, this won't work out," the last girlfriend finally cried, giving up. "You're never home when I need you. What am I supposed to do all those months when you're away? Well, I'll tell you what I'm *not* going to do. I'm not going to sit around here waiting for you to decide to come home."

Jody, who stayed home and worked a nice, safe, nine-to-five job ended up with the straw widows while the smoke-jumpers went out like Lancelot to joust the flames. Pettitt could go right down the list of jumpers divorced or who were confirmed bachelors because of the job—George Steele, J.C. Curd, Don Mackey . . .

It was hard to give up fire fighting. Parachuting and fire fighting. It was Tim Pettitt's kind of life, offering him job satisfaction, something 80 percent of American workers failed to achieve. He exalted in stopping a fire in its blackened tracks. He liked being outdoors where he felt free. He even liked the sweat and aches of backbreaking physical work. Assholes and elbows.

He liked his comrades. They were rough, self-confident men. Women, too, the three or four there were in the smokejumpers. Fire season was the center of life for most committed wildland firefighters. During off-seasons, they chafed for lack of action. They felt the loneliness gnawing in their restless bones. They marked off the days on their calendars, waiting for that call: "It's the season again. Are you ready?"

Ready? Is a pig's ass pork? Does a bear shit in the woods? Can Superman save the world?

Marking off the days waiting for life to begin again. Waiting for that moment of exhilaration and completeness when a man *knew* he was a whole man, when he linked his past, present and future to the elements of air, earth and fire.

"It's like I'm up there by myself and don't have nobody telling me what to do," Pettitt once tried to explain. "Every jump, you're really scared and you know it's marginal . . . like I might make it and I might not. Adrenaline pumps like through a fire hose. When you hit the ground, it's like, *'Wow, I survived!'* Like that. You're really happy 'cause you made it. It's a big rush. You might say it's a death rush. You can't stop talking 'cause you're really jacked up. Nobody else understands what it's like except another jumper. They're your buds. They understand."

But in this business, time caught up with you sooner or later. Time was catching up with scraggly Tim Pettitt. The little pings and pains and aches in his bones from nearly two decades of parachuting rough terrain reminded him that he had only a few good years remaining. During more recent seasons he had started taking precautions to extend the time he had left. These days when he jumped he padded himself so well he looked like a spaceman.

Jumpers hung their gear in a little open-faced shed on the ramp next to the jump planes. The heavy outsized suits with their Elvis collars hung on individual pegs like empty astronauts with the Bell helmets and face masks arranged on a shelf above. When the fire bell sounded, a jumper had two minutes to get suited up and on the aircraft. The younger jumpers made the getaway time by using only the heavy outer suits with soft pads at the joints. Pettitt added an inner stretch suit with hard pads to protect long bones, joints and especially the spine. He also stuffed more soft padding into his outer jumpsuit and used athletic knee and elbow pads.

"How's the old bones holding together?" the young bucks sometimes chided him.

Pettitt responded with his sad half-grin. "Harder and tougher and seasoned with age."

That wasn't exactly true. A season or so ago, before he took his extra precautions, he thought he broke his back. He and another jumper parachuted onto a small two-man fire, a two-manner, in Utah. The jump spot was a tiny clearing surrounded by fir trees. Although a square parachute had a natural forward velocity of twenty miles per hour, the wind was even stronger. It pushed him away from the jump spot.

Green forest rushed up at him. Alpine firs are extremely brittle trees. He exploded into the forest canopy with a sound like gunfire as the trees snapped and splintered underneath his weight. He hurtled down through them. Branches and boughs grabbed and snatched and jerked at his body.

His parachute collapsed. Sudden fear gripped his heart. He thought his chute was going to streamer down with him through the trees to the ground sixty feet below.

The parachute flared, however, in a last flutter of wind and draped over the pointed peak of a fir. It jerked Pettitt up short. It bounced him off a tree trunk. Then he hung like a fish on a line, trying to catch his breath. His body felt like he had just survived a run through the Cheyenne gauntlet of death. He stared down at the forest floor. It was still forty feet below.

Smoke wafted through the forest, but the flames were distant enough not to cause him immediate alarm. His first concern was getting out of the tree.

He finally took a deep breath and groaned, "Damn!" He reached behind to feel for the tree trunk. Something snapped higher up. He dropped another two feet.

If the parachute canopy broke free now—look out below because, ready or not, he was coming through. He knew of a guy who committed suicide by jumping out a fourth floor window. That was only forty feet.

Cautiously, he felt again for the tree trunk. He couldn't reach it for the bough that held him out and away. That meant instead of using the tree he had to tie off on the parachute and use it as his anchor point. Then hope and pray it held.

He scarcely dared to breathe. He fingered the nylon-webbing letdown line from the thigh pocket of his jumpsuit. He snapped one end of it into the rings of his parachute harness and the other end to the parachute risers. He released his right capewell; that left him hanging by one riser.

He tested his anchor point by bouncing with his weight. The tree creaked and groaned, but it held.

"So far, so good," he muttered. Outdoorsmen who spent time in solitude often talked to themselves.

He reached for the second capewell.

"It ain't the jump that kills you. It's the fall. . . ."

Clichés, he noted dryly. But how could you expect original thinking at a time like this?

He released the last capewell and now hung from the parachute only by his lowering line. He tested the anchor point a second time.

"Solid as a dollar . . ."

He started down the line hand over hand.

Suddenly he heard it. The brittle cracking of wood giving way.

"Oh, Jesus!"

The first breaking sounded like a firecracker. But then an entire string of firecrackers went off. Pettitt's weight on the parachute rent the fir in a long white gash clear to its heart.

Pettitt scrambled down the line like a monkey on a rope, trying to reach the ground before the top of the tree came down on top of him.

The line lost its tension. It fell away from him.

He tumbled. Slowly at first. Then he picked up speed as he smashed down through the fir. He grabbed desperately to break his fall. The effort twisted and crabbed him while the springy boughs slapped him around like a ball.

He was a goner. He knew it.

He landed on his back, hard. Excruciating pain took his breath away. The top of the tree with the parachute still entangled in it thudded down next to him. His lungs gasped for breath. Great sheets of raw white pain clawed at his spine. He *knew* he had broken his back. He saw himself in a wheelchair for the rest of his life. Some kindly old woman in white would come around to feed him soft Cream of Wheat because he couldn't feed himself.

How the hell could he fight fires from a wheelchair?

He lay there until his breath returned. A bar of bright sunlight shining down through the trees almost blinded him. He moved his head.

"All right!" He reveled in the small accomplishment.

He waited ten minutes until the pain abated. He wondered where his partner had landed, if he were also hung up in the trees.

He focused his eyes on his boots. They lay motionless with his feet in them. He assumed his feet were still in them; he couldn't feel to be sure. The ground, however, felt soft on his back. His eyes focused on his left foot. It had to move.

He *willed* it to move.

It moved. A miracle.

He moved the other foot.

"Thank you, God. *Thank you, God!*"

The spring in the tree boughs had slowed his fall enough that landing on a cushion of accumulated pine and fir needles had saved him from more serious injury. His bruises simply became more twinges and morning aches from time to time to remind him of man's temporal existence.

Since firefighters earned their really big money from overtime, even a sprained ankle threw them out of the overtime race. Law required the BLM and the Forest Service to offer an injured jumper another job, but it seldom amounted to much. An injured firefighter became a liability. Overhead treated him like a leper.

Pettitt was in Nevada with George Steele when Steele smoked in and snapped himself apart. The guy was a mess. Broken limbs, cracked jaw, bloody face with its missing teeth. He went off the time clock as soon as he couldn't get up to join the fireline. Other jumpers hauled him to the rescue chopper.

Workmen's comp wouldn't begin until after he got out of the hospital. Government red tape held up paying his hospital bills; he couldn't even get his jaw fixed. He ate all his meals through a straw and complained of starving while the government shuffled the paperwork around. Finally Steele paid his own bills in order to get his jaw repaired.

A mistake, Fate, or, eventually, even ageing bones knocked firefighters out of the wages. Last year a jumper got caught in a tree and spent the rest of the season in traction. One time a jumper named Hall leaped out of an airplane without hooking up his static line. He survived through luck and quick reflexes but became known from then on as "Free Fall Hall."

So many fires in the west this year threw firefighters a windfall in overtime. Before coming up on the list for Colorado, Pettitt made eighteen fire jumps and one "pounder" in Utah where he had to walk in. Pounding into a blaze was for the line troops. Elite troops *parachuted* in.

Pettitt thought he might make enough money this season to put him up easy for the winter—if he didn't crash in and break something. Every year as he grew older, it seemed, his pucker factor increased. Fire fighting—and especially smoke jumping—provided a precarious existence.

Fate and the rotation list controlled a firefighter's life during the season. Fate and the rotation list sent Pettitt to Colorado where he immediately began jumping fires. After each demobe, he and the others returned to the jumpers shack at Walker Field to check out their equipment for the next alarm. You took care of your equipment, it took care of you.

Underneath the trees between the shack and the ramp where the twin Otter posed like a startled bird ready for flight, Pettitt pulled the crumpled nylon of his parachute from his red packout bag. He held it short by the risers and let the breeze lift the canopy above his head like a kite while he checked it for rips, tears and abrasions before repacking it.

The colored parachute looked gay and alive. It seemed to be panting with energy and joy. It also seemed pitifully inadequate upon which to hang a man's life.

12

THE SUN AT 6:30 A.M. ON TUESDAY, JULY 5, HAD not yet eased above the mountains that walled in the Colorado River when Incident Commander Butch Blanco launched his initial attack on the Storm King Mountain fire. His bold little assault force consisted of seven firefighters. No more were available.

Storm King had already been "monitored" for more than three days, in spite of directives from the district fire management team promising that "we will not monitor fires, but suppress them." The team hadn't counted on an outbreak of lightning fires erupting over the Fourth of July holiday weekend. All it could do in response was issue a message through the Local Area Network: "Due to the prolonged fire danger and fire incidents, it is necessary that all personnel be available to support fire suppression action when called upon by Grand Junction Dispatch."

Firefighters translated the message to plain language. It meant District didn't have enough troops to go around. Even if firefighters took off a few hours to eat and sleep, they should be prepared to leap out of bed to respond to the next threat. Soldiers of war received little rest. Especially when the enemy controlled the offensive.

Blanco felt fortunate to have rounded up six fighters to take with him under the circumstances. Squad boss Michelle Ryerson canted her head to regard smoke curling off the top of the ridge above them. It beckoned, challenged. The hike from I-70 up the east drainage to the blaze promised to be a steep hot slog. The temperature so far was about 70 degrees in the shade, but above on the ridge at seven thousand feet the thin air let the sun's fierce rays burn through.

"This how you maintain your Jane Fonda figure?" one of the men teased Ryerson.

Ryerson responded with a good-natured laugh. Attractive in that wholesome outdoor way that required no makeup, at least not while she was still young enough that her skin benefited from the sun, Michelle Ryerson felt little self-consciousness in squad-bossing male firefighters. She earned her position the hard way—on the firelines. The kidding she endured from her largely male counterparts carried with it the affection and respect of younger brothers toward their sister. She was at ease with herself and with her life that Tuesday morning at the base of Storm King Mountain. She felt her blood pumping with exhilaration at the thought of action on the ridge.

She brushed her sunburned hair up underneath her yellow plastic helmet. The first rays of the new sun burnished a scattering of freckles across the bridge of her slightly snubbed nose.

"Let the workout begin," she joked. "We'll start with the high steppers."

The crew humped into packs containing food, water and personal gear, then shouldered shovels, Pulaskis, two heavy-duty Stihl chain saws and extra fuel. Neil Shunk brushed sweat and cast a look of dismay into the east drainage.

"It's gonna be the hike from hell," he said.

Brian Rush stretched his back to settle his pack. The acrid taste of smoke bit the back of his throat.

"More like the hike *into* hell," he said, not realizing until later the prophesy of a casual remark.

The small attack element set out, Blanco in the lead. It climbed hard through the shrub and rock fields. The joking and horseplaying from the highway soon settled into labored panting. The heavy chain saws moved up and down the line. Women as well as men took their turns at carrying the saws. Women firefighters accepted without complaint their share of the labor. Otherwise, they were *out*.

Brad Haugh and Michelle Ryerson swapped off in running point with Blanco or in bringing up drag. Between them labored Neil Shunk, Brian Rush, Loren Paulson and

Janie Jarrett, all young and in good shape but still breathing and sweating hard from the climb.

The east drainage was narrowest where it emptied into culverts underneath I-70. As it widened and steepened and thickened with brush, slab-sided Blanco in his canary fire suit ranged ahead, seeking the best avenues up the ridge.

"Butch may be old," someone grudgingly complimented the leader, "but that old guy'll walk our asses into the ground every day of the week and twice on Sunday."

Not long after the little force began its assault, Grand Junction District Fire Manager Rich Arcand driving east on I-70 to an early-morning meeting in Glenwood Springs pulled his car off the highway. He was responsible for 2.1 million acres of public lands, including Storm King Mountain.

From the highway near the exit to the Canyon Creek Estates, Arcand observed the fire on the ridge for a few minutes. It was still a ground fire of relatively few acres, apparently isolated high above human habitation. It crept through sparse fuels, out in all directions from its small black heart, moving generally in a northeasterly direction toward the Storm King peak. No one lived on or near the peak.

"It doesn't seem to pose any real threat at this moment," he commented later in strategy meetings with other BLM officials. "But it needs to be handled."

Midmorning, about 10:00 A.M., found Blanco's attack element gaining the crest of the ridge. Wads of smoke trapped in the stunted trees below the crest tasted juniper-bitter to the tongue. Smoke dried out membranes. With a few tired whoops of relief, the firefighters broke through the brush. The ridge spine was fairly clean and so knife blade narrow it permitted panoramic views on all aspects.

Janie Jarrett complained of having sprained her ankle. She lowered her pack and dropped into the dirt next to it, reaching for her water bottle.

"Ten minutes," Blanco said. He had been waiting for them, studying the fire gnawing on the steep western aspect of the ridge while he waited. Except for smudges of sweat-mud on his broad face, he appeared as fresh as when he started the long climb.

While the crew members rested and drank, they took their first look around. They seemed to have sprawled on top of the world, maybe even on God's own front porch. Gray smoke traced a thin film across the sky, but the sky was still dark blue, space-blue. Their helmeted heads touched it. No one spoke for a long few minutes out of a kind of reverence. Those who cope regularly with the powers of nature develop reverence for it.

Storm King Mountain dominated the north. It loomed, it frowned, it towered, it overwhelmed. Legend had it that Storm King controlled the weather. The ridge spine upon which the firefighters rested snaked toward it, a bare thin serpent wriggling through the brush for about four hundred yards. It dropped into a broader, flatter saddle at the foot of the mountain before merging with it.

West Glenwood Springs lay in the valley to the east, a scattering of strip malls and expensive motels and houses jammed between I-70 and the mountains. To the west, one ridge over and at the foot of it, developers had built the Canyon Creek Estates along Cabin Creek Road. The Colorado River glinted jewels in the sun to the south as it raced I-70 through the gorge.

All this terrain lay around the feet of the firefighters on the ridge. It was like they sat on a huge topographical map. The only thing that marred the grandeur of mountains and sky, forest and river was the fire. It slowly belched smoke from lower down toward the west drainage. It had grown from about thirty acres to fifty acres during the past two hours.

Blanco emptied a water bottle down his parched throat and drew Ryerson and Haugh to the thin shade of a juniper to discuss tactics. Work priorities, safety procedures, escape routes. The IC took a stick and drew in the dirt. Here was the ridge, here the mountain, here I-70 and here the fire monster on the western slope of the ridge.

Question. Should they go on the attack direct or indirect?

An indirect attack meant they had to trudge downhill, anchor and build fireline *uphill* to squeeze off the *flanks* of the fire. A direct attack started at the ridgetop and scraped fireline *downhill* to cut off the *head* of the slow-moving fire.

Blanco decided on a direct attack. Later, he was criticized for the decision. But at the moment it seemed the best course of action to stop the fire as quickly as possible.

He laid out safety zones on the ridgetop and just over the crest where a fast-traveling uphill fire would have to slow before starting downhill.

"Escape route is up the fireline and over the ridge," he said. "At least until further notice. Priority is to cut a helispot so the choppers can get in with reinforcements and supplies. I'll have a looksee at the fire and scout a fireline."

Thick vegetation and incised washes and gulleys obscured a view of the fire from the ridgetop. No flames were visible, just smoke.

Ryerson assembled the squad to start work on a helicopter landing pad. Blanco slogged off downhill through the PJ toward the blaze. A freshening breeze touched his left cheek. Weather forecasts for the week called for a cold front to move in from the west. A cold front meant winds. Winds meant a faster-traveling fire.

Blanco frowned and glanced at the sky. Still clear and blue through the smoke haze.

The fire burned out from its blackened heart on all aspects. Flames measured only about six to eight inches in height. They crawled through ground fuel that consisted mostly of dried grass clumps underneath the trees. Occasionally, flames discovered ladder fuel and torched a tree to make a short, slow run. Mostly, however, the fire kept its teeth and nose to the ground and avoided crowning.

Blanco followed the edge of the fire, studying its progress, its fuels, trying to predict what it would do, say, in the next twelve hours or so. It moved so slowly at this stage that he could have sat down in front of it to eat lunch. It was a gentle fire, a not-very-dangerous fire.

It gnawed its way northeasterly toward Storm King. Between the fire and Storm King, however, Blanco discovered potential danger. Four great patches of gambel oak grew along the western aspect of the ridge and wrapped up and over the crest in several places. Each patch ranged in size from about ten acres to sixty acres. The shrubby trees were six to twelve feet tall and grew dense and continuous. A mat of leaves and litter three inches deep covered the ground underneath the shrubs.

A late frost in the spring had little effect on the oaks. They appeared green and growing. Blanco stripped off a handful of leaves and crumpled them to check moisture content. The leaves crackled in his hands. Once fire nibbled its way underneath the oak thickets, it would further dry out the leaves to nothing more than tinder.

A gambel oak blowup in 1976 in Parachute, not thirty miles away, killed three firefighters.

A deeply thoughtful IC made his way back to the ridge crest. He stood on a boulder and pointed out the oak patches to Ryerson and Haugh. The gambel stood out lighter colored among the deep green of the PJ.

"If it's possible," he said, "if it's not too late already, we must cut the fire off from those thickets. They could go up like that."

He snapped his fingers. "Like that."

13

BLANCO'S YOUNG CREW SET TO WORK AFTER A quick lunch to provide energy—a five-minute lunch dug hurriedly from backpacks. Ryerson selected two of the crew to help her finish the helipad on the ridge spine. The helispot was a flat area not much larger than a dining room table, just wide enough to catch the skids of a Bell Ranger. Blanco and the other three firefighters began building hand line.

They anchored the fireline near the helispot and ranged it

downhill. They cut it two feet wide and scraped down to mineral rock, bumping up and passing each other and bumping up again as they worked. Brad Haugh and Neil Shunk donned leather sawyer chaps and cut out canopy ahead to clear a path for the fireline and prevent aerial spotting and slopover once flames reached the line. Pulaskis and shovels clanged in the rocky loam. Chain saw buzz echoed in background accompaniment.

It was mind-numbing, backbreaking work. The ridge was as steep as a New England rooftop.

Blanco occasionally scouted the fire to check its progress. The fireline would have to be built through patches of oak since the flames were already too near to be cut off from them. He still wasn't overly concerned. Only a light breeze rattled the leaves. The fire remained on the ground, its flames still short and slow.

Upon returning from one of his scouting missions, he detected a lull in chain saw activity. Haugh kicked in disgust at a worthless lump of metal that had once been a saw.

"The drive sprocket broke," he complained. "This'll slow us to half pace."

Then the other saw broke. The sawyers joined the hand tool squad.

"We'll never catch the fire at this rate," Haugh pointed out. "There's not enough of us—and now we don't even have saws."

Blanco remained in constant contact with Grand Junction Dispatch through his hand radio. His requests for reinforcements filtered through WSFCC.

"I'd like to have a hotshot crew and a helicopter," he requested. "Progress is slow with what we have. We're not going to be able to stop the fire."

"Everyone's still tied up at Paonia with the Wake fire," came the weary reply. "We've ordered more hotshots from out of state, but they haven't arrived yet. Jumpers are starting to demobe from Wake. Maybe we can get you a load of jumpers by later this afternoon."

"We'll take them," Blanco hurridly accepted.

Was it his imagination or had the rising smoke assumed a

slightly steeper angle toward the northeast, indicating a swelling wind? Smoke drifted over the gambel oak patches.

"How about aircraft?" the IC requested.

Dispatch must have detected a slight desperation in his voice. Paul Hefner at WSFCC ordered two tanker runs on the Storm King blaze, the first at 3:00 P.M. and the second at 5:00 P.M.

A lumbering red P-3 made the first run. It circled high and to the north of Storm King. It dropped altitude over Canyon Creek Estates on its bombing final and came in low and roaring across the west drainage. Blanco pulled his crew off the fireline. He wanted the first dump on and ahead of the end of the fireline to support its construction.

Pink afterbirth squirted from the airplane's belly.

"Look at the sonofabitch piss!" a ground pounder cheered.

Fugitive bellowed into a cloud, then erupted in pink mist before most of it landed on the fireline. Whatever stuck together splatted in the woods with the sound of a cow unloading on a flat rock and rivuleted down the slope in little oddly colored brooks.

"That one didn't do much good," Blanco radioed the P-3.

"Winds are getting gusty aloft," the pilot responded.

It *wasn't* Blanco's imagination. The wind *was* picking up.

"That ridge is so steep most of the retardant is going to run off," the pilot said. "We might do better dropping right on the fire itself."

A DC-4 unloaded directly on the flames during the 5:00 P.M. bombing run. It flew a lower final to prevent less air dispersion of the retardant. The weight of a ton of thick wet Fugitive loosened rocks and boulders. A miniavalanche thundered down the ridge to the bottom of the west drainage and threatened to further avalanche onto busy I-70 traffic.

"IC, I recommend a chopper with a bucket," the DC-4 pilot declared. "A chopper would be much more efficient."

Lacking functional chain saws, unable to wrangle a helicopter and bucket off the Wake fire, Blanco's exhausted firefighters found themselves waging a losing battle. By 5:00

P.M. less than four hundred feet of handline cut down the west face of the ridge. Active flames were approaching the line and bluffing to make an end run around it to the oak thickets. Blanco and Ryerson put their heads together.

"We're not accomplishing anything," Ryerson argued. "It'll be dark before long."

Blanco pondered. He was as stubborn as any Marine; someone once said of him that the word *retreat* did not appear in his vocabulary. Still, he had his firefighters to think of. They were without adequate tools and sufficient support. He accomplished nothing by driving them into the ground.

"Okay," he finally agreed. "It's out of here for the night so we can repair the saws. We'll start again at daybreak."

Downslope, the fire monster flapped and yawned and stretched and cracked dead branches on the ground with the dreaded sound of breaking bones.

"Goddamn him, he's taunting us," someone grumbled. "He knows he's won the first fight."

Blanco was still on the radio. "Don't give up yet," he snapped.

Dispatch had just radioed him the news. There should have been bugle charges in the background, a swell of drums and horns. Dispatch said, "IC, smokejumpers are on the way. You should have a load of jumpers on the ground within the hour."

14

EACH YEAR DURING THE WINTER THE U.S. FORest Service and the BLM sent out letters to their smokejumpers setting dates for them to report for refresher training. WAEs (When Actually Employeds) were guaranteed at least six months and one day annual employment; regular temps who had not yet worked themselves up to

WAE status were not even guaranteed a letter. Once the jumpers reported for refresher, they relinquished their lives and destinies to the National Fire Control Center in Boise and to Fate, God or coincidence, according to one's beliefs. During the season they seldom knew where they might sleep at night or where they might work the next day. They became pawns on a giant chessboard spotted with flames.

"Don't come into this business seeing only the adventure and romance," tough trainers scolded rookies in jump school. "The only job in the world harder or more dangerous than this one is that of soldiers in actual combat. If you got any illusions about it, now's the time to take them outside and stomp 'em flat. Listen to me, kids: *You can get killed in this business*.

"The first thing that can happen is your parachute malfunctions. If you don't learn what to do about that in rookie school, you can drop three thousand feet to your death. Even if it works okay, you can fly into the side of a cliff and break your neck. A spruce can splinter when you land on it and ram through your guts."

Brent "Big Johnson" Johnson listened to such a welcoming speech on April 28, 1992, at the BLM jump school in Boise, Idaho. He and ten other rookies—ten men and one woman—filed silently, even a bit apprehensively, into the small briefing room at the school. The trainer did nothing to ease their apprehensions.

He wore a blue "Smokejumper" ball cap and a fitted BLM shirt. His body looked as though it were chiseled out of Sawtooth granite. He looked like he could tuck any recruit in the class underneath one arm and jog with him to the birches on top of the hill outside the compound and back and work up not much more than an appetite. After warning the rookies that hell was what they could expect for the next four weeks, he lapsed into all the reasons why they should not become smokejumpers.

It could get them killed in various and grotesque ways.

"The worst death imaginable," he said, "is to get caught in a blowup and burn to death. You don't want to see what a fire can do to living flesh, so I'll tell you about it.

"Flames poison the air and superheat it so that it cooks your lungs. It gives you edema and you drown in your own lung fluids. You'll probably be dead before the blaze reaches you—but God help you if you're unlucky enough to still be alive when you start to burn. . . .

"You're going to be called upon to risk your lives for people you've never seen before, for *their* lives and *their* property. For that risk, you'll start out getting paid about nine dollars an hour. Plus overtime. You'll get lots of overtime during a good fire season. But you can lose it all if you get your leg broke or your neck broke and end up a carrot for the rest of your life. Uncle Sugar will give you Social Security. You can't expect much more than that."

He paused for effect, looked over the rookies with his critical eye. Johnson dared not take his eyes off the front. Neither did anyone else.

"If you have any small injury at all when training starts, you're not going to make it through," the DI continued. That was how Johnson already thought of him—the DI, drill instructor. John Wayne, maybe, or Clint Eastwood. "If you're hesitant or have doubts about your ability to jump out of a perfectly good airplane, then speak up now because you're not going to make it."

Brent Johnson had no doubts. He already knew the fire monster, had cast his destiny to the smoke by working summers with the Blueridge Hotshots in Arizona, his home state. He was twenty-eight years old that spring and in great shape. Every inch of his six-foot-plus frame was classic Westerner, from the loose thatch of light brown hair and chiseled jaw to the worn and rugged logger boots. He was quiet-spoken and introspective, a perfect model for Owen Wister's gentle but tough hero in *The Virginian.* His hobby was bird-watching. He possessed an abiding love for the outdoors and an even deeper love for God. He often carried a Bible in his backpack.

Brent and his older brother Brian had grown up competitive but inseparable after their parents divorced when Brent was in the fourth grade. There were just the two rough boys, their mother and the Great Arizona Outdoors. Brian enlisted in the army not long after he finished high school and volunteered as a paratrooper for the U.S. Army Special Forces, the famed Green Berets. He stayed in Special Forces and constantly urged his brother to enlist and join him.

"I can't do that," Brent said. "I'd like to parachute, but I can't enlist."

"Why not?"

"I can't."

Something about the gypsy in his soul required more freedom, less structure and more access to wild and lonely places than even the Green Berets offered. Most smokejumpers, as well as others of a similar breed, possessed an inherent aloneness in their souls that demanded communion with aloneness.

After completing high school, Brent bounced around here and there across the West competing in triathalons, sporadically showing up for classes at the University of Arizona and fighting fires during the season. Whatever niche God had planned for him eluded him until he attended tech school to become an airplane mechanic and met a tanker bomber pilot from Montana. The guy teased young Brent with hairraising tales about the escapades of smokejumpers he had known.

"Brent, you're built for it," the pilot said. "It's the life for a guy like you who stays in good shape and has a gypsy in his soul."

The Bureau of Land Management ran two smokejumper schools, one at Boise, Idaho, and the other at Fort Wainwright, Alaska. The U.S. Forest Service ran five or six more scattered about the West in places like Missoula, Montana, and Redding, California. Johnson applied to all of them. One morning in early April he received a telephone call.

"Brent Johnson? Your application has been accepted for the next smokejumper rookie school."

"Great!"

He paused.

"Uh, which school is this?"

"The next one."

"I mean, *where* is it?"

"Boise."

Now that he had been accepted and arrived to start training, no tough-talking DI was going to frighten him out of it.

"Have I scared you shitless yet?" the DI asked, curling up the edges of his hard lips. "I won't say a word if you get up right now and walk out of here. Hell, I wouldn't blame you for a second if you did. I won't even *look* at you. You may be the only one in the bunch with good sense."

None of the rookies got up and walked out. They almost never did. They came here to cast their destinies to the wind and Fate and the U.S. Government's National Fire Control Center.

The DI grinned a truly evil grin. "Any questions before Hell Week begins?"

"One," piped up a female voice. "Where's the bathroom?"

15

THOSE FEW RECRUITS WHO ATTENDED MILITARY parachute school before enlisting with the smokejumpers claimed the fire service rookie schools were much tougher, even though they were patterned after Fort Benning's U.S. Army Parachute School. The smokejumper school was four weeks long, while Fort Benning's was three. The U.S. Army required five parachute jumps using the uncomplicated military round-canopy Dash-One in order for its troopers to win their wings; smokejumpers made eighteen to twenty jumps during training. They jumped sophisticated steerable wings.

The army drop zone was a flat grassy field over a mile

long and nearly that wide. Smokejumpers shoe-horned themselves into tree-surrounded clearings not much larger than the area covered by the average American house.

Hell Week both at Benning and at Boise consisted mostly of physical training and conditioning. "Units" training followed. Future parachutists learned to exit an airplane in flight by using ground aircraft "mock-ups," how to deploy their canopies, how to land successfully and cope with any emergencies. Actual parachuting began after the second week. The BLM moved its rookies to Alaska to rookie jump out of Fort Wainwright near Anchorage.

In between parachute training, smokejumpers endured long classroom sessions studying techniques and strategies of battling flames and the role of the smokejumper.

"We are strictly initial attack," trainers stressed. "We carry everything we need with us when we go in. That makes us low-maintenance. We're fast. We can reach a fire and put it out before it spreads enough to require overhead teams and expensive tactics. We're very cost-efficient. That makes us indispensable during budget cuts."

Students lived in military-type barracks during training. Each morning at 5:00 the DIs slammed open the barracks' doors and sounded wakeup that would have made any Marine DI proud: "All right, girls. Drop your cocks and grab your socks. Fire is nipping at your asses."

Females lived in separate quarters. Johnson assumed they were awakened more genteelly. Kathy, the girl who asked about the bathroom after orientation, was the only female in Johnson's class of eleven rookies. Not all eleven would make it through the course.

The first morning of training began in the crisp mountain air of dawn with a mile-and-a-half run into the Boise National Forest. The run ended with push-ups, pull-ups, sit-ups and a three-mile pack-out. Superb conditioning was essential. Fire fighting was hard physical labor. Often, due to lack of helicopters and roads in many parts of the West, firefighters fought flames day and night for two or three days and *then* they had to load all their equipment—chain saws, extra fuel, sleeping bags, tools and whatever else—into their pack-out bags and hike out. The weight of an individual pack-out bag was about 110 pounds, not much lighter than the average weight of the three female smokejumpers currently on active duty. A three-miler was a long pack-out in Colorado or Arizona where ranch and logging roads webbed the countryside, but twelve-milers were common in Montana and the North Cascades.

Kathy was taller and more muscular than the average woman. She tucked her brunette hair into a ponytail, flashed a grin that sparked with good humor in the square jaw of her tanned face and easily made the runs.

"That girl can *move!*" one of the men gasped with both surprise and reluctant approval.

The rookie training day also ended with a run and more calisthenics. The class made five-mile runs to the birches at the top of the hill outside the compound by the end of the first week. They dropped for one hundred push-ups, then ran five miles back. They ran in-line one behind the other. An instructor jogged at the head of the formation to one side. At his command, the last rookie in line sprinted past the other runners and joined the DI. The DI asked him a question drawn from classroom instruction.

"How many square feet in a Quantum?"

If the rookie answered correctly, he took his place at the head of the line. The DI repeated the process by barking for the next trainee.

"Rook, what's your fifth Standard Fire Order?"

"Remain in communication with crew members, your supervisor and adjoining forces, sir."

"Wrong. That's your sixth. Get down for ten."

The errant rookie dropped for ten push-ups. Then he had to spring up and overtake the fast-moving line in order to take his place at its head. The instructor continued questioning the rookies throughout the ten-mile run. Push-ups and sprinting to catch up soon sapped the strength of any rookie caught unprepared. He dared not lag behind for fear of being evicted from the course.

"Rook, who made the first fire jump?"

"Earl Coolley and Rufus Robinson, sir."

"Good. Next?"

"Rook, when and where was the first fire jump made?"

"Winthrop, Washington, sir. In 1939."

Ed, a young guy built like a tank who lived in Boise, developed shin splints on the second day's run. On the third day he hobbled and lurched through the entire run. On the fourth day he lagged far behind. Brent Johnson gestured for him to "Come on!" Equal portions of pain and determination wrote themselves huge across the kid's square farmer's face.

"I won't quit," he told Johnson. "My leg might fall off, but I'll make it on one leg if I have to."

Instructors called Ed out of class after the fifth morning's run. He was gone by that afternoon. Johnson paused in front of the empty bunk. It was stripped, the mattress folded back on itself.

It wouldn't be the last empty bunk.

Kathy had no problems with the runs and the physical conditioning. She often kept up with Johnson on the free runs. She led the class academically. Her only problem surfaced after the evening meal one day when she and Johnson and a couple of the other students strolled out to the mock-up field. They hesitated at the base of the forty-foot tower.

"What's wrong, Kathy?" Johnson asked.

The lines on her young face had frozen into a mask of fright as she looked up at the tower.

"Kathy?"

Her face turned pale.

"Nothing," she said.

Rookies studied parachute dynamics, the proper wear and use of jump equipment, how to select jump spots, how to load onto an aircraft. Johnson packed so many cargo bundles that he could do it with his eyes closed. Into each rectangular cardboard box went food, water, sleeping bags, break-down shovels and Pulaskis, maps, tree climbers and maybe a chain saw and fuel. The fire packs were attached to small round cargo chutes, which were dropped low to the jumpers once they were on the ground. Each pack contained sufficient supplies and gear to sustain two firefighters for two days.

Rookies also studied jump history, chain of command, fire behavior and pack-outs. Always, every spare moment, they practiced emergency procedures. All through the day—at lunch, on the runs, in the classroom—instructors suddenly shouted out the name of an emergency. It was just practice, but the trainees' hearts pounded from adrenaline. What was practice *now* might be *real* in a week.

"Backlock!"

"Spin!"

"Blown panel!"

"Tangled lines!"

"Tree landing!"

"Water landing!"

"Highline landing!"

Any damned thing could happen. As soon as a DI barked out the emergency, rookies leaped to their feet and panto-mimed going through the correct procedure. Whatever was called for: cut away the main and deploy the reserve; tuck in arms to protect your face and cross your ankles to keep a splintered tree from ramming up your ass. One of the rookies suggested an emergency procedure of his own.

"Pray," he said, "and then bend over and kiss your ass good-bye."

"Emergency procedures must come as second nature," instructors preached. "You're falling at one hundred twenty miles per hour. At that speed, folks, you don't have time to think about what you're going to do. You must react on raw instinct—or end up on earth like a smashed strawberry."

Another student washed out because he couldn't get his emergency procedures down. Johnson walked by the new empty bunk and avoided looking at it.

The rookies also practiced their getaway times. They had to don their jumpsuits and parachutes and be ready to climb onto the airplane within two minutes after the sounding of an alarm. They went through the procedure at least one hundred times.

"Hit it!" someone yelled and started the timing.

They scrambled into their heavy one-piece coveralls with the Kevlar padding, into their boots, helmets and face masks. Then came parachutes, reserves and PG bags. Snapping buckles, jerking loose ends, securing, tying down, pulling together . . .

"Countdown! Thirty-two seconds . . . thirty-one . . . thirty . . . twenty-nine . . ."

"Got it!"

"Huh-uh, Johnson. You fucked up. Your helmet strap isn't tight."

Jump procedures became routine before the rookies ever climbed into an airplane. In his dreams Big Johnson practiced with RAM-air parachutes he had not yet flown. Instructor monologues raced through his head.

"The RAM-air with its hollow cells produces a twenty mph forward speed on a calm day. That means if the wind is twenty mph and you're running downwind, you'll hit the ground traveling forty mph. You're going to plow up the mountainside with your face. . . .

"If you're flying into an open ridge, go into a glide and transition into a flare at the last moment. But if you're dropping into a hole, you don't have that option. You'll have to come in steep with deep brakes and hold. If you come in too steep, you'll stall the canopy and drop out of the sky."

The rookies knew how the jumping was done. A spotter located the jump spot somewhere off the fire's flanks, if possible. The pilot circled the jump spot at about four hundred feet AGL (Above Ground Level) to let the jumpers look it over for rocks and snags and other obstacles. Then the ship climbed back to fifteen hundred feet to release the drift streams to test wind direction, velocity and behavior.

All jumps were made at three thousand feet AGL. Two jumpers hooked up their drogue static lines to the overhead cable. They either jumped together as "wind dummies" to further test the wind, or one jumped alone. He sat in the door, legs hanging out into space. The other jumper stood next to him.

"Get ready!" the spotter shouted.

A hard slap on the shoulder meant *"Go!"*

When the wind dummy landed, he radioed the circling aircraft, giving corrections for wind and advising on hazards, flight approach and anything else that might affect the other jumpers. He might hold up a colored wind streamer to help guide the rest of the stick on their landings. No more than two parachutists jumped on each subsequent pass until all were inserted. The first jumper on the ground became fire incident commander unless someone else was already assigned.

"We can do it," Johnson said.

"Aaargh!" said the others.

"Piece of cake," Kathy said.

Someone observed that she got sick to her stomach just thinking about parachuting. Even standing at the foot of the forty-foot tower made her pale. She wet her lips, but they remained dry. She stared up four stories at the small structure mounted on stilts. Its door represented the open door of an aircraft. Cables ran past the door and were anchored in a mound of soil one hundred yards away downfield.

The tower was the last step before the airplane. It was from it that rookies learned to exit an aircraft and experienced the feel of parachuting. One by one they hooked their harness risers to the cables and plummeted out the door on command. After a "free fall" of about ten feet, the cables jerked them up short, simulating the "parachute" opening. As they slid down the long cable to the mound of soil, they practiced toggle control and prepared for landing. Instructors shouted out emergencies and tested the students on their reactions.

The door at the top of the stilts looked tiny and far away from the ground. Kathy murmured her fearful opinion that from *up there* the ground looked even farther away.

"I suppose you've all guessed it by this time," Kathy finally admitted. "I'm terrified of heights."

The others looked at her, then looked away, not surprised by her confession. This girl proposed to parachute from an *airplane?* Inevitably, someone pointed out the obvious: "You don't jump from an airplane while it's on the ground."

Kathy set her pale jaw. "I can do this," she said. "I *will* do it."

She refused to look up at the tower again. She walked around pale over the weekend before the Monday that started the dreaded tower and jump weeks. The rooks finally had to put theory into practice.

"You gonna be able to go out that door when it's time?" Johnson asked her.

"I have to."

Big Johnson climbed the tower stairs at the head of the line when the big day arrived. Kathy straggled tight-mouthed and tense at the end of the line.

"We'll winnow the wheat from the chaff starting today," promised the DI with the granite torso.

Johnson stood in the door looking down at the DIs four floors down. The day had not yet drained the red out of the morning sun.

"Jump!"

Johnson hurtled into space, concentrating on body position, on counting before pulling the release handle to his "main parachute."

"One-thousand-one . . . one-thousand-two . . . one-thousand-three . . . one-thousand-four . . . one-thousand-five . . . *Five seconds . . .*"

Pull! Pull the main!

It *was* a piece of cake.

Rookies gathered at the foot of the tower when Kathy took her position in the door. They saw her eyes fix on the horizon. She would not look down. Her eyes glazed over like hardened glass.

"Get ready!" the "spotter" commanded.

Kathy gripped the edges of the door. Death grips.

Hard slap on her shoulder. *"Go!"*

She froze in the door. Trembling started in her arms and edged into the rest of her body.

"*Go!*"

Johnson and the other rookies shouted encouragement from below.

"Kathy, goddamnit! Get your pretty ass out of that door! Don't think about it, Kathy. Do it!"

The grueling runs, hours and days of closeness in the classrooms, the stress of challenge and the triumph of accomplishments had built the class into a solid team. The fires of hardship and impending danger had forged the rookies into a closeness most of them had never known before and might never know again. Only people who faced danger as a part of their lives understood those kinds of bonds.

Kathy's classmates *willed* her to jump out that door.

"*Kathy!*"

They saw the effort it took to steel her mind against her fears. It was a physical effort as well as a mental effort. Her eyes remained riveted on the horizon. She drew in a deep, deep breath.

And she jumped.

Even the instructors cheered.

In the best of all worlds, the brave young woman would have made it the rest of the way. But the world of reality is not a novel. It is simply reality. Kathy never overcame her fear of heights. She went out the tower door again and again, but she froze again on the cable and barely remembered her name, much less the steps in her emergency procedures.

One other student washed out before her. He succumbed to fatigue, lost his drive, and then his bunk was empty. The men left quietly when they flunked out. Failure embarrassed them. Kathy, however, packed her bags while tears streamed down her cheeks. She hugged everyone and cried some more. Then, head hanging, tears washing her pretty face, she left.

That was the last anyone saw of her.

Seven survivors out of the original class of eleven flew to Alaska to make their qualifying jumps at Fort Wainwright.

They looked over an old army cargo plane, a Sherpa, that would take them aloft the next day for their first jumps. A DI drove them out to check the landing zones. The "large spot" was an open meadow about three times the size of a football field.

"When you can hit this one with no problem," the DI said, "we'll give you the 'small spot.'"

That evening after chow, Brent Johnson slipped off alone. The wild Alaskan tundra began almost at the barracks' door. He buttoned his light jacket against the crisp night. Stars shined brighter here than anywhere else in the world, brighter even than over the Arizona deserts. Johnson had already fallen in love with this wild and lonely land.

He felt content, whole. Jumpers believed in this thing called Fate. Fate had been good to Brent "Big Johnson" Johnson to bring him to this point.

A voice interrupted his thoughts. "Thinking about tomorrow?"

One of the other rookies had also ventured into the darkness. They stood silently shoulder to shoulder, looking into the night past the rugged upthrusting of mountains to the jumps they would make and the fires they would battle. Their eyes lifted together to the skies above the mountains. Johnson recalled a saying he liked. It wasn't from his Bible, he didn't think, but it seemed to fit.

All men die—but a few learn to live before they die.

16

THE FIRE MONSTER HAD SO FAR DEVOURED three houses but no lives during his outbreak on the mesas above Paonia. Tanker pilots Wilson and Dahl bombed the Wake fire fourteen times in three days. Helitack Rich Tyler fell into bed dead-tired each night from hours of ferrying firefighters and making bucket drops. On Tuesday afternoon, July 5, with the Wake fire under a fire management team, George Steele and the other smokejumpers demobed to Grand Junction to get ready to sky-attack Storm King Mountain or one of the other blazes on the western slopes. Their names went back on "The List."

Smokejumpers arriving from Montana, Idaho, Oregon and other western states dumped their gear beneath the trees in front of the jumpers' shack at WSFCC. Their names went immediately on The List.

The List made determinations on who went where. Names came up on lists to boost from Washington to Idaho or from Arizona or New Mexico to Colorado. Names rotated to the tops of the lists and whoever's name came up next caught the next boost or the next fire jump. The List sent Tony Petrelli, George Steele, Tim Pettitt, Brent Johnson, among others, to Colorado during the 1994 fire season. Where and when they jumped depended upon The List. It was that simple—or that complicated—according to what one believed about it.

Either coincidence in a random, unplanned and unstructured universe haphazardly determined the makeup of a particular list—or Fate, orderly and predetermined, manipulated it with his bony fingers and guided individuals to their inescapable destinies.

Had smokejumper Don Mackey foreseen the future the afternoon of July 5 when he stepped from Casa jump plane 117BH at Walker Field, he may have taken one look at the thin streamers of smoke rising from the mountains to the east and climbed right back into the airplane. But, of course, it is seldom within man's power to see the future. Besides, Mackey wasn't built to run away from anything. His friend and fellow jumper, Quentin Rhoades, always thought of Mackey as having the "right stuff."

Mackey's imposing appearance came not so much from his physical stature—he was somewhat short of six feet—as from some inner strength. At thirty-four years old, he had wavy sandy hair that sprayed down over a broad forehead. Hazel eyes, or brown or blue according to the way light struck them, slanted out of an intelligent face tanned and lined from long years in the sun. When he grinned, which was often, it was an infectious thing that transformed him instantly into a reckless, younger Burt Reynolds looking for mischief.

"His love of the outdoors and hunting and being with his friends was what brought him to smoke jumping," said his friend Melissa Wegner, a member of the Bitteroot Hotshots.

It was Mackey's eighth year jumping fires. Born in Sacramento, California, he moved with his family to Montana's Bitteroot Valley in 1968 when he was eight years old. The lure of wildfire hooked him in 1985 when he volunteered to help fight a Montana forest fire. Two years later he became a smokejumper with the U.S. Forest Service's Missoula detachment.

Eight years and he had suffered no serious injuries.

He stepped down from the Casa onto the sun-steaming tarmac in front of WSFCC. Seven other jumpers followed him out and unloaded their gear. They had been pulled off a fire near Santa Fe that morning to reinforce firefighters on Colorado's western slopes. Mackey had heard that another booster of nine jumpers would arrive that evening, followed by a contingent of hotshots from Oregon or Washington.

He blinked against the afternoon sun and glanced at his watch: 3:15 P.M. Christ, it was hot. He shouldered the long red PG bag containing his gear and strolled across the ramp to the Ops building. A tanker bomber was taking on Fugitive in front of it. Quentin Rhoades carrying his own gear fell into step with his friend. Behind them ranged the other six jumpers, including Sarah Doehring, one of only three women during the past seven years to have endured the rigorous training to join one of the most elite bands in the world.

Laconic George Steele was repacking his chute and gear for the next alarm. He watched from the tree shade in front of the jumpers shack, picking out the several familiar faces he had gotten to know over the years. He knew Mackey and Sonny Soto and Rhoades. He didn't know Doehring. Most of the jumpers knew Mackey. Big Johnson liked the guy; Tim Pettitt had made jumps with him.

The newcomers arrived dressed for action—old jeans or army camouflage BDUs or Nomex fire-resistant trousers still black-stained from previous fires. Their logger boots were scuffed and cracked, like they had trod a hundred miles through hell. The smokejumpers, crazy, reckless, the best of American youth, goosed each other and shouted playful insults and challenges, as young, wild, physical things will do. They were free and independent spirits, true Westerners liberated by ancestors whose pioneer spirits had provoked them to cross the Mississippi for the unsettled lands beyond.

On the flight over from Santa Fe, Mackey seemed touched by one of those periods of deep sadness that caught up with him occasionally after his divorce from Rene last November. Mackey was a tough guy with that macho way of hiding his emotions. Yet, sometimes the crust cracked when Mackey was with Rhoades or some of his other jumper friends. Sometimes, late at night when the fire fighting was over and they were coming down after a few beers, Mackey talked about it. Losing Rene had rubbed Mackey's heart raw.

"I love her," he said simply after spring refresher training started.

Divorce was the smokejumpers' disease. Mackey sipped a beer. He seldom drank much, but he sipped his beer and looked at Rhoades. Looked around the table where he felt emotionally safe with his own kind. He talked about the divorce.

The job had driven his wife away. That had to be it. Rene always dreaded the long separations, the waiting, the uncertainty of never knowing when and *if* her husband would come home again. War wives grew apart from mates shipped overseas during Vietnam and Desert Storm. Smokejumpers left their mates and went to war *every* year.

"It's like we have to get reacquainted each autumn when you come home again," Rene said. "Your own son and daughters hardly know you sometimes."

Mackey talked about his hurt that one time and he seldom talked about it again.

"It's either her or the job," his friends said.

Chasing fires, jumping out of airplanes, it was addictive. It was a job for pioneers who suffocated from a routine nine-to-fiver.

"The fire gets in your blood," jumpers said. "You want to go out and defeat it."

"It's an adrenaline rush," they said. "It's also falling down cliffs, dodging dead trees, rocks falling on you, breathing thick smoke and not knowing where you are."

It was *smoke jumping*. It wasn't just what you did; it was what you *were*.

Mackey wasn't sure he could have saved his marriage even if he quit fire fighting. He remembered an old saying: *I wouldn't be me if I became what you wanted me to be.*

Unlike some jumpers' ex-wives, Rene held no grudges after the divorce. Her lifestyle, after all, didn't change that much. Even before the divorce Mackey mounted the steel bird each spring to go out and joust fires and she and the three kids might not see him again until November. She remained in Hamilton, Montana, after the formal parting—she and her thirteen-year-old daughter from a previous marriage, along with Mackey's own four-year-old son and his daughter who would turn six on July 7. Mackey was a good father to them—whenever he was home. Rene always spoke fondly of him; maybe she still loved him even if she couldn't live with that Gypsy in his soul.

"He's as much a dad to his stepdaughter as to the other kids," Rene said. "He's an excellent hunter. He loves traps and collects them. He's an excellent carpenter. He loves smoke jumping and he's good at it. He's really good at it. He's good at everything he does."

Whenever Quentin Rhoades saw the sadness in Mackey, he knew Mackey was thinking of Rene and his children.

"What's the day of the week?" Mackey asked as the jumpers trudged toward the WSFCC Ops building. You often lost track of time fighting fires.

"Tuesday," Rhoades said. "Yesterday was Fourth of July. We missed the celebrations again this year."

"My daughter's birthday is Thursday," Mackey said

softly, as though reminding himself. His eyes lifted from the desert flats toward the sudden brown swelling of the Rockies to the east. "On Thursday we'll probably be up there ass-deep in the devil's playground."

"Have you called your daughter?"

"I will. One way or another I'll get to a telephone on Thursday to wish her Happy Sixth Birthday."

The resolution appeared to lift his sadness.

Smokejumper coordinator Rick Blanton met the incoming jumpers in the Ops building. Stress sweat greased his brow.

"Get your jump gear ready," he barked immediately after greetings.

"Well, *buenos dias* to you too," quipped Sabinio Archuleta.

"You want overtime, you'll *get* overtime in Colorado," Blanton shot back. "We have an outstanding jump request from the Storm King Mountain incident. Your names are already at the top of the list."

Archuleta flashed white teeth. *"Amigos,* it's show time!"

It was indeed just a matter of whose name came up when that determined who went where. The List selected a stick of eight jumpers for the first airborne assault on Storm King because the jumpers arrived at the right moment. Blanton manifested the jumpers: Don Mackey, jump supervisor; Keith Woods; Quentin Rhoades; Sarah Doehring; Sonny Soto; Sabinio Archuleta; Kevin Erickson; and Eric Shelton.

He gave them their prejump briefing outside in the shade while pilot Kevin Stalder and jumper-spotter Sean Cross prepared the DHC-6 Twin Otter for flight. He told them that District had an IC, Butch Blanco, and six firefighters on the mountain, but they were about to retreat for the night due to equipment problems. The fire had now grown to at least thirty acres and was still moving on all aspects. It posed no immediate threat to structures. A cold front was expected to blow through tomorrow.

"Winds?" Mackey asked.

"Keep listening to the Weather Channel," Blanton advised.

Scarcely two hours after the jumpers from Santa Fe arrived in Grand Junction, they suited-up and chuted-up and, looking like moon walkers, crawled into the narrow-tubed body of the BLM's Twin Otter. They sat on hard plastic seats facing each other, so close their knees meshed in the aisle. Stalder revved up the engines and released brakes. Sean Cross, the spotter, occupied the copilot's seat. He turned in his harness as the aircraft taxied for takeoff. He threw up his hands to attract the jumpers' attention above the roaring hum of the engines.

"ETA to the fire," he shouted, "is twenty-five minutes."

"Aaargh!" the jumpers responded, adrenaline already pumping. "Let's *do* it!"

It was what they had trained to do. They were born to rise in the air on artificial wings like Icarus and unite air, earth and fire, three of the world's four natural elements. In Greek mythology, Icarus flew so high that the sun melted the wax that held his wings together and he fell into the sea and drowned.

17

THE AFTERNOON AIR LAY CALM AT ALTITUDE. Below the Otter, the browns of the flats around Grand Junction gave way to darker foothills splotted with green. The green thickened and bunched into the craggy high reaches of the Rockies. South of the aircraft's flight path rose a thick column of smoke from the Wake fire at Paonia. Ahead, in the distance, more smoke smudged the peak of Storm King. The fire there had been elevated in status and assigned its own fire case serial number; it was now known officially as BLM District Fire V-891.

The pilot picked out I-70 and followed it toward Glenwood Springs. Don Mackey sat next to the jump door. As supervisor, he would also double as wind dummy and go out the door on the first jump pass. He rested his chin in his hands on top of his reserve parachute. Rhoades sat across the aisle between Shelton and Soto. Mackey's helmet and thick-wired face mask blocked Rhoades' view of his friend's face. Mackey gave him a thumbs-up. Rhoades felt rather than saw the Bert Reynolds grin. Rhoades grinned too. It was good to have the old Don Mackey back.

The thudding of the engines made conversation difficult. It thrust each jumper deep inside himself where he faced the little animal fear that always squirmed out of hiding just before a combat jump. Everyone had his own way of coping with it. Most of them felt the urge to make contact with another human being before the ultimate aloneness of leaping into space. Erickson gave Sonny Soto's knee a tap with his fist. Sarah Doehring rested her hand on Woods's arm. Mackey lifted his head to look out the little window in the fuselage behind him. He thought of what he might get his daughter for her birthday.

Tanker-127 came up on the VHF channel. The plane was returning to Walker Field after its 5:00 P.M. drop that started the miniavalanche off the Storm King ridge. Butch Blanco had sounded strained at the failures of the drops. The old slurry that misted and put out fires would have worked much better than the Fugitive.

"Terrain is exceptionally steep at the fire," T-127 radioed the Otter full of jumpers. "I doubt if bombing it did any good; the stuff just rolls off. You're going to have a tough time finding a place to drop jumpers."

"Tanker-127, thanks for the intel," Cross the spotter replied over the channel. "We can stick jumpers into some mighty small places."

He rode the copilot's seat with his hands folded in his lap. He peered ahead through the wide windscreen toward Fire V-891. Rugged terrain up ahead.

"If we *can't* find a jump spot," he commented to Stalder,

"you'll have to land at the Glenwood airport and unload them there."

He cast a guilty glance at the ready jumpers behind him. Jumpers hated pounders. *Walking* into a fire was almost insulting.

Ten minutes away. Cross contacted IC Butch Blanco on the radio.

"The fire's still on the ground and not rolling," Blanco advised. "It's not posing much of a problem at this time. We've been fighting it for over five hours, but both our chain saws are now down. We're pulling out for the night for resupply and repairs, but if you *can* get jumpers in, we can sure use 'em."

Cross noted the smoke rising from the ridge ahead was gray-white instead of black. That was a good sign. It meant a slow-moving fire. Gray smoke rolled up lazily in a thin column. The column bent slightly toward the east with the late-afternoon westerly breeze. Winds that had been fairly stiff aloft not a half-hour ago were now light.

The plane approached from the west with I-70 below. Cross caught his first relieflike view of the fire and the terrain in which it burned. He estimated the blaze at about thirty or forty acres. The black of the burned area lay heavy about midway down the ridge. It spread slowly like spilled ink. Although from the air he saw few active flames through the smoke, Cross pinpointed the young monster's head creeping northeasterly upslope toward the Storm King peak. Its flanks and tail backed slowly downslope toward the west drainage.

The narrow etch of the uncompleted fireline ran off the tiny cleared space of the helispot on the ridge spine. Apparently, Blanco and his crew were attempting to cut off the fire from thick patches of lighter-colored green. Gambel oak stood out clearly from the darker green of the PJ.

Blanco's firefighters in their canary yellow shirts and helmets created bright patterns in the greens and browns below. In their retreat they had dropped off onto the eastern slope of the ridge into the east drainage. They paused upon hearing the aircraft's approach, their faces cast heavenward. Shadows from the summer sun's fall behind the mountains oozed into the drainage, slowly filling it.

The Otter made several low passes while the spotter and his jumpers scanned for a jump spot. They dismissed outright the helispot. It was too small, even for daredevil smokejumpers. The terrain on both sides fell off steeply and was cluttered with deadly obstacles.

"I can feel a pounder coming on," Kevin Erickson murmured, discouraged.

On the third pass, Cross pointed out where the ridge lowered and flattened into a saddle at the base of Storm King. From the saddle south the ridge spined as it approached the helispot.

"Let's take another look," the pilot said.

Cross left the cockpit and clambered into the rear of the crowded aircraft where he joined Mackey at the open door. Stalder circled the Otter and came around at five hundred feet AGL for a final observation pass. Mackey and Cross leaned far out the door into the wind to study the saddle. It passed beneath them. The fire was about a half-mile south-southwest.

"It's fairly flat and clear," Cross noted, shouting to be heard. "We can try it if the wind's right."

The plane made a fifteen-hundred-foot AGL pass for the wind streamer. The streamer fell almost straight down, fluttering gaily.

"We can do it," Mackey decided.

Erickson gave a sign of relief. Sarah Doehring volunteered to wind-dummy the first pass with Mackey. Cross helped them hook up and sit in the door. Mackey sat on the airborne platform, feeling the wind ride his boots back toward the tail of the airplane. Just another jump. He had had eight years of jumping and fire fighting.

The fire monster knew Don Mackey as a formidable enemy.

Mackey let his mind relax for a minute, only a minute, to enjoy the flight and the cool air at altitude and the grandeur of the Rocky Mountains passing below his feet. He felt alone and at peace, his mind sharp and clear and focused. This was Don Mackey's life.

"I'll wait to hear from you on the air/ground FM before dropping the rest of the stick," Cross yelled into the jumper's ear.

Mackey and Doehring together disappeared from the door. Easy jump. Mackey landed exactly in the middle of the saddle. Doehring flew a bit long of it, but still within acceptable limits.

"There's hardly any wind on the ground," Mackey radioed Cross. "You might tell the jumpers to hold up high when they come in to keep from drifting."

The remaining six jumpers reached earth safely. The Otter made several more passes to allow Cross to kick out the cargo chutes. Firefighters broke open the firepacks as they landed and distributed tools. They stowed excess gear in their red pack-out bags and hung the bags in trees to keep them safe from ground fire. Mackey used his hand radio to discuss tactics with Butch Blanco. Blanco remained at the helispot in the rear of his own troops' retreat until he knew the jumpers had landed safely.

The two leaders decided Blanco's direct attack was still the best approach to controlling the fire. Mackey and his squad would pick up Blanco's fireline and continue building it downslope into the west drainage to cut off the flames.

"We're pulling out, but we'll be back at first light," Blanco concluded. "The fire looks like we can catch it. It could become a problem if it bleeds into the drainage bottom and gets into the oak thickets. Good luck."

Otter 490AS dipped a wing in salute and set a course into the low sun toward Walker Field. Cross cast a last look at the activity in the saddle below before radioing his situation report to Grand Junction Dispatch. Eight smokejumpers on the ground. The elite had arrived. The enemy stood little chance against such determined and skilled troops.

By 7:00 P.M., still with two hours of good daylight remaining, the smokejumpers were tooled up and ready to put the fire out of its misery. As Mackey led them in a file up the ridge south from the saddle, they heard an occasional boulder bouncing down from where heat displaced it. A juniper torched, flaring in the smoke. Young, virile and confident, the jumpers charged into battle. The lines were drawn.

The fire monster waited, poised, grumbling and snapping and popping in the woods.

18

TAKE AWAY THE GLAMOUR OF THE PARACHUTE and fire fighting consisted mainly of hard labor the likes of which even convicts rarely endured. Mackey's smoke-jumpers, chain sawing aerial fuels and hacking fireline, worked to extend the boundary started by Blanco's crew.

Blanco, who had established a command post in Glenwood Springs, spoke to Mackey several times by radio during the afternoon and evening. Mackey was acting IC. As commander on the scene, he made the tactical decisions. Yet, even remarking, "I didn't feel the smokejumpers needed additional guidance," Blanco couldn't help pacing the floor and stepping outside now and again to cast anxious eyes toward Storm King Mountain. Blanco took his job seriously.

Although the Storm King blaze was small and slow-moving, several things about it troubled him. At the top of his concerns had to be the patches of gambel oak and the fire eating slowly toward them; flammable debris lay thick and heavy beneath the oaks and the trees grew so thickly in places that a man could hardly walk through them. Secondly, only eight firefighters remained on the mountain overnight, too few to handle the fire if it should get into the oaks and crown. They were on a direct attack, cutting fireline downhill. It bothered Blanco that the flames lay below them and when the fire monster charged he charged *uphill.* An unexpected change in wind velocity and direction might whip a blazing flank around the fighters in a sneak attack, encircling and trapping them in its pincers.

Blanco had been assured he could count on additional firefighters on Wednesday and perhaps an additional reinforcement on Thursday. Steve Hart, IC at Paonia, expected to control the Wake fire and free his troops within the next day or so. More than twenty smokejumpers had already demobed back to WSFCC late Tuesday afternoon. Blanco felt further encouraged to learn that an additional nine jumpers from Santa Fe had boosted to Walker Field at 10:00 P.M. and had bedded down in Grand Junction motels to rest up for early morning action on Storm King. The twenty-man Prineville Interagency Hotshot team had also been jerked off a lower-priority blaze in Oregon and flown to Walker Field to reinforce Colorado troops. The hotshots had arrived at 6:00 P.M. They were also fed and bedded down for the night. Blanco wanted them too.

"Hold what you can," Blanco advised Mackey over the air. "Don't take any chances. We have more jumpers and perhaps a contingent of hotshots on the way tomorrow. We should also start receiving firefighters from the Wake fire. We'll have that sucker stomped flat by tomorrow night."

The fire on the mountain kept its nose and paws to the ground. Approaching night calmed the winds even more. The blaze spread its black like a gradual cancer in the forest. By 8:00 P.M., even though the fire was slow-moving, it had nearly doubled in size from twelve hours previously. More than fifty blackened acres lay encased in a ring of fire.

Keith Woods leaned on his Pulaski for a quick breather. Tools banged against flintrock and sandstone, accented by the angry buzz of chain saws. The red of the fire reflected the red of the dying sun.

"The fire's picking up speed," he noted. "It's outrunning us."

"Then work faster," Sonny Soto challenged. "Don't you read what the press says about us? We're the storm troopers on Storm King Mountain."

Night fell on the mountain. It fell like a black cloak. No moon illuminated the mountain pinnacles. They rose black against the star-lightened sky. They seemed to stand in silent mock judgment over the puny efforts of the gallant band of young firefighters.

Using helmet lights and the firelight itself for illumination, the jumpers hacked away at the forest in a race against time. Firelight reflected an eerie red on the underbelly of the slowly boiling column of smoke. Dancing flames cast the fighters' shadows deeper into the forest, as though trying to expel them. Flames continued to crack in the forest with the sound of bones breaking. Loosened heated rock tumbled in unseen runways to the darkened bottom of the west drainage.

Mackey repeatedly scouted the fire. Ash and soot blackened his face. His high cheekbones glowed back the red of the approaching flames. Normally gifted with a wry bursting sense of humor off-duty, he became all-business in battle. He kept looking up from working to the scattering of lights to the west where Canyon Creek Estates nestled in the valley far below. They glittered hard like pinholes in a black cloak. Behind him, to the east, the lights of West Glenwood and Glenwood Springs sheened against drifting smoke.

Saving people and their dwellings was what fire fighting was all about. It could be a grim business at times. Mackey knew that residents in the valleys below were coming out of their houses to cast apprehensive eyes toward the mountain to gauge the fire's progress. Losses at nearby Paonia were all too fresh in their minds.

"If the fire gets a good hold underneath the oak patches and we get a strong wind in that cold front tomorrow . . ." the jumpers made a point of mentioning to Mackey.

"I know," Mackey said.

His voice grew taut.

"We could get a crown reburn . . ."

"I'm aware of it."

"That oak'll blow like a torch all the way to the top. The fireline won't hold shit."

"We'll do what we can. We'll widen the fireline when Blanco returns in the morning."

As the night progressed, glowing tongues of ground fire licked their way into the outer fringes of the gambel oak. They couldn't be stopped. Flames came up on line, emboldened by the abundance of fuel. They crawled up underneath the shrubby trees. They cracked and popped happily. They heated the air. They kiln-dried the low, thick crowns of the oaks. The green leaves, already dehydrated from drought, curled and cracked.

Mackey returned from a scouting mission, climbing heavily, his expression weary and resigned.

"Don?" Sarah Doehring asked quickly.

"No use," Mackey said. "It's already crossed to the west. There are active flames in the oak. Sarah, it's beat us tonight."

19

THE JUMPERS LOST THE RACE ON THE WEST slope. Mackey decided it was far too dangerous to continue work at night in the oaks. After a discussion with the others, he withdrew his small element to the ridgeline. They began cutting a new handline parallel to the ridge spine to prevent the blaze spreading east.

The slope proved steeper near the ridgeline than farther below. They worked in the dark with only their headlamps to guide them. The firefighters maintained precarious balance by gripping small trees and roots with one hand while they hacked away at the ground with the other. Cries of "Look out below!" and "Heads up!" punctuated the night as troops dislodged boulders and rock scree.

Shelton, Archuleta and Doehring were struck by flying rock. Mackey studied the soot-stained faces of his fighters.

They reflected the weary lines of a day of travel, a hazardous parachute jump and the grueling hours of hacking away at the mountain in the darkness.

Sarah Doehring spoke up when some of the others would not because of male macho pride.

"We're going to take injuries," she pointed out. "It's crazy working on this ridge at night."

Mackey knew it. He hated admitting defeat. They all hated it. The initial attack had failed. The fire kept moving, growing, eating deeper into the oaks. Nothing less than an extended attack force could stop the fire monster now. Eight firefighters fighting *this* blaze in the middle of the night was like pissing into a volcano to put **it** out. They had all underestimated it.

Mackey radioed Blanco's command post. It was 11:10 P.M. "Is it possible to lay on *two* Type I crews for tomorrow?" he asked.

Forty more troops. Type I crews, hotshots, were infantry ground pounders. Aside from smokejumpers, they were the most experienced and highly trained of all wildland firefighters.

"We're lucky if we get the *one* shot crew in the morning," Blanco replied. "But I'll do what they all keep telling me: I'll *try.*"

The exhausted jumpers gave up at midnight and withdrew to the cleared helspot.

"We won't be worth a damn tomorrow when the real fight starts," Mackey said, "unless we try to get a little rest."

They wrapped themselves in space blankets and poncho liners and whatever else they dug from their PG bags and tried to grab a few winks. The night air at this altitude, above six thousand feet ASL, smelled of frost, even in July. Sonny Soto cuddled into his covering and found a rock to lean against. He gazed downhill toward the fire. He could not see the flames from here. Occasionally a lone tree torched brightly. *That* he saw. Sleeping so near a fire made him uncomfortable. He shivered. He never thought he would miss the warmth of a good wood fire in July.

"Build a campfire," someone suggested, eliciting a tired spatter of soft laughter.

Someone snored. Erickson snacked. Soto closed his eyes and tried to sleep. Doehring watched Mackey as the leader stood silhouetted on the ridgeline against the eastern stars. There was now a moon. It glowed palely through the pall of smoke that hung above the ridge. Doehring knew Mackey would be thinking of the fire and how best to defeat it. Now, late at night when he was tired and lonely, he might also be thinking of Rene and of his daughter whose birthday he would miss on Thursday.

Combat troops often thought of home during lulls in the action. Especially at night.

"Nothing is forever," Mackey remarked once after his divorce. "You should never expect *forever*. All you got is one day at a time. There comes a day in all our lives when there will be no tomorrow."

It was after midnight and in the early morning hours of Wednesday, July 6. A freshening breeze scouting in advance of the predicted cold front whispered noisily through the dry oaks. It gently fluttered the covers of sleeping smoke-jumpers.

20

THERE WERE A THOUSAND WAYS TO DIE WHENEVER a blaze swept through the forest, wildland firefighters said—and each way was more horrible than the last. Sometimes you did everything right and the fire still got you. That was Fate. Fate always played a role. It made you wonder, like it made helitack Rich Tyler wonder when he drove the chase truck that day ten years ago, why Fate selected some and left others. Why two of you might be side by side, doing everything the same, and the fire monster snatched up the other guy and left you.

Virtually every firefighter has had his close calls. Smoke-jumpers by virtue of being smokejumpers as well as fire-fighters had more than their share. A good jumper could take a square Titan or Raven or Hercules parachute and fly it around the sky and land with the precision of an eagle perching on a dead snag. Parachutes were reliable most of the time—if the winds cooperated, the chute functioned properly without blowing a panel or tangling up in its own lines and the jumper didn't get thrown into a spin or back lock or land in the trees or in the fire.

It really *wasn't* a natural thing to jump out of a perfectly good airplane. There was *always* a risk. *Always* that one slim chance of something happening that wasn't supposed to happen. The fall never killed you; it was the sudden stop at the end.

Perhaps tempting Fate was what smoke jumping, what firefighting, was all about. It kept the adrenaline pumping.

"I wish you could have the feeling of your first jump and keep it forever," John "J.C." Curd said. "In a true sense, jumping never gets old. But you really wish you could capture the excitement of that first jump and keep it."

When the adrenaline flowed, life took on an intensity so keen that the environment assumed a texture almost palpable. Colors seemed brighter—the sky bluer, the earth greener. You felt like you could fly or leap tall buildings or run faster than a speeding train. You *felt* everything—wind in your face, the rough texture of your underwear, the memory of the first time you kissed a girl or made love. You felt blood pounding in your body. You felt your heart and lungs. You felt the day you were born—and at the same time you looked into eternity. Everything in your life from the day you shrieked out of the womb focused on that one inexplicable moment in time when you hurtled into space to fly. *Fly.*

Those who fight for their lives know an intensity of life the meek and timid shall never know. That was how Vietnam combat soldiers expressed the feeling.

J.C. Curd had made a total of 310 parachute jumps when

his name came up on The List that hot dry summer of 1994 and he boosted from Nevada to fight fire on Colorado's western slopes. At thirty-five years old, Curd stood six-three and broad-shouldered with blazing blue eyes, blond hair and a groomed mustache to match. His photograph should have been in the dictionary under the word *Smokejumper*.

For him, fire fighting proved a good way to get into the backcountry far away from people and the civilization that blighted nature. He got paid for hanging out in wild places. What more could he ask from life?

Unlike his friend George Steele and some of the others, Curd had never been seriously injured. Scrapes and bruises, of course, but never even a broken bone. Still, when he received his letter each spring and added his name to The List, he was aware that, in fire fighting, there *were* a thousand ways to die—and *he* never forgot that he almost experienced one of them.

Brent "Big Johnson" Johnson and Curd were both from Arizona. The BLM and the Forest Service liked smoke jumping rookies to break in on the great open tundra of Alaska before they drifted south into the Rockies and the Cascades and the Sawtooths. While Johnson made his Alaskan jumps to complete rookie school and then returned to the Lower Forty-eight, Curd remained in Alaska for the first five years of his fire career.

Airborne firefighters in Alaska at that time used old twin-engined Volpar almost exclusively. The boxy-looking aircraft held twenty jumpers at a load in its narrow belly and flew an airspeed of about 120 mph. Parachutes were also less than modern. Jumpers had not yet gone to square sports chutes. They jumped antiquated government-surplus T-10s, the same thirty-five-foot rounds used by the military. They were modified, however, to make them "steerable" by removing a partial panel. A "steerable" compared to a modern RAM-air square-wing chute was almost like comparing Wilbur and Orville Wright's first airplane at Kitty Hawk to an F-15 fighter plane. A jumper hanging below a T-10 was more or less at the mercy of the four wind gods.

One afternoon Curd scrambled out of Fort Wainwright on a four-manner to a ten-acre ground fire in thick vegetation. At jump altitude, three thousand feet, ice caked on the Volpar's silver skin. Sleet painted rind-ice on the drop-down step jumpers used to launch themselves into the gray sky. Curd braced himself on the step just one inch away from eternity. Snow and sleet flew past the airplane's wing and tail, stinging him through his padded jumpsuit like pellets fired from air rifles.

The earth crept past below in patches of dark green fir and spruce scabbed against the gray-green face of the rolling tundra. The fire burned in a great valley overgrown with timber. It had gone aerial at one end. Healthy winds whipped scarlet bands of flame through the treetops.

As soon as Curd's T-10 slammed open and grabbed air, the jumper knew they had fucked up in estimating the winds and selecting a jump spot. He drew around to face the wind, but the wind still pushed him backward toward the crowning head of the fire. An anxious glance down and back told him the bad news. He was going to land directly in the flames unless he took extraordinary measures.

To hell with the steering toggles; they were only marginally useful at this point anyhow. He released them and grabbed both risers. He tugged them almost to his knees. That pulled down the front edge of his canopy to release air out the back and give him additional forward speed.

The parachute sluffed and popped. Air rushed past as his drop accelerated. He tried to gauge his descent and forward track by measuring the speed of his boots overlaid against the earth below.

He was still drifting away from the jump spot and *toward* the fire. He was being sucked like a falling leaf directly into the flames. Rising heat singed the insides of his nostrils, burned his throat. Hot ashes swirled around him. He gasped for air as smoke and fear filled his lungs.

He stared deep and long and with rising terror into the fire monster's red gullet. The monster licked his awful chops in anticipation.

He jammed his handful of risers against his knees. The action bent him double hanging from his harness. It increased his rate of fall almost to the point of plunging out of the sky.

He dropped almost straight down.

It was his only chance.

He exploded through the conifer canopy not fifty yards ahead of the fast-running flames. Boots catching the tip of a spruce flipped him upside down and threw him crashing head down through the trees.

The ground rushed at him.

At the last moment, just before impact, his parachute caught and held. It checked his fall, but the spring of the limb upon which the chute snagged banged his helmeted head hard against the ground.

Everything went black.

When he came to, he found himself still entangled in his parachute lines and hanging upside down. The top of his helmet tapped the ground from the spring of the branches that suspended him by his parachute. He hardly had time to congratulate himself on his good fortune, however, before he realized the presence of even greater danger.

Still groggy, he heard what he thought to be a freight train closing in. Ice water replaced the cobwebs in his brain. He had almost forgotten about the fire in the excitement of his landing. Thick smoke bloated with poisonous gases eddied and sniffed around in the forest. Distant smoke-muted flames glowed at the trapped jumper like the gaping mouth of hell.

Within a few minutes, maybe no more than three or four, the monster with its flaming teeth would close on him.

Curd struggled desperately with his lines. The more he fought with them, the more entangled he became. Like a fly snarled in a spider's web.

"J.C.? Answer us!" echoed a call from deep in the forest. "Where are you, man?"

"Here! Here!"

The snapping and roaring of the avalanche of approaching flames and the trapped jumper's own pounding heart smothered his response. He still felt weak from the fall on his head. His eyes turned wide and white-rimmed toward the fire bounding through the tops of the trees toward him. Its intense heat seemed to suck the moisture from his body.

He fought the web that trapped him. Fought with a strength and intensity born out of desperation. *Don't let me die here trapped like a fly. Not like this.* Exhaustion, thirst, fear all warred inside his body, causing it to writhe and bounce and twist.

There could be a death no more horrible than to go up in flames. Curd knew how it would happen. Firefighters seldom talked about it, but they all knew how it would be.

Dying by fire began with naked terror as the monster charged in for his final bite. Gases ahead of the blaze robbed the air of oxygen, causing the victim to wheeze and gasp for breath as red and blue darts shot across his eyes. Lungs filled with fluids to repel the awful heat. If the victim failed to drown in his own body fluids, heat sucked out his breath and blood and finally his consciousness. It seared out his life, if he were lucky, before the flames reached his body and barbecued it like a steak dropped into coals.

Curd had a flash image of Gisborne's squirrel caught in the Half Moon fire.

Not like this!

He took a deep breath of the hot air. He had to concentrate. Panic killed.

He focused on his right hand. He eliminated everything from his mind except extricating himself one step at a time. It was like his hand moved in slow motion. It freed itself from the tangle of parachute lines and reached for the emergency capewell release on his chest. He felt suddenly so detached from his surroundings that even his hand could have been someone else's. The hand grasped the capewell.

The capewell opened, releasing him from that side of his harness.

He ignored the charging fire and reached for the opposite capewell. It opened. He tumbled free of the parachute and the tree that held him. He leaped to his feet and ran from the flames that sounded like a train emerging from a tunnel. He didn't look back.

J.C. Curd, Don Mackey, Butch Blanco, Tony Petrelli, Tim Pettitt, Rich Tyler, Andy Wilson, Brent Johnson, George Steele—most of the firefighters boosting to the western slopes of the Colorado Rockies that fire year seldom looked back as The List chose from among them. You never saw Death lurking ahead. It was only when you looked back that you saw the thousand faces of what Death could have been.

21

WHILE DON MACKEY'S CREW FOUGHT TO HOLD the fireline on the mountain Tuesday night, only to finally give up and seek a few hours' sleep, Butch Blanco's own little band repaired chain saws and geared up to return to Storm King at first light. Blanco intended spiking out on the mountain until he extinguished the fire. He hammered at District and WSFCC on the phone or the radio until after midnight. Field commanders whose primary concerns were stomping out fires and taking care of their fighters often became frustrated with branch overheads whose concerns sometimes seemed misplaced. The ongoing feuds between the Grand Junction Fire District and the resources center at WSFCC frequently trapped field commanders in the middle.

"See this?" a firefighter asked facetiously, displaying one fist. "That's a rock. See this?" Displaying his other fist. "That's a hard place. See this?" He stuck his head between his two fists. "This is Butch Blanco."

Butch Blanco, if anything, was apolitical. He focused on fires and fighters and equipment. He had what one critic called "a direct action mentality." He simply wanted to do his job and be supported in it without becoming the pawn of the overheads' power jockeying.

To be fair, however, he conceded, resources *were* at a premium on the western slopes. His fire was still in the initial attack phase. Other fires had priority. He had to be satisfied with anything he could get.

"I need people and I need air support," he complained to Pete Blume at Grand Junction Dispatch. "This is no small fire anymore. It doubled in size today. I want *two* hotshot crews."

"I'll get back with you, Butch."

Overheads battled it out among themselves over which resources went where and which fire *deserved* first attention. Colorado State BLM Director Bob Moore was painfully aware of the conflicts and the deleterious effect they had on firefighters from the top of the chain down to the ground pounders in the field. The conflicts dated back to 1980 when WSFCC was established as a resources coordination center.

"It's a fairly general attitude that some resource specialists and managers are reluctant to support aggressive initial attack actions," Moore groused, at first in private and then publically. "Management was not too involved early on until it was obvious we were into a bad fire year. It's only recently that top management started to focus their attention because it was so obvious."

"Leadership in this state sucks," retorted Mike Lowery, who ended up acting as co-manager with Paul Hefner at WSFCC. "State fire management officers don't have a clue about what's going on. Extremely frustrating. Forest Service is no different."

Attitudes of dissent and rebellion at the top carried all the way down the chain of command. Dale Longanecker, whose name appeared on Wednesday's jump list, said he would add a nineteenth Watch Out Situation to the Firefighters' Bible: "When you don't receive the resources that you need or you are debating with the dispatcher about the resources that you need. We need more of everything. I understand there are a lot of fires in the area. Still, dispatch seems to be placing more value on houses than on lives. As far as I'm concerned, houses can burn as long as people have been evacuated."

Matthew Black Eagle, a Sioux Indian hotshot from Montana, was less introspective.

"This is the biggest clusterfuck I've ever been involved with," he asserted. "Clusterfuck."

Storm King IC Butch Blanco largely ignored the infighting and backbiting. He had lost Sam Shroeder and his crew even before the fire fighting started. Mackey and the jumpers replaced Sam. The fire on the mountain kept growing. Blanco needed additional troops; he *had* to have reinforcements if he were to have more than a fart's chance in a whirlwind of stopping the blaze before it became a real threat to the folks living at the base of the mountain.

Pete Blume kept his promise and got back with Blanco.

"There'll be a helicopter and *one* shot crew ordered to the fire at oh-six hundred hours in the morning," he promised.

"Is that all I can get?" Blanco asked. "Is this a commitment?"

Blanco assured him it was a firm commitment.

22

ON A LARGER SCALE, THE NATIONAL INTER-agency Fire Center in Boise, the Pentagon of fire forces, also suffered problems with resources. During one of the most disastrous fire seasons of the century, demands for help assailed the Fire Center from all sides. The Center played big board with its resources, robbing from here to reinforce there, shuffling troops about rapidly to meet fire monster probes, counterattacks and assaults.

"Every goddamned thing west of the Mississippi is afire,"

lamented one director. "It's hell. It's Armageddon. We need to bring back the draft—but instead of putting 'em in the army we put 'em in the fire fighting services."

Smokejumper Jack "Captain Jack" Seagraves missed the call on Tuesday, July 5, that summoned a number of his friends and fellow firefighters to Colorado. At age fifty-one, Seagraves was like George Steele and Tim Pettitt—a smokejumper troglodyte. But he refused to give it up. He even purchased a new cellular telephone so he could be more easily contacted.

It was the new telephone that screwed him over. It rang, but he couldn't figure out how to work the damned thing before it stopped ringing. By the time he learned the Center was trying to raise him, he missed the last flight to Colorado. In such trivial ways do some men avoid Fate—or, perhaps, it is in such ways that Fate makes selections.

Irritable at missing muster, Captain Jack found himself working the operations board at the smokejumper base in McCall, Idaho. He erased seventeen smokejumper names from Santa Fe and moved them on the board to Grand Junction. Among the nine jumper reinforcements deplaning at Walker Field late Tuesday night after Don Mackey and his seven firefighters had already parachuted onto Storm King Mountain were James Thrash and Roger Roth.

The two friends sauntered into the Ops Center at WSFCC shoulder to shoulder. Jumpers gathered in a knot around them. They were all laughing and talking. Thrash kidded Roth about an Arizona blowup in dried chaparral that occurred a week or so earlier. Roth had outrun the fire. He unhinged his long legs and took off ahead of the flames through the chaparral.

"Remember the Roadrunner?" Thrash joked. "That's ol' Roger. He looked like a skinny chaparral chicken. *Beep! Beep!* Where's that damned coyote?"

You could laugh about the close calls, afterward. Roger Roth laughed easily, his big infectious Michigan grin spreading across a lean face that remained boyish at thirty. Straight brown hair capped the top of his head like a bowl.

Everything Roth did, he did with youthful exuberance. "He doesn't endure life, he embraces it," his minister said of him.

Like Brent Johnson, communion with danger and the rugged outdoors kept instilled in Roth the quiet spirituality of his upbringing. "When you're standing in the doorway of the airplane preparing to jump," he once observed, "you're close to God."

"Roth was real lucky in that Arizona fire," said jumper John Freshwater in a sober moment. "Apparently it was a real volatile fire and he got out of it. Lucky."

Roth's buddy Jim Thrash was fourteen years older than Roth. He was lean and rangy, slab-sided and rawboned on a frame that could only be described as a classic Westerner's build. In contrast to Roth who joked a lot and spoke in enthusiastic bursts, Thrash came across as more soft-spoken but with the same humor, only toned down. His humor was that enduring and solid variety like the Idaho mountains he called home. It was subtle and underspoken, like Mark Twain's. Thrash even presented somewhat of a Twain appearance in the full light-colored beard he liked to wear and his slouchy old hat that had long ago seen better days.

He snapped the suspenders that held up his ratty jeans as Rick Blanton entered the downstairs coordination center to greet the new arrivals. A smile played on his lean face in spite of the long day and the late hour.

"Who you tryin' to rile now?" one of the other jumpers asked. Thrash enjoyed baiting people into friendly arguments.

"It's still Roth," he said. "He's so *easy.*"

"But *fast. Beep! Beep!*"

"He's not even fast—except when he's scared. Right, Rog?"

Roth laughed. "It was time to get fast. I set the new one-hundred-yard-dash record. I've been asked to train Olympic hopefuls."

Thrash had smokejumped for fifteen years and had parachuted into hundreds of forest fires. In many ways, he

113

represented the heart of the McCall jumpers. His cool head in a crisis was legendary. Recently, he started talking about retiring: settling down with his wife, Holly, and their two children, a boy and a girl, and getting a *real* job. The fire summers seemed to be getting longer, his aging bones stiffer in the mornings after a night on the ground.

Some time ago, a journalist for *Playboy* magazine interviewed him for an article.

"Tell me about smokejumpers," the journalist asked, not very creatively.

Thrash pushed off his sombrero and scratched around in his hair. His eyes twinkled.

"Smokejumpers are pretty much expected to be tougher than a two-dollar steak," he declared. "If you were looking for a common thread, it would be that they all like adventure. They're adrenaline freaks willing to risk their limbs landing in a one-hundred-foot-tall ponderosa pine or fighting two hundred mph cyclonic winds and fire so hot it could burn your skin from one hundred feet away. Otherwise, we have all kinds from ultrareligious family men to drunken welfare types and everything in between."

His dark Mark Twain humor surfaced when the interviewer pressed him about the dangers inherent in his profession.

"Probably the most important thing out there is that you never want to come down to your last option," he said.

"What's your 'last option'?"

Thrash produced a small reflective blanket he kept folded and readily available in a pouch on his PG bag. It weighed about one pound and, when unfolded, was a six-foot-by-three-foot rectangle. It resembled a poncho made of fire-resistant aluminum foil bonded on fiberglass cloth with a nontoxic, high-temperature adhesive. The U.S. Forest Service started work on developing the shelters in 1958 following two decades of fire fighting tragedies. By 1976 they were mandatory for wildland firefighters.

"If you have to deploy a fire shelter, you are in a situation you don't want to be in," experienced firefighters drilled into rookies. Shelter deployment was a last-ditch effort to save life. It was a tool designed for desperate situations.

"If you are ever trapped," hotshot Matthew Black Eagle liked to explain to new fighters, "the first rule and the most difficult to follow is not to panic. While flames are raging and other crew members may be screaming for help nearby, stay levelheaded and remain under your shelter. It doesn't do any good for you to get yourself killed too. Few of you will ever have to use one, but if you do it might provide you the one thing nobody is ever guaranteed—another day of life."

Thrash demonstrated how the thing worked for the *Playboy* reporter. Ideally, firefighters should first clear the ground upon which they were to lie of all combustible debris to keep fire from burning up to and underneath them. The shelter had strips sewn underneath it for handholds. The user lay facedown on the ground and drew the shelter over him, reflective side up. He secured the corners and edges with his hands and feet and waited for the flames to pass. It trapped air underneath which allowed the fighter to breathe. The aluminum foil reflected 95 percent of the heat of a fire—up to a certain temperature.

Temperatures inside a forest fire could reach more than 2,000 degrees Fahrenheit. A human being could live on prolonged exposure to temperatures of only around 150 degrees. No human could live, fire shelter or not, in the full heat of a forest fire. If the cloth temperature of a shelter reached 500 degrees, the adhesive broke down and the foil and fiberglass separated. But, of course, the victim would have long since expired by then for lack of oxygen. Fire sucked in and burned oxygen, suffocating the victim and searing out his lungs with superheated carbon dioxide. Most fire casualties succumbed to asphyxiation before the flames ever reached them.

"Fire shelters," Thrash said, "are our 'last option.'"

Firefighters referred to them as "portable ovens" or "potato bakers."

"We have our little jokes," Thrash said. "Like, we always

carry an apple out there for use in that last option situation where you hear the roar of the flames coming up a canyon and your partner looks at you and you look at your partner and you're both thinking, 'We're taters.' If it comes to that, you crawl inside your fire shelter, stick the apple in your mouth and wait."

The *Playboy* writer couldn't be sure if Thrash were joking or not. Thrash could laugh about such things. It was his firefighter's black humor that kept thoughts of danger pushed back to a comfortable level.

Now, as Rick Blanton hustled into the coordination center, Thrash and Roth dropped their small travel bags. The center was walled with maps and banked with telephones and radios. An unmade cot occupied the back of the single room. Blanton looked rumpled and used and impatient. He had been briefing arriving jumpers and hotshots throughout the day.

"Okay, guys, let's hold it down and get this over with," Blanton said. "I'll get you guys to bed as soon as I can. We have all kinds of requests for your services starting at oh-dark-thirty in the morning."

That was no surprise. It had been the same story all over the West since early April.

"We have red flag watches and warnings for tomorrow," Blanton said. "We're forecasting dry thunderstorms with strong and gusty winds. They should arrive in our area around two o'clock P.M."

"That means a good blaze," someone commented.

"They'll whip up better than a good blaze," Blanton agreed.

"Think overtime," Thrash advised, still with his quiet grin.

"Think bed." Blanton sighed. "The way things are going, you may not see clean sheets around here again until Thanksgiving."

The Prineville Hot Shots unpack their gear in the Canyon Creek subdivision shortly before a wildfire killed nine of their members on Storm King Mountain July 6, 1994. David Frey photo, *Glenwood Post*.

Tanker bomber dropping "fugitive" onto Storm King blowup. Bernard Boettcher photo, *Glenwood Post*.

Ram-air parachute used by BLM smokejumpers. Bureau of Land Management Great Basin Smokejumpers.

A Chinook helicopter fills a dump tank with water to put out hot spots on Storm King Mountain. Casey A. Cass photo, *Glenwood Post*.

Jumpers "In the door." Bureau of Land Management Great Basin Smokejumpers.

Nadine Mackey, mother of fallen Missoula smokejumper Don Mackey, plants a tulip near the site where her son perished in the Storm King Mountain fire. Casey A. Cass photo, *Glenwood Post*.

Victim: Don Mackey, smokejumper. Public domain photo.

Retreating from a blowup fire. Bureau of Land Management Great Basin Smokejumpers.

The burnt corpse of a squirrel stands frozen in its tracks on Storm King Mountain a week after the fire raced up the hillside. Casey A. Cass photo, *Glenwood Post.*

Smokejumper Eric Hipke suffered burns in daring escape from fire. David Frey photo, *Glenwood Post.*

Fireline and location of deaths of twelve firefighters on Storm King Mountain. Photo by Bureau of Land Management, public access.

An American flag stands at half mast above the spot where twelve of the fourteen fallen firefighters died July 6, 1994, west of Glenwood Springs. Casey A. Cass photo, *Glenwood Post.*

The Storm King Mountain fire in its infancy. Shot July 2, 1994— four days before blow up. Casey A. Cass photo, *Glenwood Post.*

Victim: Kathi Beck, hot shot. Public domain photo.

The granite crosses are laid side by side on Storm King Mountain before placement. Casey A. Cass photo, *Glenwood Post.*

Victim: Roger Roth, smokejumper. Public domain photo.

Victims: (L to R) Tamera Bicket and Scott Blecha, hot shots. Public domain photos.

Firefighters stand in shock as the Storm King Mountain fire that claimed the lives of 14 firefighters rages out of control. David Frey photo, *Glenwood Post.*

Victims: (L to R) Bonnie Holtby, hot shot; Jim Thrash, smokejumper; Jon Kelso, hot shot. Public domain photos.

Victims: (L to R) Levi Brinkley and Doug Dunbar, hot shots. Public domain photos.

A line of 14 hearses drives through Glenwood Springs with Storm King Mountain in the background. Casey A. Cass photo, *Glenwood Post.*

23

LIKE EVERYONE ELSE IN COLORADO THAT SUM-
mer, residents of the valleys at the base of Storm King
Mountain were acutely aware of the fires burning on the
western slopes of the Rockies. They were even more aware
of the fire that burned on the mountain above them. The
"Ten O'Clock News" on Tuesday night aired clips of the
Wake fire at Paonia. They showed one house erupting
in flames and a red-and-beige airplane releasing retardant almost on the rooftop of another house while fire swept
up a nearby ridge toward it. Still other clips showed
smokejumpers parachuting onto a mountain, helicopters
making bucket drops and tearful victims lamenting their
losses.

"Whatever else," concluded a TV anchorman, "it is *war*
in the Rockies this summer."

A Colorado map flashed on the screen. Little red flames
marked the locations of dozens of active wildfires. One of
the tiny flames pinpointed Storm King Mountain. The
commentator skimmed over the fire, lumping it in with
several other fledgling blazes which he said firefighters were
either monitoring or should have under control by the end
of the next day.

The weather forecast that followed the news called for a
cold front to blow through the Rockies on Wednesday
afternoon, bringing with it the dreaded dry lightning storms
that had already ignited so many fires. Winds might become
locally gusty, but Colorado could expect no much-needed
rain.

Scattered populations in the two-hundred-thousand-
dollar houses at Canyon Creek Estates, in the Mobile Home
Mountain Park, in West Glenwood and in the RV parks
along Mitchell Creek slept lightly that night. They kept

117

getting up to make sure the fire had not spread down the sides of the Storm King ridge to their backyards. They had watched it growing throughout the day even as firefighters battled it. They studied it and attempted to predict what it would do. Some of them actually resented the fire. It was more than an act of nature; it was a malevolent being with *personal* motivations to destroy.

Some of them resented Storm King Mountain for the way it dominated their lives. The mountain was more than a weather predictor. It was like it also predicted the future through the weather.

In the winter, it snagged the snow clouds and displayed them before they reached the valley. People below looked up at them and shivered. Spring came and Storm King grabbed the rain clouds and teased its subjects with them. It browned first with drought, a reminder to those below of how much life depended upon moisture. It caught the bolts of dry weather lightning and rumbled and growled and scolded the people in the valleys for their transgressions against nature. Winds previewed its rocky ribs and hissed in the PJ and ponderosa pine and gambel oak thickets, causing sudden mood changes in the human population below.

Man has studied Mother Nature, read her, appeased her, thought to predict her whims and at times even tried to control her pernicious temper. But he has never dominated the bitch. In a chaotic world of cause and effect, things happen which seem random and unexpected to man's limited understanding. SHIT HAPPENS goes the message on a popular bumper sticker. Sometimes it seems Mother Nature throws a tantrum just because she knows she can, just to make puny man kneel and pay homage to her powerful and unconquerable will. Mother Nature through her winds and rains and mountains remains earth's pampered and willful mistress.

On Tuesday afternoon, thin cirrus clouds had appeared high in the dry skies above Storm King Mountain, slender silver threads blown long and pale and gone virtually unnoticed as scouts for the approaching cold front. The mountain, it seemed, issued its warning, but its subjects were preoccupied with different clouds, those composed of smoke.

The fire had undergone a big change from Sunday morning when Glenwood *Post* reporter Nan Johnson first noticed it burning in a single tree. She saw the smoke now from her home seventeen miles away. It was mostly white, still a slow-moving fire, but it bent near the top in the freshening winds aloft and started to flatten off a bit. It swayed like a dancer keeping beat to some old Barry Manilow tune played slow.

Residents nearer the fire cast cautious looks at the ridge. They drove home from work or from the grocery store and paused for a moment in their driveways to watch the cloud that hovered threateningly above their lives.

"It has gotten bigger," Jack Bohannon said to his wife.

"What?" She knew what he was talking about. Everyone in Canyon Creek Estates was talking about the fire.

"It has grown."

"It'll soon be out. They're up there fighting it now."

Through binoculars, the yellow combat coats and helmets of the firefighters glowed like colorful ants amid the dull greens and grays and browns of the mountain ridge. They flashed brightly through the slow rolling of smoke. Flames themselves remained largely invisible to spectators in the valley, except on Tuesday night when they reflected orange against the underbelly of the smoke.

At 10:30 P.M., Doug Hanks was driving home from New Castle, approaching West Glenwood on I-70.

"I thought West Glenwood was on fire," he told his neighbor.

"Not yet," came the nervous reply.

Karen Haff stood outside on the front lawn of her Canyon Creek home for a last appraisal of the fire before she went to bed. She picked out a growing ring of flames eating out a larger circle on the ridge. Smoke undulated gently against a sky full of stars. Surely firefighters had it all under control. She went to bed not feeling as secure as she should.

24

(AP)—In Colorado, two dozen fires continued to burn. More than 8,000 acres have burned during the past few weeks.

In Arizona, a bright orange helicopter hovered over a tiny man-made lake in the desert while its snorkel sucked up 1,600 gallons of water in 40 seconds.

Then the 1960s-vintage Sikorsky "Sky Crane" lumbered off toward the Rincon Mountains above Tucson to bomb a stubborn wildfire, part of a massive multiagency attack on fire burning throughout the West.

Federal officials said half the 34 major fires in the region appeared contained or nearly contained. But firefighters on the ground weren't ready to declare victory, particularly amid desert brush dried to tinder by last week's record siege of hot weather.

"Every time you put it out and it looks like it's out, it keeps going," said Charles Guernsey of Lake Charles, La., who works on a chopper ground crew and was fighting his eighth fire this summer in the West.

The National Interagency Fire Center in Boise, Idaho, reported that as of Wednesday, the 34 fires burning in nine western states had scorched an estimated 150,000 acres of forest, brush and grassland. More than 30 homes and outbuildings have been destroyed, said spokeswoman Pat Entwistle.

About 7,000 firefighters, 175 fire engines, 38 helicopters and 32 air tankers were on the firelines in Arizona, New Mexico, Colorado, Wyoming, Montana, Idaho, Utah, Nevada and California.

And 1994 is shaping up as a bad year; fires have burned an estimated 1.3 million acres so far, compared to the five-year average for this date of 874,648 acres.

Things could get worse soon . . .

25

FIREFIGHTERS ASSIGNED TO FIRE V-891, THE Storm King fire, stirred early on Wednesday. Don Mackey glanced at the luminous hands of his watch. Shortly after 3:00 A.M. His bones and muscles ached from lying on the cold ground.

Downridge from the jumpers, fire still popped bones and colored the underside of the smoke to the reddish orange hue of a festered wound. A cool breeze from the west rustled the night and breathed against Mackey's cheek. It gave him a quick start. Those hours before dawn should be the calmest. Even the wind should be sleeping. Mackey twisted his head back and forth to catch the breeze on both cheeks one at a time. He estimated its speed at about ten mph, perhaps a bit less.

He shifted to rest his back against the gnarled trunk of a pinyon pine. He drew his blanket around his shoulders and, utterly without good humor, peered into the fire-tinted darkness before dawn. Even a perennial wit like James Thrash, had he been here, would have found little in the situation to joke about. The Burt Reynolds in Don Mackey was not up to his usual mischievous standards.

The other jumpers were also restless. Erickson and Sarah Doehring stirred in their bedding. Sonny Soto lay curled up for warmth; he drew up his knees until they almost touched his chin. Woods using a jutting of rock for a windbreak snored long and rhythmically. Someone else moaned.

"Who pulled off all the cover and kicked me onto the floor?" someone complained in a feeble attempt at comedy.

He went unanswered.

Presently, jumpers separated themselves from the dark earth. They rose like dark shadows out of shadow and began preparing coffee over heat tabs. They opened cans and freeze-dried packages of spaghetti or ham and eggs or whatever they had for a mostly cold breakfast. There was little talking. An owl somewhere deep in the east drainage went *t-hoot t-hoot?*

"*T-hoot* do you think it is?" someone grumbled. "*T-hoot* to your feathered ass."

T-hoot t-hoot?

Mackey listened to the owl. Owls were lonely birds. Owls perched on spindly dark branches at the gates of ancient cemeteries and questioned *t-hoot?* of the spirits.

Jumpers gathered silently around their supervisor. They squatted wrapped like Indians against the morning chill, eating listlessly and gazing downslope toward the fire. They could not see flames from here on the top, just their glow reflected against the smoke and backlighting the spiny tips of trees. The fire seemed to have grown since midnight. It had the breeze feeding it oxygen.

"If it should blow," the jumpers pointed out to Mackey, "it'll run upslope and through the saddle. There goes all our gear."

They had cached their red pack-out bags containing parachutes, jumpsuits and excess equipment in trees at the jump spot.

"The gear'll be all right until after daylight," Mackey said.

"What're you having for breakfast?" Doehring asked him.

A little bit of Burt Reynolds broke through in a grin. "How about hotcakes and maple syrup, sausage, eggs over easy, orange juice and cold milk?"

Doehring held up a can. "How about chili con carne?"

A half-century of full physical living had made Butch Blanco's morning muscles stiff and sore. The narrow hard cots at his temporary headquarters hadn't done his body much good either. Forest fire fighting was a young man's game.

At 4:30 A.M., Grand Junction Dispatch summarized the day's projected weather for him over the telephone. The forecast called for more of the same except for the cold front still expected to arrive in the afternoon. A "cold front" this time of year generally dropped the normal summer temperatures two or three degrees.

Winds of ten to twenty mph by 11:00 A.M. should bring increasing high clouds. The winds were expected to intensify to fifteen to thirty mph by 1:00 P.M. and shift to the northwest and gust to thirty-five mph by 3:00 P.M. Daytime temperature highs at altitude would probably drop from about 90 degrees to the mid or upper 80s.

"Unfortunately," predicted Don Cuevas, local National Weather Service forecaster, "conditions will continue mostly dry for the next five days."

Blanco gathered up his small force before daybreak. It now consisted of twelve firefighters, up from the seven of yesterday. He had picked up five more from local resources, but then lost one when Janie Jarrett's sprained ankle from the day before grounded her for the day. Janie helped drive the eleven remaining firefighters to the entrance of the east drainage off I-70, then returned to the BLM offices in Glenwood Springs to work the command center. By late afternoon, the command center would be the busiest office in the state of Colorado.

Blanco's crew members carried heavy packs containing not only their tools, chain saws and fuel but also food, water and sleeping gear. The IC intended they stay on-site until they strangled the fire to death. Darkness lay in the east drainage, as though in hiding from the red maw of the fire above on the other side of the ridge. The troops lounged around on their packs, catching a few winks before the day's labors commenced, while Blanco, Mike Hayes and Todd Abbott set out ahead to scout a new route and tie-in with Don Mackey's smokejumpers.

As soon as there was enough light to see, Michelle Ryerson and Brad Haugh saddled up the main body and pushed into the narrow mouth of the east drainage. Repetition of the climb, this the second morning in a row, made it no easier. It was still three-and-one-half hours of toil through thick PJ and tumbled boulders.

Storm King Mountain scowled down upon them in warning, its face touched bloodred by a rising sun unseen at lower altitudes. Smoke from the ridge gathered at its summit like a ridiculous crushed hat worn on the head of a fat man.

26

RUSTY-HAIRED KENT HAMILTON IN THE AIR CO-ordination Center at Walker Field knew forest fire fighting literally from the ground up. He had started as a regional Forest Service employee and firefighter in California, worked his way up to a hotshot team, then volunteered for the elite of the elite, the smokejumpers. In the same way a recruit soldier started out in basic combat training before wending his way up through the infantry to reach the airborne, a wildland firefighter often started his career as a part-time ground pounder working for the Forest Service seeding pines or building roads and only fighting fires as a sideline. Most forest firefighters learned their basic skills at the local or regional level and then perfected them as members of hotshot crews.

As national rather than local resources, hotshots and smokejumpers lived a professional rodeo cowboy existence from about April or May until October, hopping from fire to fire the way a pro bull rider hopped from rodeo to rodeo. The fire circuit normally started in Arizona and West Texas and New Mexico, the more arid Southwest where, after the thaws and the spring rains, the sun turned white-hot and made kindling of the chaparral and palo verde and PJ. Fire might break out in April on the lowlands south and east of

Flagstaff and then follow the thaws and the drying out up through Colorado and Idaho and Montana to Alaska and then back south again as the autumn snows and rains brought the northern fire season to a close.

Hamilton cradled a telephone receiver between his chin and his shoulder while he used his one good hand to move colored pins around on a huge wall map of the Grand Junction Fire District. The other arm hung in a sling, the result of his having crashed onto boulders hidden in tall grass at a jump spot in Washington's Wannatache National Forest earlier in the season. A broken clavicle grounded him for the rest of the year. He would be riding a goddamned desk until September or so, pushing colored pins around on a map. One color designated tanker aircraft and their locations, another pinpointed helicopters and jump planes and Air Attack command aircraft while a third color kept up with smokejumpers. Hotshot locations and destinations were kept on a separate map upstairs. The Air Coordination Center handled only air resources.

"I always thought I had had a safe career," Hamilton sometimes mused, "but then I think, wait a minute. I've been burned, badly, had a hernia operation and broken my clavicle."

Burn scars crept out of his shirt collar and his right shirtsleeve. He was about thirty years old. He thumbed his green "smokejumper" ball cap with the wings sewed on it to the back of his head. His scraggly reddish beard combined with his lanky build to lend him the appearance of Shaggy on the TV cartoon series "Scooby Doo."

He drawled into the phone, "It's a four-manner then. We'll see what we can do as availability comes up."

He hung up.

April Hamilton shuffled quickly through a sheaf of manifests, checking for him on jumper availability. She was Kent's only compensation in having to lay out the rest of the season and miss the overtime race. It was she who helped wrangle him a position with her at WSFCC after his injury. At least they would be together for the rest of the season.

April was blond, short and just plump enough to make

her cute. Kent had met her in Alaska about two years ago. Both worked out of the Alaskan Fire Service base in Fairbanks, he as a smokejumper, she as dispatcher. Since firefighters lived a Spartan military existence, sleeping in a barracks, eating at a common chow hall, the two young people were often thrown together. They didn't begin dating as much as they simply started hanging out together. Romance among forest firefighters frequently began on common ground as friends and buddies before it blossomed. Sometimes, as with Kent and April, it led to marriage.

She finally went to the computer and located information for her husband.

"I was afraid of that," she said. "There won't be any jumpers available until maybe tomorrow when they demobe off Sinbad."

Kent shook his head. WSFCC had more requests for services than it could accommodate.

"Maob District won't like it," he said, "but I'll have to call 'em back and tell 'em they'll have to wait."

Fires were triaged according to terrain and fuels, size and location, firefighter accessibility and threat to structures. Larger, more menacing blazes were attacked first. Other fires, such as the initially small one at Storm King Mountain, were "monitored" simply because of lack of resources.

Hamilton paced the office for a moment. He glared at the offending arm that had thrown him out of action.

"Damn," he murmured. He glared out the window toward the airfield. A DC-4 tanker had just filled up with Fugitive and was taxiing for takeoff. "I need to be out *there*—not stuck in this goddamned office."

Firefighters *belonged* on the front lines. Assholes and elbows on a fireline. The rear area was for the REMFs, the Rear Echelon Motherfuckers, the sick, lame and lazy.

Hamilton fretted. His wife smiled slightly and rolled her eyes. Her husband's career traced a perfect example of the forest firefighter's life. Restless Westerners seeking adventure and action and deprived of new frontiers became firefighters, drawn to the profession as career soldiers were drawn to combat. Hamilton had started out modestly in 1983 as a member of a U.S. Forest Service fire engine crew. Fire engines were severely restricted. They attacked along roads or other accesses and provided structure protection and support on the periphery of larger fires.

Three years after joining the Forest Service, Hamilton suffered a near-fatal encounter with the fire monster.

"If I had to make a list of the ways I had to die," he mused afterward, "being burned to death would be at the very bottom of the list. It would be below being skinned alive or cut into pieces until you bled to death. I can think of nothing more horrible than burning yourself into a crispy critter. Imagine this. Imagine sticking your hand into an open campfire. Take it further. Imagine yourself *being* the campfire. That's what it's like."

In retrospect, his burning had been a foolish and careless accident. The fire hadn't even been a wildfire. Hamilton's crew was instructed to control burn a landfill dump in the Sequoia National Park in California. Out of the landfill protruded rotting stumps of redwood and oak. Soil and trash partially covered them.

"It'll be a bug-bear to get them stumps lit," the crew foreman observed. "Hamilton, see if you can soak them with gasoline."

Another crew member had torched a test burn at one end of the dump. It was a small fire confined to its own area. Hamilton and another worker paced off about thirty yards from the fire, a safe enough distance under most circumstances, and began emptying jerry cans of gasoline onto stumps.

The entire episode was freaky. It shouldn't have happened, but it did happen. Unrecognized by any of the crew or the crew foreman, gasoline fumes oiled the calm morning air. They spread by osmosis. The small open flame sucked them toward it like smoke and fumes drawn up a chimney.

Bent over a stump, Hamilton sloshed gasoline from his can. Suddenly, the air exploded. The test fire thirty yards away shot a stream of flame through the gasoline-saturated air. It was like a flamethrower going off. Hamilton had only an instant before it engulfed him. His stunned senses recorded the head of the flames bursting directly at him like a meteor.

He screamed as his body flared like a torch. Red-blue tongues of fire sprouted instantaneously from his body. They cracked and popped, blossoming around him like the live petals of some evil flower.

Most such victims went instantly insane from panic and bolted to their deaths, running at such frantic speeds that no one could catch them until they dropped dead. A freak accident set Hamilton afire; another mishap saved his life. As he recoiled from the fiery attack, he tripped over one of the stumps that had precipitated his misfortune in the first place. He dropped to the ground in a writhing, screaming ball of flame. Fellow firefighters kept their wits. They pounced on him and rolled him in the dirt, extinguishing the fire.

He escaped with third-degree burns on his right arm and back. The nylon strap of his backpack melted into his flesh. He was to bear ugly scars from the flames, but he survived. Quite a few professional wildland firefighters bore burn scars.

Many firefighters might have given up their profession rather than risk a repeat encounter with the dreaded fire monster. Not Hamilton. A year after his narrow escape, he advanced from a Type II firefighter to a Type I by enlisting with the Arrowhead Hotshots headquartered in King Canyon National Park, California. As much as he later loved smoke jumping, it was working with the hotshots that captured his heart. Even today he missed the camaraderie of his old hotshot crew. His heart beat a little warmer each time he jumped onto a fire and shots hiked in for reinforcement. Shots were mostly younger than other firefighters, they were louder and more boisterous in a good-kid sort of way. Bonds Hamilton formed with the members of his hotshot crew remained unbroken.

Smokejumper Roger Roth, who had outrun one fire in June in Arizona and whose name on The List had bumped him to Colorado on July 5, had been one of Hamilton's comrades on the Arrowhead Hotshots. The two ex-teammates always caught up on old times and old shot friends whenever they met on the circuit. They shook hands and embraced warmly. Both missed the hotshots sometimes.

"Buddy, have you run across any of the old shots lately?"

"I saw Big Jim up in Idaho first of the season. McCall accepted him for jump school."

"He's giving up the hotshots?"

"The shots is for the young kids. How about Annie? Heard from her?"

"Annie quit too, I heard. Got her masters and Ph.D. and somebody told me she's teaching at the University of California. The Arrowhead's almost an entirely new crew now."

"They don't stay too long, most of 'em."

"Those were the good days, buddy."

"Those were the good days."

Unlike smokejumpers who tended to be individualists and semi-loners, hotshots traveled together like an extended gypsy family, as close to each other as Army Rangers or an Army Special Forces team. The twenty of them even had their own gypsy buggy. It was a big truck with an enclosed bed containing tools, bedding, food and even folding chairs with the individuals' names inscribed on them, like movie directors had. The shots became as attached to the buggy as to their own homes. It *was* their home during the summer. The only times they abandoned it was to fly to distant fires. Federal regulations required all hotshot crews to headquarter within two hours of a jetport.

Hotshots during the 1994 fire season used their jetports frequently.

Other than smokejumpers, hotshot crews, hand-picked for physical fitness and dedication, were the most highly trained of forest firefighters. Each recruit received more than eighty hours of training before being cast into the war against forest fires. Teams had a tendency to be as brash and bold as squirrels in a park. They blended a Marine-like intensity with the nonconformity of a rock-and-roll band. Because of their training and daring and because they thrived on the thrill of attacking the heart of a forest fire with shovels, axes and chain saws, they often received the most dangerous assignments.

Hotshots devised their own weapons. In addition to the half-ax, half-hoe Pulaski and the half-ax, half-rake McLeod, the Arrowheads devised a "rhino tool" by bending a shovel blade to the angle of a hoe. The Los Prietos Hotshots swore by their "Super P," a Pulaski with a hoe blade almost twice as wide as a standard P.

The order of tools changed with the terrain. Scraping tools were most effective in thick duff, for example, while digging or chopping tools might be required for heavy ground growth.

Chain of command in a shot crew flowed downward from the superintendent to the foreman to the squad bosses. Sawyers and tool bearers formed the squads. The most bitching job on any crew was sawyer. Chain saws led the attack. Big powerful tools out on point. Few Lead Ps or First McLeods sat back very long thinking they were cool while hearing the throaty *rrrrr!* of the chain saws out ahead. Everyone on a shot crew aspired to be a sawyer. Sawyers were the elite among hotshots.

Hamilton and Roth, like all recruits, started out as tool bearers with the Arrowhead Hotshots. The key to advancement within the hotshot crew and within the fire service itself lay in training and experience. Each firefighter carried a Wildland Fire Suppression Curriculum card, a "Red Card," that listed his qualifications. His Red Card and his "Task Book" tracked his career as he took classes and courses in subjects ranging from the use of portable pumps to fire behavior calculations, from fire forces organization to the duties of an incident commander or division group supervisor. An individual's fire assignment depended upon the qualifications tabbed onto his Red Card.

His assignment also depended upon such unexpected events as an injury. Kent Hamilton would be riding a desk for the remainder of the season because one bad jump left him with a broken clavicle. A friend of his from Alaska caught a fishhook in the eye and broke his neck the previous spring. He was on his way to work air dispatch at WSFCC. Together they would ride out the season and wait until next year. Their names would not rotate on the jump list with those of Don Mackey, J.C. Curd, Roger Roth and the others. Hamilton planned to make up for lost overtime this year at Squaw Valley where he worked winters as a ski patrolman.

One thing Hamilton remembered about his old friend Roger Roth in retrospect that 1994 season was that Roth was one of the slower runners on the Arrowhead Hotshot crew. He wasn't the slowest, but he ran farther back than the middle of the pack.

"Maybe he's picked up some speed," Hamilton said. "He outran that Arizona fire, so I guess that proves you can do it if you have to."

27

FIREFIGHTERS FROM ARIZONA, NEW MEXICO AND elsewhere mingled in apparent confusion at Walker Field's Western Slopes Fire Coordination Center. Tankers hadn't yet started flying their missions for the day. Wilson's and Dahl's P2V and Gary Towle's DC-4 sat parked among other aircraft on the ramp near the Fugitive tanks. BLM's Bell Ranger 93R was still tied down on the tarmac beyond; helitacks Rich Tyler and Bob Browning gave it a preflight in preparation for the arrival of chopper pilot Dick Good. The smokejumpers' Twin Otter also sat parked with an open parachute door in front of the little scramble shack containing the jumpers' gear. Word spread that Air Ops had laid on another full stick—eight jumpers—for Storm King Mountain later in the morning.

Smokejumpers underneath the trees in front of their headquarters shook out chutes and packed air drop bundles. They goosed each other and made jokes and showed off for the benefit of female hotshots, who cast coy looks in their direction. Tony Petrelli and Roger Roth checked the bulletin board inside for their names on the jump list. George Steele, his experience and seniority making him a supervisor, caught up on paperwork in the back office.

"Looks like we're skying-up for the next jump," Roth said to his partner, Jim Thrash. He gazed out across the desert flats toward the mountains. "I'm ready," he said.

Thrash grinned. *"Beep! Beep!"*

Four separate hotshot crews from four separate states outside Colorado, each team wearing its own distinctive uniform, clumped according to team integrity on the browning lawns around WSFCC while they awaited assignments and transportation. Sporting blue T-shirts and forest green trousers, the Prineville Interagency Hotshots gathered in the morning sun between Ops and the jumper shack. Yesterday morning, the Fire Center had withdrawn the twenty-firefighter team from a fire in the Winneman National Forest outside Klamath Falls, Oregon, and ordered it to fly immediately to Grand Junction. Hotshot Levi Brinkley telephoned his mother.

"We've already been to hell," he said, referring to a previous raging wildfire in California which the shots had fought for several days. "Now, we're going to heaven."

A thin smoke haze from the many fires in the mountains veiled Walker Field as the hotshot flight landed at 6:00 P.M. Tuesday. Rick Blanton at WSFCC repeated his quick briefing and sent the shots to dinner and rest for the night.

"Be back here ready to go at six tomorrow morning," he told them.

The small town of Prineville, Oregon, population six thousand, prided itself on its young firefighters as much as it prided itself on local high school football. The Prineville

Hotshots based at the Ochoco Forest headquarters was founded in 1980. It was one of about sixty hotshot crews in the nation and one of the newest. The crew in the summer of 1994 consisted of fifteen men and five women. Three of the hotshots were permanent Ochoco Forest workers while the other seventeen were season "temps."

"These are mostly college kids home for the summer," explained Prineville Mayor Todd Vallie. "For them, the epitome of success is to get on a shot crew."

Oregon Governor Barbara Roberts later commented on sending the Prineville Hotshots to Colorado.

"We do our best for each other when we do it across state lines to help each other," she said. "My late husband said only two things matter in life—time and love. How you spend your time and how you spend your love tells who you are. Those hotshots are young people who give both a commitment of time and love, and who give a professional responsibility."

Prineville Hotshots Superintendent Tom Shepard and his foreman, Brian Scholz, went inside the Ops building to check with Hefner or somebody upstairs about the day's operations. Since aircraft space limitations had forced the team to leave behind some of its gear, the two men had been on the phones since first light trying to obtain tools from Grand Junction District to arm their hotshots. They had been assured Colorado would resupply the team upon its arrival at Grand Junction.

"We were *told*," Shepard growled, growing increasingly frustrated, "to leave our own tools behind—that you'd have some for us here. Where the hell are they?"

Scholz shook his head. He was a short, solidly built man in his thirties with a thick mustache and short-cropped hair. He stepped outside to explain the delay to the others.

"I'm not too sure they know *what* to do with us," he said. "Go get coffee, naps, whatever. Just stay close by, ready to go."

"That's our middle name—R-E-A-D-Y," quipped Doug Dunbar. "What's their middle name—R-E-T-A-R-D?"

Dunbar, twenty-two years old, was on his fifth summer as a wildland firefighter. With some regrets, he intended this to be his last year. He would finish his degree in business administration in the fall with luck and leave the hotshots behind to go into the corporate world. Dunbar's dad often boasted others to boredom about the accomplishments of his strapping blond son.

"Doug's the kind of human being that society ought to have," Randy Dunbar bragged. "He's a good worker. He's a good, kindhearted kid. Any parent would be proud to have a son like Doug."

Doug was close to his father. He kept him apprised of the shots' movements during the season. Just before his flight took off from Kingsley Air Field in Klamath Falls on Tuesday afternoon, Doug telephoned home.

"We're heading to Colorado to put out a fire," he explained.

"Glad you called, son. I always like to keep track of where you are. Be careful."

"Piece of cake, Dad."

While the shots waited, Kathi Beck, Mike Simmons and some of the others explored for soft drinks and snack machines. Rob Johnson, twenty-six, and his younger brother Tony, twenty-three, wandered over to the parked Otter and peered inside through the open jump door. Jumper Dale Longanecker saw them and came out.

"I can fix you up with a parachute," he joked.

The brothers laughed.

"We'd thought about it," Rob admitted. "But now . . . I doubt it."

As with Dunbar, Rob Johnson was in the summer of his last fire fighting year.

"One more year," he promised his younger brother when they received their report-in letter that spring. "I have to have just one more year with the shots. They're hard to give up."

Tony was the outgoing brother. Along with his lanky build, Rob had a certain taciturnity which cast him in the mold of a young Gary Cooper. During the winters he audited lift tickets and ski school receipts at the Vail ski resort. He so rarely talked about himself that coworkers at Vail Associates thought he had already given up fire fighting to become a full-time certified public accountant in Oregon.

"He's so quiet," a Vail CPA said of him. "He's not the Rambo-type at all. It took a long time to get to know him, but once you do you find he has a great sense of humor."

Scott Blecha and Jon Kelso, both twenty-seven, also planned to quit the hotshots at the end of the season. Blecha was a wide, muscled man with a beard whose after shadow no amount of shaving eliminated. Straight brown hair dangled freely over a broad forehead, accenting active dark eyes which twinkled with constant unsuppressed humor. Tamara Bickett came over and threw a companionable arm around his thick shoulders as he caucused with Kelso, Tom Rambo and Alex Robertson. They chortled over jokes and funny, exaggerated tales of fire fighting and firefighters.

"He always makes people laugh," was the way Blecha's girlfriend described him.

"What are you doing, Scott?" Tami Bickett prodded. "Telling filthy, disgusting dirty jokes again?"

Blecha laughed, a deep booming sound that made everyone around him laugh.

"God, Tami," he said. "I'm so sorry I forgot to include you. This one is really *filthy*. You'll love it."

Hotshots were family. They laughed and fought and cried together. Male or female learned to take whatever came without getting their feelings hurt. It was tough on them if they were thin-skinned when they joined up. But they'd get over it.

"I'm really going to miss you when you go, big boy," Tami said. *"Really."*

She threw her free arm around Kelso to include him.

"I'm going to miss both of you," she said.

Blecha had completed his BS in mechanical engineering in the spring before he reunited with the shots for his last season. He planned to go on to graduate school in the fall.

For just an instant, a veil of sadness sheathed the fun in his dark eyes. He glanced away. Then he looked back and smiled softly.

"You're just saying that because of my Greek body," he cracked.

Jon Kelso flashed a wide boyish grin. Hair mopped around his head. He resembled Huck Finn who had somehow made it into adulthood. Or maybe a friendly Andy-of-Mayberry type. People introduced to him half-expected him to kick the toe of his boot in the sand and mumble, "Aw, shucks." Before going away to college to earn his degree in wildlife biology, he had lived his entire youth in tiny Prineville isolated and safe from the corrupting influences of a Portland or Seattle or Los Angeles.

"Jon Kelso," said his friends, "will always be lovably small-town."

Levi Brinkley, who had phoned his mother about "going to heaven" in Colorado, looked around WSFCC with the same curiosity he explored Horizon Drive after the hotshots' arrival last night. He was one of the newest shots, having quit his construction job in Boise in the spring when he learned Tom Shepard picked him for the crew. Word about his acceptance spread rapidly in his hometown of Burns, Oregon. As in Prineville, everyone in Burns knew everyone else. People remembered Levi as the firstborn of a set of triplet brothers born on Halloween 1971.

"Trick or treat?" was one of the town jokes. "And here come Mrs. Brinkley's tricks."

"Most people remember when they were born—these three wild little boys," said Carol McDonald. "His mother tells the greatest stories."

Brinkley stood with Dunbar on the edge of Walker Field. WSFCC squatted on the southern edge of the runway isolated from the airport's main terminal. Heat devils squirmed out of the desert that stretched from the airport east toward the stark, brown rise of the mountains.

"Funny," Brinkley observed, "how heaven can look so much like hell."

A single school bus drove up around 8:00 A.M., creating a flurry of excitement. Brian Scholz counted his hotshots and called the roll: Kelso, Blecha, Brinkley, Rob and Tony Johnson, Rambo, Robertson, Dunbar, Kathi Beck, Bonnie Jean Holtby, Bickett, Terri Hagen, Kip Gray, Mike Simmons, Bill Baker, Brian Lee, Louie Navarro, Kim Valentine. Everyone present, all twenty, including Shepard and Scholz. Present and ready to go.

Except there was only one bus to haul four shot crews, eighty firefighters and their equipment, to several different fire sites. Tom Shepard looked grim.

"Stand down, people," he barked. "I'll try to find out what's going on. If anybody knows."

He telephoned Grand Junction Dispatch.

"We're here," he grumbled. "Now what are you going to do with us?"

"Prineville? Oh, you're going to Storm King Mountain. Butch Blanco is IC."

"When? We could have damned near *walked* there by now."

"We got a lot of fires," Dispatch alibied.

The hotshots waited some more while overhead tried to sort out the use of the one bus or acquire others. The five Oregon women in their blue Prineville T-shirts congregated in a chattering cluster on the ramp outside Ops. They were, without exception, athletic outdoors types with that wholesome sun-browned look of women accustomed to seeking sunshine and fresh air. They were attractive and feminine while at the same time possessing the same sense of adventure as the men. They readily melded into the rough-and-tumble world of healthy males. In their childhood, they were the tomboy girls who learned to climb trees and race bicycles as well as change the diapers on a doll. As hotshots, the women generally agreed they had the best of both the female and the male worlds.

Women first joined U.S. Forest Service fire fighting crews in the mid-1960s. They had to work hard, harder than the men, some said, to win spots on the hotshot teams and earn the respect of their fellow firefighters. Like the males, they carried packs that weighed forty pounds, swung Pulaskis and McLeods for twelve to fourteen hours a day and cut down trees with chain saws. By 1988 they accounted for 12 percent of Forest Service firefighters, then expanded their percentage to 40 percent by 1994. The head firefighter in the U.S. Forest Service is a woman, Mary Jo Lavin.

"They've been challenged and met the muster," said Dennis Pendleton, a Forest Service branch chief in Washington. "A firefighter is a firefighter. When you call for ten or twenty, it doesn't matter the gender. It's whether you can do the work."

The most senior female on the Prineville Hotshots was Tamara "Tami" Bickett, 25. She joined the U.S. Forest Service in 1988, the same year she graduated from high school in Lebanon, Oregon. She resembled a more robust version of actress Marilu Henner.

"That's all Tami ever talked about, was wanting to be a firefighter," said her high school friend Teresa Gentry.

In high school Tami had been a strong, competitive athlete. Her spirit carried over with her into the hotshots. Two years ago she was injured in a fire and assigned to work in a Forest Service supply office while she recuperated. She bitched and groaned about the inactivity so much that her doctor finally released her to go back on the fireline.

"Young lady," he warned, "take it easy. It doesn't do anyone any good to be so dedicated that it gets you killed."

Tami's friend, twenty-one-year-old Bonnie Jean Holtby, also had tenacity. There was a stubborn set to her square jaw that might have been unattractive except that it disappeared almost completely whenever she flashed a wide grin as open and readable as a Judith Henry Wall novel. She stood tall enough at five-feet-eight to have played basketball for her Redmond, Oregon, high school team. She also ran track and cross-country.

"She wasn't gifted with a great deal of speed," said her high school coach Jim Erickson. "But she worked hard for everything she got. She had that really strong character and integrity. Some kids gain a lot of success just by sheer talent. Bonnie didn't have that talent, but she was a dedicated hard worker. She's special that way."

Although Terri Ann Hagen at twenty-eight was the oldest woman on the hotshots, this was her first year chasing fires. She had needed the money to continue her studies at Oregon State University where she would soon complete her degree in entomology, the study of insects. Summers in the outdoors where she might collect insects from different places appealed to her, as did the adventure and the camaraderie of other young people.

Before this year, she spent her holidays and summers drawing and collecting blood at Central Oregon State Hospital in Redmond. She and the manager of the hospital lab, Steve O'Connell, became good friends. He liked to tease her. He called her the "Go Girl" because she couldn't seem to stand still. She was always on the go, vivacious and energetic and laughing, full of life and busy living life.

"She was always bringing these strange and exotic insects into the lab," O'Connell said. "My kids still have some at home. She was so excited about being accepted by the hotshots."

Kim Valentine, twenty-three, was a rather shy and awkward brunette who had also needed a summer job to support college. Polite and friendly, she nonetheless seemed reserved to some of the other firefighters and a bit standoffish. She had not been a star athlete or anything to help her conquer an innate shyness. She once said she wished she could be more like her friend Kathi Beck.

"Kathi is always pushing the envelope," she said. "Life to her . . . Well, she goes out and grabs it like there's not enough to go around."

Kathi Beck was twenty-four and the most daring member of the Prineville Hotshots. As tall as Bonnie Holtby, she was broad-hipped and muscle-toned with a long aquiline nose that perked up on the end, dark eyes so intense they almost crackled and full, straight lips that spread mischievously across her pretty face.

"She lives on the edge," her father described her. "We're dubious at times, but her love for adventure overpowers our concerns."

Kathi sky-dived, skiied and climbed rocks. One year she climbed Mount Hood in Oregon, then flew to Thailand to climb. She was a psychology major at the University of Oregon and a reserve soldier in the U.S. Army National Guard. Her mother liked to talk about Kathi's achievements.

"She's got great determination," she said. "As a little girl, she might be ill with the flu, but she'd still insist on going skiing."

"Kathi must drive her parents crazy," Doug Dunbar observed. "If I had a daughter or a wife like her, I'd lock her up for her own safety and my sanity."

But for all her daring, it was another unrelated trait that most endeared Kathi Beck to the other hotshots. The only thing that came close to challenging her passion for the outdoors was her golden heart and her love for her fellow man. Kathi was the team's Mother Teresa, its confessor. She was the one person on the crew to whom the others felt safe in expressing their deepest emotions. They discussed with her their fear of death or their jealousy over leaving a lover behind or virtually *anything* and knew it would be kept strictly confidential.

"I don't see how she's got enough room inside to hold that great big heart of hers," said Rob Johnson.

"Kathi is a free spirit," her mother said, smiling. "She is a beautiful person, and so kind. I always thought she would be written up in history books because she is so unique."

The young men and women of the Prineville Hotshots, robust and browned and healthy, mingled in easy comradeship and waited for the overheads to decide what to do with them. Blecha and Brinkley chuckled over a story about how a flare-up in California scorched Kelso's eyebrows, causing him to "run away calmly."

Kelso laughed with them. "Big flames, big fun."

After two or three hours waiting, however, putting in

"ramp time," patience wore thin. Word spread among the hotshots: "It's a big rat fuck. They don't know from a frog's ass what to do with us. Who runs this goat roping?"

"Is it chow time yet?" Brian Lee wanted to know.

"It will be before we get out of here."

Even big Scott Blecha yawned with boredom. He stretched out on the grass next to Jon Kelso and used his yellow helmet as a pillow.

"Wake me when the world's on fire," he said.

The Prineville Hotshots cooled their heels, their destinies hanging on something as routine as the availability of buses. Back home in Prineville, a long line of cars led by a black hearse and black limousines eased through the gates of the town cemetery and halted before a fresh open grave. The town was burying a sixteen-year-old local boy who plunged eighty feet to his death from a cliff on June 30.

"When tragedies happen to a family town," said the minister, "it affects each of us in our hearts."

28

The (Storm King) fire remained active throughout the night. RAWS data shows little or no relative humidity recovery. The fire had flanked 1,000 feet by the time fireline construction began at 1000 hours that morning. The fire in the litter under the gambel oak was moving laterally at a rate of about 70 feet per hour and backing down the slope at a similar rate.

BLM assessment (Wed, July 6)

THE SUN HUNG HIGH IN THE EASTERN SKY—IT was about 9:00 A.M.—when Butch Blanco and his advance party of Hayes and Abbott broke out of the scrub PJ on the wall of the eastern drainage. Sweating heavily beneath their backpacks, the three men scrambled up the last steep stretch of rocky terrain to the ridge summit. Chain saws burred angrily off their right flank, from down toward the saddle at the base of Storm King. Mackey had his smokejumpers busy building fireline along the top of the ridge to stop the fire's eastern advance and provide a safety zone in the east drainage.

"This fire's getting big," Abbott said, surprised. "Much bigger than when we left last night."

Separate smokes curled up from small patches of gambel oak the jumpers were burning out at the fireline to "neutralize" it as fuel for the main blaze. A pall of heavier smoke from below clumped in the stunted mat of forest like fiber caught in the teeth of a cotton gin. Morning breezes stirred it occasionally. The fire monster cracked and popped relentlessly through the oak cluster not a quarter-mile below. So far, the blaze remained on the ground. Blanco drew in a deep breath filled with acrid smoke.

It was going to be a long day.

"Smokejumpers do more work before nine A.M. than most people do all day long," a jumper chided Blanco, parodying an army TV recruiting ad.

Blanco chuckled good-naturedly. He held high regard for smokejumpers.

"But we do it better," he joked back. "And we do it longer."

IC Blanco and Jumper-in-Charge Mackey squatted on their haunches at the ridgeline to discuss strategies and tactics. Blanco drew from his water bottle. Mackey swiped off his helmet and chewed reflectively on a twig. He had already scouted the fire this morning, but scouting it on foot was a bit like the old story of how a blind man describes an elephant by feeling it. He only "saw" one piece of the elephant at a time and he could never be sure how the entire elephant really looked.

"We need to take a gander at the fire from the air," Mackey said, explaining that he had already asked the helicopter assigned to them to bring a long line to retrieve the jumpers' pack-out bags and fly them to safety. "Just in case the fire makes a run," he added uneasily, glancing downslope toward flames hidden in oak brush.

WSFCC had offered the helicopter for only four hours. Storm King firefighters could use it as an aerial observer.

"We'd like to use it to also ferry up a hotshot crew," Blanco radioed Dispatch. "We do have a shot crew en route?"

"That's the promise—but they haven't left Walker Field yet."

"What's the holdup?"

Dispatch didn't know. "Transportation," he guessed.

"See if you can speed 'em up," the IC encouraged.

Unknown to the fighters on the mountain, District Fire Management Officer Pete Blume telephoned Paul Hefner at WSFCC. Blume had toured the Wake fire at Paonia shortly after daybreak and found it well on its way, finally, to being controlled. "The other fires in the district are being taken care of," Blume assured Hefner. "Storm King Mountain is now our number-one priority for resources."

His word should release more troops and equipment for use at Storm King. It was just a matter of time. Both Blanco and Mackey hoped reinforcements arrived before the scheduled cold front and its winds that afternoon.

The force on the mountain now consisted of nineteen firefighters—Mackey and his jumpers for eight, Blanco and his crew for an additional eleven. The two leaders heard Michelle Ryerson and the rest of Blanco's fighters scrambling up the last stretch of slope. They collapsed for breath on the ridgetop.

"Give them fifteen minutes rest," Blanco told Ryerson, "then let's get it on. Time's gold."

Together Mackey and Blanco scouted the ridge, gesturing and talking and planning as they walked. Mackey pointed out where the fire had overrun the line Blanco's crew started on Tuesday down the west flank. Considering that the fire was not moving all that fast yet and was still a ground fire with short flames, the two leaders decided on a dual attack to pinch off the fire monster's head. At least that was the plan until they got a chance to take a longer look at the fire from the air.

Blanco would go indirect on the ridgeline, widening the fireline jumpers started last night. That line lay anchored at the tiny helispot and led northerly along the top of the ridge toward Storm King Mountain. Blanco would also cut a second, larger helispot about two hundred yards north of the first one, near the saddle onto which Mackey's smoke-jumpers had parachuted yesterday afternoon. While the first helispot *could* receive a chopper the size of a Bell Ranger, getting in and out of it would prove tricky. Blanco's fireline would connect Helispot 1 with Helispot 2.

The smokejumpers planned to go direct and work a new fireline down the west slope ahead of the creeping fire. The two firelines would eventually form a kind of triangle to channel the blaze into a corner and kill it. Designated escape routes—just in case *something* happened and fire-fighters had to get out quickly—were the firelines them-selves which led either up the ridge or along the ridge into the east drainage. Clearings here and there, one of which was Helispot 1, served as safety zones.

Blanco clapped his big hands at his resting crew.

"Let's get it on," he shouted. "Our plan is to get the fire lined and tied off."

Kevin Erickson was one of Don Mackey's squad leaders. Shortly after work began on the revised plan, he drew Mackey aside and pointed downslope toward the gambel oak. Much of it had already been underburned. Fire-dried leaves caught the freshening breeze and rattled like skele-tons.

"I don't like our going down in there," he said.

Mackey leaned on his Pulaski. He studied the sky. Still blue through the haze of smoke with only a transparent stripe of high cirrus here and there. He studied the smoke cloud. Gray and not black or brown.

"The fire's not burning too active," he said. "What would your option be, Kevin?"

The two men talked tactics for a few minutes, finally coming to the same conclusion.

"I have to agree that a direct attack is the best way," Erickson conceded. "That oak just makes me a little nervous, that's all."

"It makes *me* nervous," Mackey agreed.

Erickson hesitated. Chain saw buzz and tool clanking forced him to raise his voice.

"Who *is* the IC here anyhow—you or Blanco?" he asked.

"You got me. You want it?"

"Yes."

Mackey smiled. "We'll see what happens."

29

WSFCC ASSIGNED RANGER HELICOPTER 93R TO the Storm King fire. Hotshots and jumpers still mingled around the Ops building in casual disorganization when the chopper lifted its skids off the tarmac for the half-hour flight to Glenwood Springs. Dick Good flew the little whirlybird. His helitack crew consisted of Steve Little, Bob Browning and Rich Tyler.

As seen from the airfield, the sun had not yet popped above the Rockies. The morning light shone clear with that lovely translucence only mountains and deserts provided. Thin, high cirrus scouted the sky in advance of the coming cold front. Sunrise began above the airfield at about two hundred feet.

Dick Good kicked on power to the chopper, lifted to one thousand feet and lined out toward the sun like a bee honing in on a distant orchard. He followed the shimmering ribbon of I-70 below as the interstate climbed out of the desert and followed the Colorado River upstream into Glenwood Canyon. Lanky Steve Little flew second seat with the pilot.

He gazed out the wide bubble windows as the chopper scooted along, outrunning its tailing shadow on the earth. He yawned. He seemed to be daydreaming.

It was a quiet half hour.

Bob Browning, doing his own daydreaming, sat on the canvas webbing seats with Rich Tyler in the small cargo compartment behind the pilot seats. A dazzling white sun at this altitude bent rays across Browning's tanned face and burnished copper highlights in his heavy beard. He was a slender, sandy-haired man in his late twenties who liked to talk hunting and fishing. He had boosted in from the U.S. Forest Service in South Carolina to helitack for the season. That and the fact that he was a hotshot before transferring to helicopters was about all Rich Tyler knew about him. They had been too busy to form any kind of true personal friendship.

Tyler's own meditative gaze followed the horizon. The helitack rarely took off in a chopper without thinking about that other day nearly ten years ago when pilot Jim Daugherty struck the powerline not far from here and crashed his bird, killing everyone aboard. If Tyler hadn't switched to the chase truck at the last minute . . .

The thought always crept into his head—and each time he willed it out of his mind. Sometimes he couldn't help thinking he really did live on borrowed time.

He thought of his tanker bomber friend Andy Wilson. Wilson would probably be flying at least some missions against Storm King during the day. The crazy young devil— he and Earl Dahl zipping in underneath that curl of smoke at the Wake fire on Monday!

"If you gotta go in a bang," Wilson joked recklessly, "what better day than on July fourth."

No. Wilson wasn't flying today. Tyler probably wouldn't see him again until maybe Saturday night for dinner. They had run across each other briefly last night at Walker Field after all the aircraft shut down. Bombers and choppers flew no fires after dark. The last sliver of red sun posed on the edge of the desert to the west in Utah. Wilson had dropped out the belly hatch of his P2V and hailed Tyler across the tarmac.

"That was some real dumb hotshotting on Monday," Tyler chided his friend. "You'll never get old like ol' Earl trying to be bold like me."

They laughed easily, comfortable with each other. Wilson agreed flying underneath the smoke hadn't been the most prudent act Dahl and he had ever committed. No old bold pilots and all that. But he shrugged it off and the two Minnesotans chatted easily about other things for a few last minutes. Tyler promised, "Patty'll cook us up a dinner that'll make you *beg* some unfortunate girl to marry you."

"I'm not old enough to marry."

"You're not bold enough." Tyler laughed. "You're bold enough to fly into the fires of hell, but let some pretty thing whisper marriage and you stampede like a herd of scared sheep."

"Fire's a lot safer than marriage."

The airmen walked together to the pilots ready shack where they caught up on their paperwork at the long table in the middle of the one room. Afterward, with the sun gone and only its lingering streaks remaining on the horizon, they walked together to their vehicles parked outside the gate. It was that cool, calm time after battle.

"I reckon we've got another good fire started over toward Glenwood Springs," Tyler commented. "They say people who live around it are afraid it'll be like the Wake fire. We'll probably be flying it tomorrow."

"*We?* Got a mouse in your pocket, big fella? I've been piloting that ol' Neptune sunup to sundown. I've finally got a day off. Nothing for me to do all day Wednesday except head out to the ranch and doze and eat."

Wilson and his brother owned a working cow ranch a few miles south of Grand Junction. The pilot spent holidays and some winters there; his brother acted as foreman and kept the ranch going.

"Rich?" Wilson said suddenly as the two airmen clapped each other on the back and parted.

Tyler turned. "Yeah?"

They looked at one another. Wilson finally smiled. "Nothing," he said. "It's nothing."

He turned away, then turned back again. "Rich," he said, "be careful up there, okay?"

Tyler told himself he was always careful, as careful as anyone could be considering they were all literally playing with fire. He smiled to himself as the chopper *whump-whumped* above I-70 toward Storm King Mountain. Time to get down to today's business. Good's voice came over the intercom.

"There she blows."

Smoke rose thick but still almost white from the mile-long ridge that hogbacked between I-70 and Storm King Mountain. The column of smoke twisted slightly and leaned toward the east, pushed by the drift of air out of the west. Yellow-helmeted firefighters scrambled around in the smoke on the ridgeline.

Good circled the chopper wide of the smoke. He flew above the motels and strip malls of West Glenwood and then returned and climbed a cushion of air up the east drainage toward the firefighters. Two firefighters—Tyler recognized Don Mackey and Butch Blanco—directed the arriving bird onto a tiny clearing. The helispot appeared the size of a family dining table. Boulders ranged downslope off one flank of it while a straggling of PJ ran downslope in the opposite direction.

Tyler took a second look as Good flared the chopper for landing. "You got to be shitting me!" he gasped.

Whirling blades wind-blasted PJ and kicked up dust. The skids settled carefully. Tyler jumped out to help the bird settle. The blue-and-white-and-red chopper came to a gentle rest with its nose facing uphill. Tyler always praised Good on being one hell of a flyer. The pilot cut power. He stuck his head out into the morning smoke.

"Couldn't you guys find a better helispot—like in the top of a tree?" he growled at Mackey and Blanco.

Mackey flashed a sheepish Bert Reynolds grin. He

pointed toward the saddle where Michelle Ryerson and some of her crew were kicking up their own dust building a larger helispot.

"You'll think you're landing at Denver International by the time we get back from the recon flight," he said.

Good harrumphed. The helitacks remained on the ridge while the fire supervisors took their places in the chopper to look the fire over from the air. The bird lifted off. Finding himself on the ground, Tyler looked around. Like Wilson, he preferred to fight his fires from the air. All the smoke made him uneasy. How the hell would you get out of here if things blew up?

From Helispot 1 looking toward Storm King Mountain, the ridgeline flattened out into the saddle at Helispot 2. The saddle appeared relatively flat and clear of serious timber. Beyond it rose a series of rocky outcroppings where no fire could sustain itself.

An escape route.

What could not be seen from Helispot 1 was how the outcropping of rock funneled a tangle of oak and PJ into a steep rocky chute two hundred yards past the saddle. What appeared to be an escape route was instead a dead end choked with highly inflammable fuels.

30

BLANCO AND MACKEY CAREFULLY STUDIED THE fire on the mountain from their airborne seats in 93R. They stared down into the scorch of the natural inferno. Good maneuvered the chopper upwind of the smoke column. The column rose thick and compact alongside the bird and towered above as it flattened out at altitude and drifted slowly east and north.

Mackey seemed surprised to find the fire had grown to an

estimated one hundred acres overnight. Even so, it remained a modest-size fire, grown beyond initial attack into extended attack but still not of sufficient size to warrant a designated overhead team of supervisors. Blanco continued as IC, a position he shared somewhat in practice with Mackey.

A huge and growing black spot stained the ridge's west flank. Flames crept and smoldered around the edges of the black. Fingers like spilled ink oozed among and around the lighter green patches of gambel. In places the blaze had slopped over the ridge top into the east drainage. Most of it, however, stayed on the western aspect and moved slowly along the ridge toward the mountain while also backing down into the west drainage.

Mackey pointed. With his finger he flagged an imaginary line from the ridge top down the west side of the ridge ahead of the fire's head to the bottom of the drainage. He then drew another line tracing the spine of the ridge between Helispot 1 and Helispot 2. Firefighters in their yellow helmets and shirts were working on the firelines. Blanco nodded. Neither man saw anything to cause him to want to alter the original attack plan. They made only one modification. They decided to split troops building fireline on the western aspect and place one group at the bottom of the drainage to cut line uphill; the other group would continue working downhill. Eventually the fire monster found himself tied off and defanged as the two firelines linked up.

"I'm not sure we can hold the fire without stopping the head," Mackey said.

Reinforcements would be integrated into the lines as they arrived. Soon, Blanco surmised, glancing at his watch—midmorning already!—there should be enough people on the ground working with tanker bombers and chopper water lifts to make the direct assault work.

"But if we get wind in that front this afternoon . . ." he pondered, then left the thought uncompleted. There was no need to finish it. Mackey nodded his head.

Fresh oxygen infusing into gambel oak parched by drought

and then further dried out by the heat of the ground fire created a volatile mixture.

Below, squad leader Kevin Erickson paused to look up at the low-flying chopper. He whipped off his plastic helmet to wipe sweat with his shirtsleeve. A sunburn line showed across his broad forehead. At twenty-eight, he was a lean young man, powerful-looking, with more than five years of fire fighting experience. Erickson studied fires the way an architect might study the supporting beams of a structure he was building or the way an engineer pored over blueprints of a new bridge. Erickson was instinctively careful when it came to battling the fire monster. He had never been burned or anything, like Kent Hamilton, but he realized deep in his soul that the monster could get you if you didn't watch out.

Mackey's voice came over Erickson's two-way radio. Erickson watched Mackey's face pressed against the window of the chopper circling lazily above as the jumper-in-charge radioed him the new plan for splitting the troops in half. The chopper resembled a great brightly colored grasshopper with skids. Like it had been jumped up by some kid walking through tall grass with a fishing pole.

"Kevin," Mackey instructed, "you want to take your squad down at the bottom and start cutting line uphill?"

"It looks awfully ugly down there," Erickson radioed back. "How about safe areas? Can you pick out any from the air?"

"It's not as bad seen from up here as it looks from the ground. Vegetation is pretty sparse at the bottom. I think we can get away with it."

Erickson had that cautious streak. He kept listening to the fire breaking bones, the dry skeletal shuddering of the oak thickets.

"Let's scout it out again when you come down," he suggested.

There was a short pause. "Roger that," Mackey said.

The IC wanted to take another look at the fire before he came down. Good circled the Ranger, then roller-coastered it off the ridge and slid down above the Canyon Creek Estates. The big expensive houses were widely spaced and handsomely landscaped among live oaks and ponderosa pine. Each home commanded a picture-window view of Storm King Mountain and, during the last four days at least, of the smoke rising around it.

Good landed the helicopter on the Estates' large grassy Commons to let the firefighters study the blaze from this angle and complete their fire maps. Some kids and other spectators attracted by the aircraft and front row seats to the drama being played out on the mountain hung around the Commons and perched themselves like birds on the wooden rail fence that anchored the Commons. A couple of Huck Finn towheads with freckles across their noses and bare toes digging in the soil ambled over to Mackey. Mackey grinned at them. They reminded him that tomorrow was his daughter's birthday.

"We seen the smokejumpers yesterday," they said. "Boy, that was *bad*. That was *awesome*. Are you a smokejumper?"

"Yes."

"Awesome. Is there going to be some more?"

People in neighboring homes, wondering about the increased activity, ventured onto their lawns and shaded their eyes against the sun to peer first at the helicopter and then at the smoke.

"It's about time they started fighting that fire," one resident murmured, relieved.

The towheads were more interested in firefighters and their equipment than in the potential of the blaze to wreck devastation. They ogled the chopper and the firefighters.

"You really *really* do parachute right into the fire?" an awed little boy asked Mackey.

"Well, not *into* the fire," Mackey said, laughing.

"How close?"

"Close enough. Too close sometimes."

"We wanna see it some more."

"Just keep watching," Mackey encouraged with a farewell grin. "The show's just starting."

31

CHECKING HIS EQUIPMENT REACHED ALMOST
an obsession to a jumper whose life depended upon proper
functioning of both himself and his gear. A religious experience even. The jumper was a careful person even though his
two major activities—falling from the sky and fighting fire
when he landed—attracted adventurer types, the proud and
the few, who wanted to make it clear they were not
intimidated by the universe. While on the one hand they
gloried in the recklessness and uniqueness of their profession, on the other hand, they mildly resented being catego-
rized the way Evan Kelley of the Forest Service headquarters in Missoula, Montana, characterized them in 1935
during the debates over whether or not to use parachutists
as smokejumpers.

Kelley had at first rejected the notion of dropping parachutists onto fires, arguing, "The best information I can get
from experienced fliers is that all parachute jumpers are
more or less crazy—just a little bit unbalanced, otherwise
they wouldn't be engaged in such a hazardous under-
taking."

Kelley finally came around to accepting the utility of
using smokejumpers, but he never changed his mind about
their mental balance. He always thought them a little crazy,
a speculation entertained and sometimes encouraged by
smokejumpers themselves. Only rain, snow, bird shit and
nuts fell from the sky. It was part of the image.

Tony Petrelli couldn't give a whit about image on
Wednesday morning when he joined the other smokejumpers in checking out his equipment in front of the
shack. He nodded and grunted and felt tired and sloppy
from having fought the Oil Springs fire until nearly mid-

night the day before. A McDonald's McMuffin or McWhatever on Horizon Drive that led to the airport hadn't improved his disposition much. Someone offered him a cup of steaming coffee. He felt it warm in his hands and set it down on the long table inside before heading for the bulletin board to check the position of his name on The List.

"What's with all the hotshots hanging around outside?" he asked of the small group of jumpers gathered at the bulletin board.

"Can you spell *clusterfuck,* boys and girls?" one of them said, laughing.

"We got us another fire," Hipke or Roth explained. "I guess the hotshots are waiting for a bus—and then they can pound the ground to get there. We're luckier. We've got reservations on Smokejumper Airlines."

"Heard where we're going?" Petrelli asked. His name was among the first eight.

"Your ass is on The List, Petrelli. Storm King Mountain."

"Sounds like a Viking village or something."

In addition to the seventeen jumpers who boosted in from New Mexico on Tuesday, eight of whom were already fighting the Storm King fire, another twenty-seven had since demobed from either the Wake fire or one of the other blazes on the western slopes and added their names to The List. In its random way, The List made its selections. The List and Fate—maybe they were the same thing.

"It could have been any of us selected," J.C. Curd said later. "It's all a matter of how your name came up and where it came up. Maybe if Kent Hamilton hadn't broken his clavicle in Washington, he would have been on it instead of Thrash or Roth. Pettitt might have made it, or Big Johnson, or me—it was up to The List or to other lists somewhere. That's what we all try to understand. The List controls our future."

George Steele wended his way silently to the bulletin board, nodding to other jumpers but saying little. Dragging a word out of him was like mining truth out of politicians. He stabbed a blunt finger at his name. It was down past the first stick. He grunted to himself, then strolled outside to study the weather. He noted the thin cirrus stretched high across the sky like the sheerest of veils.

Casa Jump 17, the twin-engined aircraft that had flown in the New Mexico jumpers the day before, sat fueled and ready on the tarmac in front of the jump equipment lean-to.

"The wind's coming," Steele predicted. "If you don't get a jump in this morning, get ready for a pounder. I doubt there'll be any more jumps after noon."

The List for Storm King Mountain that Wednesday, July 6, proved as consequential for those it excluded as for those it included. Indeed, it had the power to alter lives. The first stick of the day bound for Storm King was made up of Tony Petrelli, Dale Longanecker, Roger Roth, Eric Hipke, Bill Thomas, James Thrash, Michael Cooper and Mike Feliciano. Mike Tupper would fly as spotter.

"They thought they were fortunate to get a jump," Tim Pettitt said. "Everybody else that day would probably have to walk into their fires."

Rick Blanton gave the selected jumpers their final prejump briefing. He told them they were reinforcements for other firefighters already on the site. He said a cold front was on its way.

"If there's wind—and we expect at least *some*—it's going to make small fires bigger," he said. "Butch Blanco is IC. Do him a good job. He's a good guy who uses jumpers a lot. The fire is about twenty minutes out once you take off."

The Casa's windows were small and double-paned recessed to withstand pressure. Tony Petrelli grabbed a peek out one of them during the streamer pass over the burning ridge above West Glenwood Springs. He glimpsed a severe cone-shaped mountain, almost bald at the top. It loomed out of ridged and rumpled terrain that looked steep, rocky and brushy. He couldn't tell much about the fire during his brief first study, except that it had many fingers and looked messy. His lips felt dry like sandpaper. He licked them. They dried again.

A fire like that on a steep slope with fingers reaching into unburned brush made him jumpy.

The dropped streamer showed insignificant drift. Tupper the spotter worked his way back from the cockpit to pass on any last-minute intel.

"Winds are calm, about five knots from the south, southwest," he shouted above the throbbing of engines. "Wind drift looks to be about one hundred yards, straight and steady with very little turbulence. Sabinio Archuleta is going to be standing on the jump spot with a streamer. You should be able to see him when you open in the air."

Hipke and Thomas bailed out the door on the first pass. Petrelli and Longanecker snapped their static lines to the cable and edged into the open door and looked out and down as the Casa circled for a second pass. Below, Hipke and Thomas rode into the thick white-gray of the smoke on brightly colored wings. They soared off the fire to its windward flank before they toggled into the wind and, with their backs to the mountain, guided back in toward the jump spot in the saddle.

The jump spot appeared to be somewhat larger than the average house. It looked earth-brown and fairly level before it dropped off on either side of the saddle into jumbles of rock and stunted, thick brush. Someone in a yellow helmet stood on the upwind side of the spot.

Petrelli gave no thought to the fire at the moment. He concentrated entirely on the target. The Casa came around and leveled out on final at three thousand feet. Petrelli tensed.

"I'll take the side of the jump spot toward the highway," he shouted to Longanecker.

Longanecker nodded. Not even two eagles tried to land on the same branch.

It was an intense jump, what with the smoke and the narrow ridge and the mountain, but all the jumpers flew in two at a time safely on target. Archuleta stood grinning at them with his bright teeth as they landed. A long paper streamer hung fluttering gaily from his uplifted fist.

"Bird shit would have landed on your head," someone told him, joking and on a high from the flight.

"That's what falls out of the sky," Archuleta teased back.

"Huh-uh. *Heroes* fall out of the sky. Where's the bear you want raped? How come you sissies had to call *us* to put out this piddley-assed fire?"

The newcomers quickly stuffed their excess gear into pack-out bags and left the bags at the recently completed Helispot 2 for 93R to fly out. Hipke gave his hand radio to Longanecker. Billy Thomas and Petrelli ripped open the drop packs as soon as the cargo chutes landed and readied the chain saws, fuel sig packs and leather chaps for action. They started off as sawyers.

Lithe Sarah Doehring hurried up through the brush from the fireline to greet the new jumpers. She smiled at them.

"Welcome to hell on the mountain, boys. Let me show you around."

32

"I FIGURE THAT WITH SIXTEEN JUMPERS ON THE ground and a hotshot crew on its way, we can hook the fire before the front gets here," Dale Longanecker ventured.

None of the firefighters liked working direct line in thick oak underbrush so dry it chattered in sinister undertones. But choices were limited. It was either hold the fire now, here on the ridge, or face the prospect of the approaching front releasing a flaming flood of destruction onto the settlements below.

Blanco and Mackey seeded the second stick of jumpers directly into the battle forming along the west downridge fireline. Tony Petrelli cranked over his heavy chain saw. The exaggerated wink he tossed at Mackey promised, "We'll have this little fire beat down by sunset."

Sawyers led the attack in opening up a swath through the scrub on the downslope. Chain saws screamed as trees fell. Sawyers literally ripped through the smaller growth while swampers followed to clear the debris away for the hand tools. Warrior ants chopped and hacked with their Pulaskis and McLeods to clear a path down to mineral soil. The fireline was about six to eight feet wide with a scrape depth of a foot-and-a-half. Fuel along with oxygen and heat formed the three sides of the fire triangle; depriving the fire monster of fuels—starving him—was the most effective way to defeat him. Ordinarily, a fireline six feet wide halted most fires in their black tracks.

Whenever Mackey wasn't laboring on the fireline himself, he scouted the fire. Scouted it frequently, sometimes with squad leader Kevin Erickson, ranging out ahead to where Quentin Rhoades and some of the other jumpers labored near the bottom of the drainage building fireline uphill. Jumpers noticed he looked anxious. He urged them to greater effort.

"C'mon, kids. We don't want to lose this race."

"You're becoming a real slave driver, know that, Don?" Roger Roth retorted, but then grinned slightly through the ash that masked his face black.

A hot breeze stirred up-canyon. Mackey noticed it had picked up since earlier in the morning. Petrelli paused before biting his saw into the next scrub oaks ahead of him.

"No coffee breaks in this business," Longanecker chided, but he too felt the hot breeze licking at the side of his neck and cheek.

Ground flames no longer crept toward the line; they rose up on their tiptoes. Toward the bottom of the drainage, brush torched sporadically but more frequently than before. Flames bubbled, flared, like a volcano about to erupt, then fell back to the ground. Ash sifting finely through the air, like dirty gray snowflakes, settled on yellow helmets and on the shoulders of sweat-soaked yellow shirts. Smoke oozed through the forest and clung to branches.

Mackey pressed his two crews. Petrelli and Thomas flew

from tree to tree, felling them as fast as a battalion of beavers on a rampage. The rest of the line crew got caught up in the spirit. Tools rattled and clanked behind the sawyers like a rusty engine. Backs aching, sweat pouring, firefighters tore at the rocky soil.

Shortly after 11:00 A.M., Mackey climbed to the top of the ridge where Michelle Ryerson's squad worked the indirect line between the helispots. The fire exerted little pressure on his crew at the moment. Sawyer Tim Byers and his swamper Mike Hayes looked up and paused in their labors. Mackey pointed into the west drainage.

"Fire's starting to push the line up ahead of us," he explained to Byers. "Can you take your swamper and give our guys a hand?"

Byers swiped off his helmet to let the air cool his head and took a swig of water before attempting to raise Ryerson on his hand radio. After two or three tries, with no response from Ryerson, Brad Haugh's voice broke in.

"Affirmative on that," he consented. "We're always happy to lend our brethren from the sky our superior expertise."

The Glenwood Springs sawyers united with Petrelli and Thomas. The sawyer teams played leapfrog, bumping ahead of each other. Other saws screamed down below where fighters worked to push their line uphill to link it with the downhill line. A wide expanse of oak brush still separated the points of the two lines. The fire monster seemed to know that was his only escape route. He headed directly for it.

Petrelli's saw suddenly shrieked as though in excruciating pain. The chain pinched inside the heart of a thick pine and snapped.

"Damn!"

Billy Thomas volunteered to repair it. He was handier at some things than Petrelli. Instead of taking a deserved break, Petrelli reconed ahead a short distance to steal a look at the flames deeper in the drainage. He climbed onto a boulder and craned his neck.

Not far down, to his left, a forested hogback rose slightly

out of the surrounding terrain. It was smoking heavily. No flames were visible, they remained on the ground, but the darker color of the boiling smoke and the crack-popping of burning wood marked it as a hot spot.

Petrelli frowned. He looked around. He found himself under less than ideal conditions: dry aerial fuel in the tree crowns and a steep grade. A bit more of a breeze might lift the fire off the ground and into the trees. It would take a good blowup, what? about six or eight minutes to roar from the bottom of the drainage to the helispots on the ridgeline?

On the other hand, a strong runner might cover the same uphill distance in, what? ten or twelve minutes? More?

Maybe it was merely the mood accompanying such thoughts, but Petrelli found the sky suddenly overcast. It wasn't just the smoke blotting out the sun. The day *had* grown dull. A forbidding gray veil seemed to settle over the ridge. It muted out the sun, took the edge off it, until it was rheumy and red like the eye of an angry and ill god peering down with displeasure upon what he had created.

"Things look a little creepy," Thomas muttered when Petrelli returned to help him with the saw.

Together they stretched the chain around the loosened blade and retightened it.

Mackey also spotted the hot spot on the hogback and read its implications. The fire monster was trying to escape. He persuaded Blanco and Ryerson to release their other sawyer team to help clear on the main fireline downslope. The monster couldn't be let loose again. Brad Haugh and Derek Brixey joined the smokejumpers in their daring race to cut off the fire monster's head. The screaming of the chain saw combo created an odd off-key sort of excited harmony.

Suddenly, frantic shouts rang out from both upslope and downslope.

"Look out! It's coming! Get the hell out of there!"

33

FIREFIGHTERS TOOK TO THEIR HEELS. THEY stampeded uphill toward the top of the ridge, casting frightened looks back over their shoulders as they ran. It had finally happened. The fire had crowned.

The culprit was a cedar tree about forty yards downslope and to the left of the main downhill fireline. It suddenly torched, lifting earth-bound flames into its turpentine branches. It whooshed like a slow-motion explosion. Breezes grabbed some of the flames and slung them like bolts into the unburned tops of a thicket of oak.

Sky and fire united as an avalanche of flames caught and immediately charged uphill, throwing dark smoke over its head and slinging fire ahead of it. It raced fiercely through the treetops, snapping at the fleeing firefighters and blowing hot breath down their necks.

"Flank it, goddamnit!" someone yelled desperately. "Don't run from it. *Flank it!*"

You couldn't outrun a fire once it got going. Roger Roth had outdistanced one in Arizona the week before, but it hadn't been on a steep upgrade. You didn't ever want to *try* against a fire like this one.

"Flank it, goddamnit, flank it!"

Thomas and Petrelli turned abruptly left and bolted. They placed the fireline between them and the blowup. Other firefighters turned either left or right to let the flaming run pass between them. As it turned out, the run was only about five or six feet wide. From where Petrelli and Thomas turned to look back, they saw only boiling smoke and heard the crackling of the fire's rush through the treetops.

Mackey suddenly appeared, breathing heavily.

"Get your stuff," he shouted. "We're pulling out."

He barked orders into his hand radio. Strain and concern

161

wrote themselves in indelible letters on his face. He was responsible for sixteen jumpers. He sounded the alarm. *Retreat! Retreat!*

"Wait a minute," Dale Longanecker's deep drawl filled the radio. He had made the ridgeline in one supreme dash and now stood looking down on the run.

The slender thread of flames streaked between groups of firefighters. It crackled and roared like a freight train picking up speed coming down off the Rockies. It ran like a flaming snake from the one cedar tree all the way to the top of the ridge, stopping only when it reached the fireline. The fireline held.

It held, but in a final burst of defiance the fire monster tossed a blossom of flame across the line into cedars beyond. The cedars blazed. It was almost like the monster was laughing and saying, "See? If I really want to break out, your puny efforts cannot stop me. This was only a little demonstration. Wait until I *really* want out."

"The run's over," Longanecker radioed. "Repeat, it's over. We've got a slopover up here, but the run is down. I think a bucket drop will take care of the slopover."

"Hold what you got," Mackey said. "I'm on my way up."

Smoke from the narrow run dissipated. Firefighters from below clumped together on the ridgetop.

"Beep! Beep! You're making a habit of this, Roth," James Thrash chided his partner. "You got some kind of competition going? This is the second fire you've outrun in a week."

"Huh-uh. I don't race 'em anymore. I stepped aside and let this one pass, thank you."

Squad leaders accounted for their people. Anxiety and adrenaline rapidly bled out of the troops in staccato bursts of humor and grab-assing. These things were funny, afterward. Mackey and Butch Blanco removed themselves from the excitement rush and studied what they could see of the main fire. The smoke rose gray-white again as the blaze, its break for freedom thwarted, dropped back to gnaw at the ground. Some of Michelle Ryerson's fighters attacked the slopover in the cedars.

Both Blanco and Mackey had fought fire long enough to respect its tremendous power. They were cautious men. But you couldn't turn tail and run every time the monster fought back.

"We get paid the big bucks for this," Mackey mused. "We get overtime to stand up to it and drive it back into hell."

At his request, chopper 93R delivered two 250-gallon buckets of water directly onto the slopover. Helitacks Browning, Little and Tyler took turns staying on the ground at Helispot 2 while one of their number flew with Dick Good to help manipulate the bucket dangling on its long line from the helicopter's belly. The fire in the cedars sizzled viciously as it died, whipping its tails of smoke. Ryerson's fighters attacked the surviving flames. Blanco pulled in a couple of sawyers to finish the cooldown.

Smokejumpers headed back down the steep slope. They looked determined. The battle wasn't over yet, not by a long sight. The fire monster was still trying to reach the gap in their lines.

"Keep your heads up," Mackey warned. "You see anything like this again, I want all of you out of there."

Petrelli flashed a grin. "Boss, I never once hankered to be the hot dog at a wienie roast."

34

THE COLD FRONT FIREFIGHTERS HAD ANTICI-pated for two days arrived in Grand Junction seventy miles to the west of Storm King Mountain, heading east. The temperature was around ninety. It dropped by a degree or two, such was the extent of the "cold" in the front. Even more significant to firefighters on the western slopes were the winds. They increased from a steady ten miles per hour to twenty-two mph with gusts to thirty. Paul Hefner stepped outside the Ops building and faced the rise of the Rocky Mountains to the east beyond Walker Field. He stood there a long time while gusts of wind flapped his slacks and shirt.

George Steele was right in assuming there would be no more jumps today, not in these winds. WSFCC finally straightened out the transportation problem. It was just before noon. School buses arrived. Their spirits rejuvenated, the Prineville Hotshots loaded their gear into one of the buses and arrived at the Commons in the Canyon Creek Estates in time to watch 93R dump water onto the cedar slopover on the ridge. They prepared themselves and their equipment. The chopper would be coming for them as soon as it completed its bucket drops.

Another bus transported twenty-two disgruntled smokejumpers, including George Steele and Jumper-in-Charge Ken Wabaunsee, to the Commons. *Walking* to a fire or being *bused* was undignified. Birds never *walked* south for the winter.

Troops and overhead started to mass for an all-out attack on the worrisome Storm King fire. It had started out slow. Burning in only a single tree three days ago, it now had the makings of the district's next project-size blaze.

Dick Good's 93R buzzed down from the ridge and landed on the grass in the Canyon Creek Estates Common. It could transport only four or five firefighters at a time. Tom Shepard signaled to the first lift. As leader, he accompanied it while Brian Scholz stayed behind to supervise.

Scott Blecha mimicked a railroad conductor: "All aboard!"

The shots felt in rare good form after a slow morning's start. Excitement crackled among them. None sat to wait his turn on the chopper. They had too much energy. They stood in clusters and chattered animatedly. They watched the fire on the mountain. They had the enemy in sight.

The first lift took off. Rob Johnson quipped, "Once again into the breach, Horatio."

The cold front passed Grand Junction and headed for Glenwood Springs.

35

SO FAR DURING THE YEAR THE FEDERAL GOVernment had declared some twenty-five disasters in the United States, including floods in Alabama, Georgia and Florida. FEMA, the Federal Emergency Management Agency, had spent $24 million in the West alone, aiding nine states with wildfire. Colorado had been particularly hard hit by over six hundred wildfires. The state's Emergency Fire Fund contained $691,000 before the season began. By July that had been spent, plus another $6 million. Neither Colorado nor FEMA officials knew what the final count might be by the time winter cooled things down. Some were guessing the bill might reach a burdensome $15 million.

"Disaster disrupts people's lives and the economy of this country," FEMA Director James Lee Witt said. During his tenure he had toured disaster sites such as the Los Angeles earthquake, the Georgia floods and Hurricane Andrew's aftermath in Florida. Now he toured Colorado's fire sites. "Urban ghost towns are left behind in the wake of natural disasters," he said, "because no one wants to rebuild. We need to study the impact of earthquakes, floods and fires before they happen, not after."

Talk that year was on disasters and how to study, combat and fund them. Common complaints from top to bottom, from the president to the worker in the field, centered on coordination, organization and money. It seemed everyone that spring and summer was wagging his finger at someone else. James Lee Witt pointed his finger at state legislators for not preparing adequately in advance for disasters. State legislators complained about the federal government. Firefighters blamed the Fire Service and the BLM. The Fire Service and BLM blamed each other and both blamed FEMA. Firefighters bitched because government couldn't seem to afford sufficient helicopters, air bombers, fire fighting equipment, personnel and transportation.

It took chopper pilot Dick Good from 12:30 A.M. to 2:30 P.M. to ferry all members of the Prineville Hotshots from the Commons in Canyon Creek up the mountain to Helispot 2. Then he was scheduled to start delivering smoke-jumpers. He seemed irritable. He was doing the work of two pilots. No other choppers were available.

In between airlifting troops, the pilot made bucket drops and hauled cargo in and out of the combat zone. More hot spots developed as the wind ahead of the cold front continued to pick up.

"We need bucket drops," Blanco and Mackey insisted.

"Make up your minds," Good snapped. "It'll take me until dark to get the jumpers up here. What do you want first—shuttle missions or buckets?"

"It'll have to be buckets," Blanco decided.

"Fine. There's only one chopper. I can't do everything at once."

Jim Byers and several other fighters working line near the helispot overheard the exchange.

"Coordination sucks," one of them murmured. "Who runs this show? Mickey Mouse?"

"Nah. Mickey Mouse knows *how* to run things. Disney World *works.*"

"It's all a nightmare," said Jerry Usrey, a national worker who handled firefighter logistics. He was on his way from California to Glenwood Springs where, in charge of logistics for the Storm King fire, he would find himself considering such questions as whether to keep an ambulance stationed at Canyon Creek, where to get oil changes and fire filters for large fire trucks, and where to put two dozen pizzas donated by a local merchant.

"You come into a place like this and *Wham!*" he said. "Instantaneous city."

Organization of a project offense against a fire required the same coordination and support, on a smaller scale, of course, as the Allied landing at Salerno in WWII or the assault on the Normandy beachhead. As the Storm King fire gradually grew to project size, the first contingents of what would ultimately become a force of four hundred firefighters began to surround the fire. Like an army in combat, firefighters traveled and fought on their bellies. They had to have beans and they had to have bullets. However many troops manned the front lines, at least half that number was required in the rear to support them.

"A lot of people want to bitch about support," explained a weary command post coordinator. "That's because they don't know what it takes to move an army—to transport it, feed it, equip it, take care of its needs and wants and injuries and toothaches and gripes. With fires like we've had this year, you set up in Montana on Monday and then by Thursday or Friday you're setting up all over again in Arizona or Colorado. Considering the demands, the Fire Center at Boise and the regional coordination centers do a helluva job. One helluva job."

Overhead for the Storm King blaze set up a command post in a tent city at Glenwood Springs Middle School and eventually another sub-CP at Canyon Creek Estates. The CPs quickly established a logistics network while firefighters on the mountain battled the fire in hand-to-hand combat. Hundreds of details had to be arranged, synchronized and organized. Troops needed communications centers, medical facilities, ground and air transportation. They demanded food, water, portable toilets, bandages, vehicles, cots, tents, tools, clothing . . .

Coordinating all this required improvisation most line troops rarely saw and therefore seldom fully understood. For example, federal caterers flew in to feed the troops once the number of firefighters exceeded one hundred at any one site; however, it generally took caterers several days to arrive and get set up. Since fighters had to eat in the interim, command posts maintained contracts with grocery chains, restaurants and other facilities to fill in until the caterers were ready.

Arvin Leany who owned Starvin' Arvin's Restaurant in Glenwood Springs had, since May, provided over fifteen hundred meals to Colorado firefighters. He personally flew in by helicopter at the Wake fire to feed firefighters who couldn't break line even to eat. At other times, he loaded his trucks and drove them to feeding locations.

"We take the catering trucks up on location and we make sure they have a nice hot meal with a lot of liquids and fresh fruits," he said.

Fred Penoyer, manager of the Grand Junction City Market warehouse, called extra refrigerator trucks to duty to support the Storm King fire. Volunteers of the Glenwood Springs City Market whipped up twelve hundred sandwiches for firefighters, while Sue Chapman of the corporate office staff prepared crews for at least an all-nighter in Glenwood.

"We loaned firefighters a refrigerator truck to park at their command post," said Bob Hendee, manager of City Market at Glenwood Springs. "We tried to anticipate their needs. We went through an awful lot of Gatorade."

Occasionally, private employees got caught up in the excitement and threat of fire danger and joined the firefighters. One City Market worker quit making sandwiches to become a more active participant in the war.

"I was on the perimeter fire protection for fourteen hours," he said. "I looked right into that big fire. It's pretty scary seeing those trees blowing up. But I've already warned them here at the store, if there's another big fire, I've got to go."

Up on the mountain, firefighters had no time to dwell on how much money fire damage was costing FEMA or the state. They cared less about *how* overhead provided the equipment and material they needed—just as long as they received it. On the mountain there was no time for bickering and blaming and pointing the finger. The red enemy clawed at their fireline. The fire monster sent out his patrols to test the line. He probed and threatened and postured. And he built up his forces of wind and heat and flame for an all-out assault on the high ground.

Kathi Beck arched her back to relieve muscle cramps from a fast hour hacking at fireline on the ridge's west slope. She had been among the first hotshots airlifted from the

Commons below to the top of the ridge. Blanco and Mackey immediately integrated most of the shots with the smoke-jumpers along the direct attack line. Mackey's troops were being hardest pressed.

The near-desperate race to head off the fire's attack caught up Kathi in its excitement. She threw herself into the fight with such enthusiasm that even muscles hardened from mountain climbing, skydiving and physical conditioning in the Army Reserves could not keep up the pace indefinitely.

She caught a deep breath, brushed sweat off her forehead and tossed a protective look behind her to make sure Tami and the others were all right. That was when she noticed she no longer made a shadow on the cleared fireline. Like Tony Petrelli, she found something gloomy about the way tendrils of gray smoke drifted over and around her and seemed to blend against the sudden forbidding blue-gray of the sky.

She looked up, attracted by a mass along the western horizon. The sound of fire cracking bones filled her ears while a dark thunderstorm display filled her vision. Lightning cracked from its depths.

"Pray for rain," someone called out.

36

HERE AND THERE FLAMES FLARED UP LADDER fuel and made torches of trees, but for the most part the fire grumbled noisily and resentfully on the forest floor. Don Mackey constantly scouted the leading edge of the fire. He climbed the steep slope to the ridgeline and stood on a boulder and looked down upon it. Then he scouted it some more.

"Keep your eyes peeled." He stopped to caution firefighters. "This thing keeps growing—and there's a wind coming."

"Don, we're aware of the front, okay?" someone finally responded. "Don't be so jumpy. We can handle it."

Crews rotated in taking short lunch breaks starting at around 2:00 P.M. The "lunch spot," as one of the break sites was dubbed, lay about halfway up the side of the ridge. It was a small rocky clearing of about an acre or less in size, barren of ground fuels with only three or four scrub pines and an oak finding nurture within its parameters. Steep draws framed it on either side. The draws opened farther down into the drainage.

"This looks like a good place in case we need another safe area," Dale Longanecker suggested.

The other firefighters looked at him. Hotshots shifted warily.

"You never know," Longanecker said. He shrugged.

Other designated safe areas and safety zones included the two helispots at the top of the ridge. Longanecker himself briefed some of the hotshots on the escape routes. The primary route followed the unfinished fireline uphill through thick gambel oak.

It wasn't ideal, but it was the best they had, Longanecker said. It would have to do.

Some hotshots later insisted they received no safety briefings once they choppered onto the mountain. Zilch. They merely hopped off the helicopter and were immediately hustled into battle.

"It was like everything else," a hotshot charged bitterly. "We got here and they didn't have a fucking clue. There was no briefing on the weather, no equipment, no food, nothing provided. We felt like bastard stepchildren."

Ever since the jump that morning, Longanecker sniffed around like a cat with all its senses honed. Some of the firefighters overheard him voicing reservations to Mackey and hotshot superintendent Tom Shepard about how the battle was being waged. Although he agreed with the supervisors that the fire's configuration, location and rate of growth called for a direct attack, he couldn't help thinking it dangerous business to fight in the tinder-dry oak brush.

"We're inviting disaster," he said.

"This business is always dangerous," Mackey said, but he, too, sniffed around, always alert. Although he said nothing, his behavior indicated he sensed something almost sinister in the way smoke coiled in and around the trees, the unexpected graying of the sky.

A somber mood affected many of the firefighters. Usual lunch break chatter and grab-assing remained glaringly absent. Firefighters glanced uneasily at the shrinking sky. Their eyes shifted toward the fire monster who kept gnawing his own lunch out of the woods. They listened to the unsettling rattle of the freshening wind picking its way through dry leaves and branches.

No one ate much for lunch. Tony Petrelli's stomach felt inexplicably tight, the way it sometimes felt in the air before a difficult jump onto some spot about the size of a swimming pool surrounded by brittle fir trees. He snacked some and drank a lot and looked around. He attributed the dark mood to weariness, at least among those jumpers who had parachuted in yesterday with Mackey. They had fought the fire much of the night. They looked beat. Their faces underneath their helmets showed the strain. They were caked with sweat-mud and streaked with the gray ash that saturated the air.

Quentin Rhoades, Woods, Shelton and Sonny Soto broke onto the lunch spot, dropped their packs and tools and simply crashed on the ground.

"Can somebody tell me what's wrong with this picture?" Soto cracked. "Somebody die I didn't know about?"

Even the college-age hotshots appeared subdued.

"Eat worms, Sonny," a jumper retorted. "Your chute's on fire."

One of the hotshot rookies—the jumpers thought his name was Brinkley, Levi Brinkley—stared at Longanecker when the jumper mused, half to himself, "That front'll be coming through within an hour or so."

Brinkley got up from eating and ranged out toward the fire, then back again.

"Will the line hold?" he asked.

Longanecker said nothing. The fire had already made two or three short aerial runs since noon. The heat from the runs could be felt one hundred yards away. Fire had also spotted across the line in a place or two, drawing fighters away from the main assault to put out the spots.

Brinkley took his fire shelter from its pouch and looked at it as though he had never seen it before. Firefighters often joked about the shelters being "portable ovens."

"Do these things *really* work?" Brinkley asked, inspecting his shelter.

"'Taters," said lanky James Thrash with a wry lopsided grin.

After eating a little and drinking—someone even broke a few Cokes from his pack which made the rounds—the firefighters looked better. The spirits of healthy young men and women couldn't be suppressed for too long. While firefighters routinely faced the fire monster and learned to respect him, they nonetheless diminished any hold he might try to exert over them by presenting an offhanded front of exaggerated bravado. It was like whistling at midnight in a graveyard. If you laughed and poked fun at the spooky things around you, they lost their power over you.

Mackey took about five minutes at the lunch spot to gobble down a can of spaghetti before he jumped to his feet again and scrambled upslope out of sight into the trees to confer with Butch Blanco and Tom Shepard. A few minutes later Dale Longanecker paced off from the group. The lean firefighter stood in the thick light tinged dull gray by smoke sizzling off the ridge and merging with the sky. He watched infant lightning flash-glow inside a thunderstorm cloud far to the west. The cloud drifted slowly toward the north, avoiding Storm King Mountain as though shunning a plague. It took any hope of rain with it.

A few minutes later Petrelli observed Longanecker scouting a gulley in unburned territory about three hundred yards away. His yellow helmet flashed on high ground among juniper, then disappeared into the thick brush growing in the gulley.

At 2:20 P.M., Don Mackey raised Petrelli on the hand radio.

"If you have some of the hotshots there with you," he said, "send them back on the line to improve it."

It sounded as though Mackey may have spoken to Blanco and Shepard and the three decided a six-foot-wide fireline might not hold after all, considering the cold front on its way. Hotshots at the lunch spot got up and slogged off.

Longanecker called Petrelli on the radio.

"I've found a hot spot down here," he advised. "It's about ready to blow. Send the jumpers down to where I am. Can you see me?"

He stepped up on high ground.

"I see you," Petrelli acknowledged. "But I don't think making more line is a good idea. We're spread pretty thin. We're having enough trouble holding the line we have."

Longanecker paused. "Okay. Maybe you can send me a saw and a couple of diggers, but not just yet. I'm asking for a bucket drop first."

Dick Good in the Bell Ranger made one drop on the spot. Mackey interrupted the airwaves with a request for a drop near the ridgeline. Flames were spotting everywhere. Longanecker relinquished the bucket after an exchange with Mackey. Mackey's hot spot seemed more critical.

"From up here," the chopper pilot advised, "it looks like activity is picking up down there."

Petrelli, Thomas and Shelton started down through the trees to link up with Longanecker. Winds preceding the front soughed through the dry gambel oak, kicking around ashes and supplying fresh oxygen to the fire.

Longanecker's voice blasted from Petrelli's radio: "Tony, stay where you are until we get the bucket back. It's really hot here."

The three reinforcements froze in their tracks. The fire monster launched another aerial run as they watched, this one larger and more menacing than any of the other ones.

Dale! Petrelli screamed at his radio.

Flames one hundred feet tall, the height of a ten-story high-rise, rose up out of the forest just beyond Longanecker.

The fire monster stood up on his hind legs. He roared deep in his fiery gut. He rocked back and forth as though searching for victims. Then he leaped forward with astonishing speed.

"Dale! Look beside you!"

Longanecker whirled toward the sound of the charge. He had descended again into the gulley, whose timbered and rocky sides blocked his view of the approaching flames. He saw torching in the interior, somewhere across the fireline where flames were not supposed to be. He saw a boil of smoke, but he failed to see the run itself. Indecision gripped him.

"Dale, it's coming for you!"

Damnit, he could *hear* it.

He *felt* the tremendous blast of its hot breath whistling through the forest.

Which way to run?

Not uphill. No one outran a blowup going uphill.

He dashed a few steps toward his left, then thought better of it and ran to his right.

From which flank was it approaching?

He fought back terror.

Then he saw flames high-stepping through the crowns of trees below him and to his left. They operated as in a giant furnace, creating their own updraft to push them uphill.

"I see them!" Longanecker radioed Petrelli.

Petrelli shouted, "God, that's impressive!"

"Scary," Eric Shelton echoed, involuntarily retreating toward the relative safety of the lunch spot clearing.

Typically, a blowup started on the ground. It smoldered until it built up enough heat to flare into the trees. Tree canopies became the flames' racetrack. The fire raced hard and fast through the treetops until it burned enough to cause the canopy to collapse, dropping flames back to the ground where they rebuilt their intensity to start a fresh cycle. Unpredictable winds sped up the cycle.

Most runs did not last long. This one traveled one hundred fifty yards in fifteen seconds and blackened a swath about twenty feet wide that lay between the lunch spot and Longanecker's gulley. Even from three hundred yards away, the length of three football fields, the radiant heat from the flames stung Petrelli's face and scorched his eyebrows. When the monster dropped back down to all fours and then to his belly again underneath the trees, he left thick clouds of dark smoke roiling in the forest.

"Longanecker?" Petrelli's anxious voice pleading into his hand radio pierced the mantle of smoke. All across the mountain firefighters paused to listen to their radios, waiting, holding their collective breath.

A reply finally came. "I'm all right," Longanecker said. "How about there?"

Petrelli half-grinned with relief. He released his pent breath.

"It ran between you and us," he explained, almost babbling from the joy of finding his friend safe. "Dale, we don't want to come down deeper into the drainage. I think you ought to get out of there too."

"Give me a minute. I'm going to take another look, maybe get in a bucket drop. Then I'll be right up."

"Don't be too long."

37

THE LITTLE THUNDERSTORM CLOUD SWEPT around to the north and picked up speed as it disappeared, as though spurred by a jockey. Storm King Mountain seemed to have lost its fabled ability to create its own weather. Weather acted without reference to the mountain. The cold front arrived of its own accord and sniffed around the base of the peak with no more respect than a dog for a fire hydrant.

From its hellish lair near the bottom of the west drainage,

the fire greeted the front with a fiendish gurgle of delight. Flames rocked and flapped in the unstable air, like race-horses anticipating the opening of the starting gates.

Tony Petrelli glanced at his watch. It was 3:20 P.M. Dick Good and his chopper had delivered all twenty members of the Prineville Hotshots, but had been too busy since with bucket drops to pick up any of the smokejumper reinforcements waiting at the Commons in the valley below. On the mountain were forty-nine firefighters—twenty hotshots, sixteen smokejumpers, Butch Blanco's squad of eleven, and two helitacks, Rich Tyler and Bob Browning, who at the moment were functioning as chopper ground crew at Helispot 2.

And down below in the west drainage the fire monster felt the slipping of his leashes.

38

GEORGE STEELE AND THE OTHER SMOKE-jumpers who had been ignominiously bused to the fire site found themselves left out of the raging battle waged on the Storm King ridge. The chopper was occupied with bucket drops and couldn't airlift them. They surged helplessly against the wooden rail fence that enclosed the Commons in Canyon Creek Estates. Some of them paced back and forth, so nervous they could almost have *jumped* from the valley floor to the ridge. A few spat out occasional curses of disappointment. But most of them, having accepted their exclusion when The List made its selections, simply watched. Helpless.

The mountain ridge was really boiling by now. Winds infused the fire with new life. The flaming mountain dominated the little Canyon Creek community kneeling at its feet in homage. Residents arriving home from work along with those who had been summoned home by nervous spouses congregated in silent clumps at the Commons. Spectators shared a feeling that something big was about to happen.

Steele swept off his helmet and gave his assessment of the situation in his usual laconic way. "It's about ready to blow," he said.

"We could always hike in," suggested jumper Wayne Williams. He was a slab-muscled man with fine sandy hair whipped across his broad forehead by the wind. On Tuesday, he had battled fire near Craig, Colorado. By the time he demobed, it was too late to get a slot on Wednesday morning's stick to jump Storm King.

The sun rode weak behind transparent cloud cover. In a few short hours it would be dropping onto Grand Junction beyond the mountains. Darkness arrived more quickly in the mountains than on the flats. It was foolish to hike such rugged terrain with night falling.

The jumpers left Williams's suggestion hanging. Besides, they hoped the chopper might yet break loose for them.

Williams was absorbed in the fire. He leaned his elbows on the top rail of the fence. "Each fire is a living entity," he observed once in a philosophical mood.

Storm King's "living entity" carved a blackened face on the side of the ridge facing the Canyon Creek Estates. Active flame traced the face's outline and gave it motion. Viewed from the right angle through the smoke, the face in profile turned into that of a demon peering out of the brimstone and ashes of hell. The fire monster. He appeared to be laughing. Demonic laughter carved in flame that nonetheless chilled the souls of those firefighters who could do nothing but watch.

Firefighters up on the ridge had no time to indulge in philosophical cud chewing. The arrival of the cold front and its accompanying winds stirred increased activity all along the firelines. During the past half hour alone the fire had made several short crown runs south and west of the lunch spot. Radio traffic crackled like lightning. It seemed every firefighter with a radio tried to claim a piece of the air to report slopovers, spot fires and torching. Excitement and tension rippled through fighters ranging from IC Butch Blanco manning a strategic vantage point on the ridgeline to Dale Longanecker still scouting line in the west drainage in spite of his earlier close call.

Mackey requested a bucket drop downslope. Jim Byers needed one for a slopover. Ryerson demanded a bucket near the ridge spine to put out spot fires in gambel oak.

"I need one more bucket," she said, her voice drawn taut over the BLM tactical channel. "Who has priority? Who needs it worse?"

"Go ahead and take the next one," Mackey volunteered.

"It's boiling down below," the helicopter pilot chimed in. "I'll get a bucket down there as soon as I can."

Longanecker was about two hundred yards upslope from the bottom of the drainage. "Things are really heating up down here," he informed Mackey, then opened a staccato-like radio conversation with the jumper-in-charge over another possible crowning.

Mackey radioed Dispatch and asked for a tanker bomber and a load of retardant. The infantry was hard-pressed; it needed air support, heavy artillery.

Dispatch came back with, "Is the fire threatening houses?"

"Not yet," Mackey admitted.

"No tankers are available."

Mackey turned away in exasperation. He slammed his fist against his knee. Where in hell were all the tankers? Storm King deserved tankers as much as any of the other blazes burning on the western slopes.

When Longanecker learned of the refusal to assign further air support, he seethed with quiet rage. "We get *everything* if houses are threatened," he said. "But what about lives—*our* lives? Firefighter lives?"

Michelle Ryerson pulled members of her crew off the helispot line and took them and some of the hotshots to fight spot fires. Sawyer-swamper team Brad Haugh and

Derek Brixey worked with hotshots and jumpers on the fireline leading down from the top of the ridge. The rest of Mackey's jumpers and the remaining hotshots labored in thick brush on the lower fireline. Longanecker scouted line alone at the very point of the battle in the west drainage. Ground helitacks Bob Browning and Rich Tyler stood with IC Butch Blanco at the top of the ridge for a moment. Hotshot superintendent Tom Shepard joined them to talk tactics.

Lines in all their faces revealed the growing tension. Heated wind scorched their cheeks. Yellow fire clothing and helmets flashed like a flock of canaries among the dull green of unburned gambel oak and PJ and against the black of the scorched earth. Firefighters working in pairs and in small groups covered the ridge's west flank.

Chopper pilot Good's vantage point in the air offered him a crow's view of the battlefield. Black fingers stretched themselves dangerously in and around and among the firefighters. The mountain appeared to sizzle on the very edge of eruption. Flareups blew here and there like flashes from burning lava in an active volcano.

"What's it look like from up there?" Mackey radioed.

"Active," Good replied in an understatement. "It's going pretty good west of Helispot One."

It took the helicopter fifteen to twenty minutes each trip to empty its bucket, fall back to refill it either from the Colorado River or a nearby fish hatchery and return. Good had to be more careful in his approaches after the front arrived and the wind swelled. He chafed at having to add valuable minutes to his turnaround time by circling toward the east and making a direct approach into the stronger winds. No more grabbing a bucket in the Colorado and flying straight up the drainage to the fire.

So far he had made three drops since the front blew in. Two of them missed their targets. The bucket dangling on its long line oscillated in the higher winds, jerking the chopper erratically as it tried to hover above its target. Wind slashed at the downpour as soon as the bucket released its load, fanning 250 gallons of water into a broad painter's stroke against the looming front of Storm King in the background. Instead of landing on the intended flames, water splattered downslope and riveleted off without effect through unburned timber. The splash soaked Brad Haugh working one hundred feet from the drop.

"Missed," Bob Browning commented from where he watched on the site near Helispot 2 with fellow helitack Tyler and the two firefighter supervisors Blanco and Shepard. "There's too much wind."

The pilot's voice over the radio betrayed his annoyance. He sounded as though the keying of his mike interrupted heartfelt swearing.

"I'll be right back with another bucket," he promised.

Flames chewed away the base of a large dead pine and dropped it across the fireline. Fire tiptoed over the natural bridge toward fresh fuel on the other side. Jumper Roger Roth helped a couple of hotshots saw the downed tree into lengths and remove it. Mackey came by on his way downhill, carrying a cubitainer of water for troops below.

"It's come right up to the line," Roth said. "I don't think it's going to hold."

"It has *got* to hold," Mackey said.

Farther below, Mackey asked Kevin Erickson and Sarah Doehring to find a chain saw and check the entire fireline for other hot material blowing and falling across it. The two jumpers trudged off uphill to carry out the assignment. At the fallen tree occurred one of those random episodes in which Fate, or chance, redirected and changed lives.

Another cubitainer of water had been bumped down firefighter to firefighter from the top of the ridge.

"It's for the guys below," Brad Haugh explained. He and Brixey joined Roth and the hotshots at the fallen tree.

"I'll run it on down," Erickson volunteered, "if you guys will help Sarah clear the fireline."

"Keep doing what you're doing," Roth said. "We're almost finished here. I'll take the water."

Roth hefted the five-gallon plastic jug in one hand and

headed off with it downslope. Smoke swirled around him. It clung to unburned gambel on the fire-free side of the line like tufts of cotton. On the burned side it slithered among blackened sticks where a previous crown run had turned trees into charred exclamation points. A casual decision over a container of drinking water led Roger Roth deeper into the flames.

The same decision guided Erickson, Doehring and Brixey uphill away from the flames.

39

At 4:00 P.M. the fire blew up . . . As the winds reached their highest velocity, the fire reached the bottom of the west drainage, which it crossed. The fire ignited the opposite side of the drainage . . . Within seconds a wall of flame raced up the opposite ridge . . . pushed by 30 mph winds.

Interagency Investigation Team

THE WEST DRAINAGE WAS A NARROW DEEP DRAW with steep sides. It ran roughly north-northeast by south-southwest at the foot of the burning Storm King ridge upon which firefighters made their stand. At the south end it opened into culverts underneath I-70 to let rainwater empty into the Colorado River. The opposite end rose at a good grade toward Storm King which it drained. The shallowest part of the drainage occurred at the saddle near the base of the mountain which smokejumpers used as a jump spot and where Helispot 2 was located.

Even though clogged with PJ growing wild and thick among boulders as big as automobiles, the draw functioned like a natural chimney. The passage of the cold front turned it into a jet engine. Wind, entering the intake in volume off

I-70 and the Colorado River, was compressed in the ventura wind tunnel where the drainage narrowed and steepened and then thrust out the back toward Storm King with tremendous force.

Fire that for three days had remained a sleeper suddenly flexed its muscles, rejuvenated and awakened by rich oxygen. The fire monster rose almost languidly at the bottom of the drainage, at first yawning smoke into the sky with the sound of a faulty woodstove coughing and choking around a sudden infusion of wood and air. Giant smoke rings charged skyward, turning darker, a sure sign that the fire was picking up speed and not completely burning its fuel.

The fire roared and flapped and huffed dragon smoke as it worked itself up for a rampage. It escaped, howling like a jetliner picking up speed on its ground run to take off. Flames whistled and roared. Nimble as forest fairies, as ferocious as giant carnivores, they leaped the cup trench at the bottom of the fireline in the drainage and ignited the opposite slope.

An *uphill* avalanche of flame rose to the top of the ridge facing the firefighters. It made its one long destructive dash in less than thirty seconds. The fire monster chortled and flapped his jaws over the ridgetop. Then he turned. He sucked wind, creating his own weather now, his own force.

He fish-hooked and charged up the drainage itself toward Helispot 2 in the saddle at Storm King's feet. He tossed fiery bouquets ahead. He played leapfrog with himself by throwing small fires out in front and then overtaking them. Trees exploded from the heat of their own resin. They filled the sky with bursts of fireworks.

He roared his tremendous defiance: *I'm free now! You can't stop me!*

Tony Petrelli stared in awe at the raw power suddenly unshackled. Smokejumpers waiting at the Canyon Creek Commons for airlift froze.

"My God!" someone murmured in stunned reverence. That said it all.

Petrelli came out of his momentary daze. He shook it off

in the stark realization that Dale Longanecker had not followed his advice to come up out of the drainage. He was still down there!

Petrelli's hands shook; he almost dropped his radio trying to key its talk button. Frustration and fear for Longanecker's life stretched his voice high and sharp. He literally screamed into the mike: "The bottom's blown out! It has spotted across the canyon! Get the hell out of there! Get to the black!"

The jumper continued to sound the alarm. Mackey was apparently somewhere along the fireline that provided him only a limited view. He interrupted the cacophony of radio traffic, asking Petrelli, "Did you say it has jumped the main canyon?"

"Yes! Yes! It's spotted across the main canyon and it's really rolling. We're getting out of here now."

Petrelli and Thomas with him broke away from the lower fireline and skittered like spooked rabbits through the PJ toward the lunch spot. Other jumpers followed. Everywhere on the ridge the general alarm went out all at once, as though everyone awoke to the danger at the same time. Warnings flew as hot and thick as blowing ashes.

Hotshot Jon Kelso shouted through the radio at Tom Shepard, "You've got another hot spot below you. See it? Below you? It's really going."

They were voices collectively strident with immediate fear and desperation. IC Butch Blanco tried to hold things together, tried to prevent panic, but even he came across the air like a man who heroically strives for balance while witnessing the beginning of Armageddon.

He spread the alarm: "It's blowing. *It's blowing!* Everybody get out of there. Get out of the brush. All firefighters, head for the safety zones!"

From above, helicopter pilot Dick Good and his air crewman Steve Little looked down and back to the blowup. They were on a return flight to the river to get more water. The chopper's empty bucket dangled on its long line. Blasts of hot air tugged it erratically back and forth.

Good pulled collective. The chopper drew up like a bird startled in midflight. It hovered in the turbulence. Good dropped it into a slow left turn. He could hardly believe what he saw. Tyler and Browning were still down there.

The entire ridge below appeared to have gone up in a nuclear explosion.

He wasn't the only one that day reminded of a quote attributed to fire analyst Bob Walker of the U.S. Forest Service.

"People think we can manipulate and dominate nature because we're so good at building bridges and roads and things," Walker said. "But when a fire this big gets started, you can't stop it."

40

FIREFIGHTERS ON THE RIDGE WERE DIVIDED into three loose main groups with isolated individuals and teams scattered here and there—Butch Blanco, Tom Shepard and Don Mackey roaming from place to place as mobile command posts; Tyler and Browning at Helispot 2; the line scout Dale Longanecker deep in the west drainage.

Michelle Ryerson's BLM firefighters and half the Prineville Hotshots made up the first group. They manned the upper fireline. It turned out to be the safest spot on the ridge.

Nine other hotshots—Tom Kelso, Kathi Beck, Scott Blecha, Levi Brinkley, Bonnie Holtby, Rob Johnson, Tami Bickett, Doug Dunbar and Terri Hagen—were among the second group with smokejumpers James Thrash, Roger Roth and Eric Hipke. They worked together improving and holding the direct line that ran downhill west from the top of the ridge.

Farther down from this group, along the lower fireline,

the last group composed of smokejumpers Keith Woods, Quentin Rhoades, Sonny Soto, Eric Shelton, Bill Thomas, Tony Petrelli, Michael Cooper and Mike Feliciano, eight of them, felt the first hot blast of the blowup and bolted through a swath of reburn toward the nearest safety zone, that designated by Dale Longanecker at the lunch spot.

Firefighters who had never survived a blowup thought Harry T. Gisborne may have exaggerated his tales of the 1929 blowup at the Half Moon fire in Glacier National Park. Now, however, and forever afterward, they fully believed fire *could* travel fast enough to catch a squirrel or a grouse in full flight. Within seconds after flames leaped the cup trench at the bottom of the west drainage, burned up the opposite slope, and then roared up the drainage toward the saddle and Storm King, other flames slung missiles of fire into the dense, highly combustible gamble patches across the fireline below the firefighters and on the same ridge slope with them. It was a nightmare blown into shocking reality. That which every firefighter on the mountain feared most had finally occurred.

Butch Blanco shouted directly into his hand radio: "Mackey, bring everyone up from the fireline."

"Go! Run! Go!" echoed another radio plea.

Hazardous as it was, parachuting onto a fire was only transportation, a way of getting into battle. Battle itself tested a fighter's mettle. Everyone on the mountain had his courage tested that day.

Tony Petrelli led the smokejumpers' flight to the lunch spot. The grade that far down the side of the ridge was as much as 50 percent in places. It was littered with rock scree, loose boulders and felled trees. Gulches and dry washes scarred it like the gouged-out trenches made by some giant's fingers. The jumpers held together as they scrambled across the rugged hillside. They shouted and called out to each other through the swirling smoke that enveloped them. No one must be left behind.

Gale force wind estimated at forty-five mph tore at the jumpers' clothing and sent helmets flying. It howled through the trees. It whipped cries from their lips and dashed them against the side of the mountain. Because of the boiling smoke, no one could be sure where they were. They scrambled on, panting, sometimes falling to all fours to scurry up particularly steep grades, holding onto and helping each other as they fled. The only thing they were certain of was that safety lay generally uphill.

The fire chased them. And it wasn't far behind. It chased them at eighteen miles per hour through superheated air. It was an exploding inferno thirty stories tall and a quarter-mile across. Fiery tongues three hundred feet long stabbed the sky until it bled red smoke one thousand feet high.

The fire monster was coming. *God, he was coming.*

The little band of spooked jumpers burst from the brush into the lower end of the lunch spot clearing. They scrabbled across the dry wash and paused in the middle of the opening to assess the situation. They huddled in a clump for comfort. Around them gathered the winds and the red sky and the blowing ash and the booming and bellowing of the fire monster lunging upslope toward them.

Some of the jumpers thought they should circle the wagons where they were and break out fire shelters. Others wanted to continue their flight. Only, which direction should they flee? Dark smoke cut visibility down to mere yards in places.

"We might intercept the fireline and follow it up the hill if we angled back to the left," was one suggestion.

"Back toward the fire? No way," came a response.

"Look! It's going to be on us here in two minutes like a hound on a rabbit. We gotta do something. Fast."

Petrelli's face felt like it might spontaneously combust.

"I don't think the clearing's safe," he said. "All I know is I don't want to go back down to the line."

Quentin Rhoades noticed Don Mackey first. Mackey simply appeared out of nowhere. Rhoades thought of his friend's daughter's birthday. An odd thought at such a moment. It was tomorrow. Had Don called her? Christ, they were in the middle of a blowup! There wouldn't be birthdays for anyone, anymore, unless they got the hell out of here.

Mackey wore his pack and carried a radio in his hand. He flashed a lopsided Bert Reynolds grin at the jumpers that instantly reassured them. His presence had the effect of a shepherd calming his sheep. He pointed.

"Walk straight up the hill," he directed. "Walk up to the black on the ridge below Helispot One. That's a safe zone."

Indecision was over.

"Walk?" someone cried. "My aching ass. Run!"

The eight jumpers bolted. Searing winds clawed at their backs. Petrelli dropped to the tail of the file to help stragglers. When he glanced back for Mackey, Mackey had disappeared.

He's going back down the line to get everybody else, Petrelli decided. *He didn't have to come to direct us, but he did. He didn't have to go back down to the line to get everybody else, but he did.*

Quentin Rhoades also missed his longtime friend. He hesitated.

"Where is he? Where's Don?"

He yelled, shouted. Mackey couldn't go on down there. He *couldn't!*

Petrelli grabbed Rhoades. "We'll never find him in the smoke. He'll be all right. He knows what he's doing."

"It's her sixth birthday tomorrow."

"We'll remind him. Let's go. Run!"

Rhoades also had a baby daughter. *Don could have taken us to safety himself,* ran through his thoughts, along with a premonition that chilled his blood. *He could have honorably come with us and called the others on the radio and told them to get the hell out of there. But I guess he feels the only way to get them out is to go down and personally demonstrate the urgency. Sometimes a radio message seems so remote and detached. That must be why he went back. Don Mackey has saved my life and the lives of seven other smokejumpers. I want to thank him. Myself and my family are forever in his debt.*

"Hasn't he done enough?" Rhoades anguished. "He could have come with us."

"It won't do any good for all of us to get caught down here," Petrelli reasoned rightly, shouting into the smoke and roar and howl of wind and fire.

Besides, none of them were saved yet.

41

DALE LONGANECKER HELD A LIMITED VIEW OF the blowup because of his position near the bottom of the drainage. Trees surrounded him. He heard the fire as it took off howling up the slope opposite him. Flames leaped into view. They swarmed up the other ridge, then fish-hooked and charged up the drainage toward the mountain peak and the saddle. He knew he didn't want to be caught in the gambel. He took off running toward the lunch spot as the clamor of voices on his hand radio told him the fire monster had broken loose on *this* side of the drainage.

Sparks shot into the trees around him as he ran. One glance over his shoulder added speed to his flying feet. Flames as tall as a skyscraper towered almost directly above him. They threw firebombs at him. They chased him uphill through the forest and boulders and rock scree.

If he tripped and fell, the fire monster would devour him instantly. Nothing left except a charred piece of flesh the size of a roast burned in an oven.

Not a pleasant thought.

He reached the lunch spot scant yards ahead of the blaze. The clearing was deserted except for the thick roiling layers of dark smoke. He debated whether to continue running uphill through the PJ and oak. The fire settled the matter for him.

It surrounded the clearing. Walls of flame cracking and popping and hissing raced around both sides of the clearing like a thing alive and enraged. God, was it pissed off. It traveled faster than any man might run.

Wind so hot it felt like it was setting his clothing ablaze drove Longanecker deeper into the clearing. Trapped at the lunch spot, no escape in sight, he hurled himself into the midst of a small field of boulders to take what refuge he could. No trees grew nearby to provide fuel. Cheatgrass grew short and sparse in the opening.

He huddled on the ground and wrapped his head with his arms and knees and took short breaths to prevent the air from cauterizing his lungs. The day turned dark red around him before he squeezed his eyes closed to protect them. He knew now what it felt like to be thrust into an oven and the burner turned to *broil*.

"Go! Run! Get out of there!" babbled from the radio. Firefighters encouraging and warning each other.

Yeah. Right. Get out of there. It was too late for smoke-jumper Dale Longanecker. Flames two hundred feet tall and more cracked the air all around him.

Damn The List.

The List had brought him to this.

It might not hurt to pray.

In fact, it might be a damned good idea to pray.

42

AFTER LEAVING THE LUNCH SPOT AND HIS EIGHT jumpers, Don Mackey next appeared on the fireline where the nine hotshots and three smokejumpers in that group had the most restricted view of any of the firefighters on the ridge. The six-foot-wide fireline they had cut downhill ran a narrow pathway through thick foliage. A short distance from where the line ended, the slope steepened sharply before dropping into the drainage.

Trees and topography concealed the downhill flames from

the firefighters and buffered the wind blowing up out of the drainage. Although both the increase in smoke and the clamoring on the radio warned the fighters of impending danger, none of them showed any great urgency to get out. They almost leisurely gathered up their tools. Mackey materialized among them. Apparently, they assumed this run to be like all the others; it would run a short distance and then drop back to the ground. They seemed to think they had plenty of time.

"Let's go, kids, let's go!" Mackey urged.

"There's a lot of talk," Roth said, indicating his radio. "What's up?"

"We've got to get out of here now. *Now!*" Mackey emphasized. "It's blowing up."

The situation still appeared less than critical to them. Nevertheless they hoisted their packs and tools, shouldered the chain saws and took off following the clear-cut fireline uphill. It was the only escape route out of the canyon. It was steep and appeared much too long to Don Mackey who *had* seen the flames.

He stood aside to let the column pass. Bonnie Jean Holtby brought up the rear. Mackey noticed she already breathed hard and that the look she cast him, alone among all the firefighters, contained mixtures of fatigue and fright. He smiled reassurance at her.

"Run away to fight another day," he said lightly.

"Is it really coming?" she wanted to know.

"It's coming. But everything's gonna be all right. You played basketball, didn't you? Well, the goal is straight up that trail."

She was only twenty-one years old and had not yet faced the fire monster when he came unchained. The anxious look that set her square jaw said she wasn't sure if she wanted to brace him. But she smiled tentatively, bravely, and used her Pulaski as a walking stick to catch up with the other fighters.

Mackey hesitated a moment longer. The red cast to the smoke boiling out of the drainage farther down drew his eye like a magnet. He tried to raise Longanecker on the radio. Neither Petrelli nor any of the others had seen the line scout since he took off after chow. No one had heard from him since Petrelli radioed him of the blowup.

Mackey felt a responsibility for Longanecker. Indeed, for all the smokejumpers. He drew a deep breath. He had no choice. He took a step toward the drainage.

He tried the radio one last time. "Longanecker?"

Longanecker answered this time. He coughed, as though expelling smoke, but his voice sounded calm. "What can I do for you, Don?"

"Are you all right, boy?"

"I'm okay. I'm in a safe zone."

Mackey didn't bother to ask him where. He felt suddenly light and almost happy. He had accounted for all his jumpers. Doehring, Archuleta and Erickson were farther up the line; Roth, Thrash and Hipke were here with the hotshots; Petrelli and Rhoades had the rest of the jumpers busting ass for the ridgetop.

Blanco's strained inquiring voice came over the radio, asking for a situation report. Mackey could have said SNAFU—Situation Normal, All Fucked Up—but he felt too relieved for that. He keyed his mike.

"I've got the last bunch here with me," he said. "Have dinner ready. We're on our way home—and we're in a hurry."

43

AT FIFTY YEARS OLD BUTCH BLANCO WAS THE oldest firefighter on the mountain. Although his career in the service started relatively late in life, he still had had considerable experience both as a volunteer and then in recent years as a full-timer. Blanco possessed a cool head in a crisis, his superiors said of him, and nerves as solid as Mt. Rushmore. The man knew his job.

Yet, no man, however experienced and competent, prepared himself for all eventualities when it came to predicting what a fire could do. Even if he *could* predict it, he still had to lead his men into combat because fire had to be faced. Fire had to be stopped in spite of the expected cold front, the dried gambel thickets, the rough terrain and lack of sufficient personnel and air support. Ike Eisenhower couldn't pull back from Normandy just because of tank traps and steel spikes in the surf and cliffs and big guns on top of the cliffs.

Fate or merely the luck of the draw put Butch Blanco in charge when what happened on the mountain happened. Deep, unspeakable dread that quickly turned to sadness filled his heart almost the instant he saw the firestorm. It was something that happened over which he had no control, but the questions started right away. He questioned himself and the questions haunted him. But it happened and once it happened all he could do was try to get the people out.

A stand of ponderosa pine lower along the ridgeline obstructed the IC's view during the first few minutes of the blowup. He and hotshot superintendent Tom Shepard were helping the two ground crew helitacks bump water cubitainers from Helispot 2 downslope when the mountain exploded.

"We saw the smoke building—and then *Wham!* the mountain was on fire," said Derek Brixey, a twenty-one-year-old crewman on Michelle Ryerson's squad.

"I've never seen it blow up and grow like that," said Brad Haugh. "One moment we were fighting fire. The next we were fighting for our lives."

"There was no place to go," said Prineville Hotshot foreman Bryan Scholz. "We kept going up the ridge and the fire kept going up the ridge."

Blanco heard the explosion as the firestorm built. It roared like a hurricane trapped in a tunnel. He dropped a cubitainer and stared. Smoke boiled from deep in the drainage. Flames leaped into sight and raced up the opposite drainage wall, lapped over the top and started downhill again toward the Canyon Creek Estates. Other flames steamrolled up the drainage, eating out the bottom and blackening it. A third front charged up the ridge slope toward firefighters scattered all along its face. Seven miles to the east in Glenwood Springs people thought from the mushroom cloud that someone had set off a nuclear bomb.

Winds generated by the firestorm struck Blanco with the impact of a Sahara sun wind. He grabbed for the radio at his belt as the air filled with traffic. The first message he received came from Brad Haugh. Haugh and Ryerson had dropped off the top of the ridgeline to scout spot fires.

"It's spotted west-northwest of my location!" Haugh exclaimed.

"Get out! Get out!" Blanco responded. "Move up to the safe zones."

"Which one?"

"The old one," Blanco barked. "Helispot One."

"I'll start out when I have a visual on the crew below," Haugh shot back.

"Get out when you can. Repeat! Repeat! All hands, move up to safe zones. Run!"

He continued barking the same command into the radio. It became almost a litany. *"Get out! Get out! Get out! Get out now!"* Tom Shepard on the hotshot channel took up the cry. Half the hotshots near the top broke for safety. It was the other half out of sight below on the fireline that made Shepard's heart thud against his chest walls.

Flames attacked coming up the hill at one thousand feet per minute.

"We need air tankers," Blanco pleaded into his radio. Desperation sharp-edged his voice. "We're losing the fire on the side where the houses are. It's over the other ridge and headed downhill toward Canyon Creek Estates."

Motorists driving by on I-70 braked in astonishment and pulled to the shoulder of the highway or slowed to a snail's pace in the fast lanes to block traffic for miles in either direction. Many of them got out to watch. They craned their necks back and stared in awed silence, as in the presence of some passion play depicting man's final tragedy.

"They'd get out and gawk if the planet were going up in a

nuclear holocaust," complained a Colorado State Trooper dispatched for traffic control.

People broke out cameras and videos. Al Bell from Glenwood Springs came away with rare video footage. He started filming the fire on Monday, July 4, after the blaze dropped from its single lightning-struck tree and gave itself birth on the ground. He chronicled fresh segments each day.

Monday's recording showed a thin plume of smoke eddying out of dense foliage high on the side of the ridge. Tuesday's tape revealed a small swath of black ringed in red flames eating out from a center. The head moved generally northeasterly toward Storm King Mountain. The day's filming ended with two smokejumpers parachuting onto the ridge.

Bell's Wednesday filming proved the best and most dramatic evidence of how the wildfire flared into a deadly inferno. It showed how fifty mph winds lifted flames into huge torches.

"There's somebody in that canyon who's in deep trouble," Bell exclaimed.

Ironically, the most riveting still photos of the blowup were snapped by a traveling resident of Prineville, Oregon. When Bruce Meland stopped along I-70 and broke out his 35mm, he had no idea that the Prineville Hotshots from his hometown were among those cornered by the fire on the ridge. He was in Colorado covering the Pikes Peak Hill Climb for *Electrifying Times,* the electric car magazine he published. The fast-moving wildfire intrigued him. Years earlier he had written his master's thesis on how various conditions affected field burning. He took eight frames of the fire through a telephoto lens over the next fifteen minutes.

"It just happened so fast," he said. "By the time I stopped taking photos, it looked like Mount Saint Helens going off. People don't realize how massive this thing was.

"My main thought when I saw this was, 'Where are the support aircraft?' The helicopters with the water came later. The wind was blowing thirty-five mph where I was, so the fire accelerating up Storm King Mountain must have pushed the winds there to seventy or eighty mph."

News of the blowup spread throughout Colorado in a matter of minutes. U.S. Representative Scott McInnis was quick to note that the Storm King firefighters were mostly elite hotshots and smokejumpers.

"These people were not rookies," he said. "They knew what they were doing. They were some of the best we had."

He paused. "They knew they were in trouble," he said.

"It was a race against fire," said Governor Roy Romer, who had toured the Wake fire and was having his share of political difficulties balancing disaster funds and trying to keep peace among the various fire agencies.

Firefighters at the foot of the mountain viewed the blowup from a different and more personal perspective than other spectators. After all, it *could* have been any of them up there in the fire. Smokejumpers stood or knelt in small groups on the short, dry grass of the Canyon Creek Commons, their gazes riveted on the smoking ridge. Some of them perched on a fire engine and peered through a mounted telescope. They exchanged few words; those they did speak were directed almost in prayer at the yellow-clad ants scrambling around on the mountain to escape the fire.

"Go!" the jumpers uttered now and then. "God, please *go!"*

Prayers from the depths of firefighter souls. There was nothing else they could do.

Volunteer firefighter Larry White stood perimeter protection in Canyon Creek. The blowup mesmerized him for twenty minutes. Then he talked about it to try to put it all together in his mind.

"Those two winds just came in and sheared together in crosswinds and blew that thing up," he said. "Sparks and chunks of burning wood started flying. The wind just took fire bands over the tops of the trees."

Fire bands popped like lightning from treetop to treetop. Air superheated ahead of the fire provided a kind of conduit along which spontaneous flames fled.

"There are firefighters down in there," White murmured. "God help them. They're in deep trouble. . . . We're all brothers. It could be any of us."

Jumper Wayne Williams had never seen anything like it—and he was a sandy-haired veteran of twenty years' firefighting experience in the West. He roosted on the top rail of the wooden fence that enclosed the Commons. Full of nervous energy and anxiety, he slipped off the fence and paced while his eyes remained glued on the distant inferno.

That other veteran, George Steele, suddenly pointed. The broken jaw from his old injury gave him a particularly grim appearance. His entire face reflected the rigid set of his patched-up jaw. Words typically failed him. He merely pointed.

"Oh, no, Jesus . . ." someone said, sighing.

Shiny fire shelters blossomed in the smoke.

Steele fumbled with his hard hat. He stared. He looked away, then back again quickly.

Something had gone badly wrong when firefighters sought salvation in their fire shelters—their final option.

44

TONY PETRELLI BROUGHT UP THE REAR IN THE line of jumpers scurrying uphill toward safety. In places the climb proved so steep a man could stand vertical with the rest of the earth and still reach out and almost touch the hill in front of him. The exhausted jumpers urged each other on through the swirling smoke. Running and clawing and scrabbling, falling and getting up and running some more. Casting frightened looks back over their shoulders as though half-expecting the monster to leap out of the smoke and devour them.

Behind them pursued thunder as in a fighter jet taking off

in high winds. Belching smoke. Winds bellowing and hurling flaming faggots across the sky.

It was a meteor storm. It was the planet Krypton blowing up underneath Baby Superman. It was Armageddon.

And it all seemingly unfolded in painful slow motion, as in one of those nightmares in which the dreamer is chased by unspecified demons.

The jumpers were excellent physical specimens. But some of them had been in straight battle for nearly twenty-four hours after parachuting in with Mackey's stick yesterday. Long hours of toil and now a heart-pounding dash up a mountainside so steep a goat might have lost its footing strained even youthful muscles hardened by labor. Sonny Soto faltered and started down. Keith Woods grabbed him and half-dragged him forward.

"My legs!" Soto cried. "God, not now. I'm cramping. Cramping bad."

"Sonny, damnit. We're roast pig if we stop now."

Petrelli ran only a few steps behind them. He lost sight of them through ashes and smoke and sand grit and gravel and twigs and burning branches hurricane-mixed by the howling winds. A helmet went flying. It banged off a tree trunk and shot straight up, disappearing into the wild smoke. Petrelli slipped down his chin strap to hold on his helmet. Hot wind tried to suck the breath from his lungs.

The monster roared at his heels.

Petrelli almost ran up the backs of Soto and Woods.

"He's cramping," Woods explained. "He can hardly use his legs."

Petrelli's eyes flashed white. "Sonny, you *got* to keep going."

"Leave me," Soto said. "Save yourselves."

Woods tightened his grip around his friend's middle. "You're crazy, man. No way. You're going with us if I have to drag you by your collar."

They struggled on. To give up was to die.

During one of those unexpected flashbacks that occurs at such times when the mind tries to detach itself from present threat, Petrelli saw the laughing faces of Thrash and Longanecker and the other jumpers with whom he had parachuted onto Storm King Mountain that morning. Had it really only been a few hours ago, last night, that he rotated off the Oil Springs fire and made his name available for today's list?

"It's only an average fire," Thrash said as they prepared for that morning's jump. "Not even project-size. We'll whip its ass before midnight and still get in our overtime."

Who was whipping *whose* ass?

James Thrash and Roger Roth were buddies who liked to work together. Petrelli had seen neither of them since lunch at the lunch spot when someone teased Roth about having outrun the blowup in Arizona a week ago. Jumpers were always teasing him about it. *Beep! Beep!*

"Your name comes up on The List," jumpers said, shrugging, "or it don't come up on The List and you put off your wings for a while longer."

Petrelli didn't want his name on The List for wings. Not just yet. He hoped Thrash and Roth had made it out. He hoped Mackey had found them down on the line and they all made it out.

He hadn't made it out yet.

Running. Stumbling. Falling. Lungs burning. Ash raining down and singeing hair and skin. Hot embers bombarding Nomex fire-retardant shirts and sizzling angrily. The jumpers' shouts of encouragement and alarm.

"We're not making it. It's too far to the top," came a frantic bellow. "Get rid of your gear!"

A firefighter abandoning his tools in combat was like a soldier throwing down his rifle and bolting for the rear lines.

"I'm sheddin' 'em!" Eric Shelton cried.

He dropped his sig pack containing gasoline for the chain saws. Petrelli dumped his chain saw next to it; it had been holding him back. Two other chain saws and sig packs plus some Pulaskis completed the cache.

Let the fire have it all. Fuck it. The monster could have anything except their lives. They'd fight for their lives.

Surrendering weapons was the final act of a defeated

army. The retreat was now a complete rout. It jacked up the pucker factor to the panic level.

Soto crumpled from his leg cramps. Leg muscles depleted of calcium and moisture twisted his heels back toward his butt. Woods dropped next to him. His eyes were shot with fear—but he wouldn't leave a comrade behind. Woods shouted at Soto above the jet engine roar of the pursuing flames.

"Goddamnit, Sonny! *Please?*"

Soto wasn't giving up. It wasn't in his nature to give up. His white-rimmed eyes fixated on the flames roaring uphill through the woods behind as he scrabbled and clawed and tried to get to his feet and continue. But nothing he did relieved his tortured leg muscles. Nothing could make them functional. Not the firestorm closing in on him, that hurricane of flames the height of a thirty-story building. Not scorching winds so fierce they whipped gambel brush back and forth like strands of sea oats. Not the air so hot it seared eyelashes and blistered the skin and threatened to combust lungs.

Woods pulled at Soto. Yelling. It was a scene extracted directly from one of Ernie Pyle's combat notebooks. There he was, the wounded GI at Iwo Jima or Tarawa or Salerno. The enemy closed in on him, but his hometown buddy stayed. They either made it together or they died together.

Petrelli grabbed Soto underneath one arm. He and Woods bodily yanked the cramping man to his feet. Soto's legs twisted underneath him and refused to bear his weight.

From Petrelli's hand radio issued a frantic voice. Kevin Erickson's: *"Mackey? Mackey? It's spotted just below you. Get the hell out of there. Run!"*

Petrelli had no time to dwell on what might be happening elsewhere.

Woods threw an arm around Soto's waist. "I've got him now. Tony, see to the others."

"There's good, safe black up the hill," Petrelli shouted. "Can you make it?"

"Leave me here," Soto begged. "No use in the fire getting all of us. I'll deploy my shelter."

Petrelli shook his head. "There's too much aerial fuel here."

He recalled the intensity of the crown runs through the reburn during the past hour.

"Leave me."

"No!" Woods retorted. "Tony, go on ahead. I've got him. The others need you."

Such men as these were rare. They made heroics common. Petrelli slapped the men on their backs, quickly, one at a time, and then he scrambled uphill after the remaining jumpers.

Woods and Soto found themselves alone, following the shouts ahead of them lost in the boiling smoke. Soto cramped worse than ever.

"It's no use, Keith," he said. "We're not gonna make it like this."

They really *weren't* going to make it. Flames already showed through the smoke.

They fought their way into a small rocky clearing where a low outcropping of rock offered some protection. Soto had reached the end of his physical endurance. They had to make a stand.

They looked at each other. "Deploy," Woods said.

Raging hot winds tore at their shelters and threatened to rip them from their hands.

"Hurry!"

Finally, side by side, heads uphill away from the approaching fire, they managed to flop belly-down onto the ground and cover themselves with the reflective blankets. Sweat immediately soaked their clothing. They death-gripped the hand- and footholds at the corners of the shelters and heard the fire monster coming.

"Keith . . . ?" Soto said.

Any sense of humor had been burned and worn out of him during the dash up the ridge.

"Yeah, Sonny?"

They waited, hearts pounding against the rocky soil.

"Keith . . . ? Thanks, partner."

"You'd have done the same for me."

A moment later: "Sonny . . . ?"

The approaching fire hurricane all but burned out the sound of their voices.

"Sonny?"

Just to talk to each other and find comfort in companionship as death closed in.

"Sonny, do you think we'll make it?"

"We'll make it."

"Yeah."

"Keith . . . good luck."

"Good luck to you, Sonny," said Woods and then buried his face into the earth to find what oxygen remained close to the ground.

Only one hundred yards ahead, the remaining six jumpers faced the same dilemma of whether to continue their flight or to dig in. In less than eight minutes they had covered five hundred yards of terrain so steep mountain goats went around it. They were exhausted. Muscles cramped. Lungs worked like bellows.

They still had over one hundred yards to go to reach safety at Helispot 1 when it became obvious to all of them that they weren't going to make it. Petrelli looked around. They were in a small, previously burned clearing less than one acre in size. Maybe it was enough. Somebody had to make the decision.

"Deploy shelters," Petrelli ordered.

Jumpers dropped immediately to their knees and scratched the earth like frantic dogs, slinging away debris that might catch fire and lead flames into their shelters with them. Burning branches blew across the clearing with the velocity of artillery shells as Petrelli staggered from shelter to shelter to make sure everyone was inside. Red fire glow reflected against the shiny coverings. They looked like silver sleeping bags.

Or like fancy body bags.

Petrelli was the last to cover up. He lay on the ground at last and restricted his world to a space the size of a large oven. He recalled hearing somewhere how firefighters who survived blowups in their tiny foil shelters never forgot the sound of flames sweeping over them. The experience haunted their nightmares for the rest of their lives.

Funny though, he thought, how when a man's life diminished to almost nothing in the face of danger he felt so vital. He lay with rough blackened cheatgrass against his cheek. His eyes focused on pebbles and a charred twig at the end of his nose. A red ant darted about as though it too knew what was coming.

Petrelli had never felt so alive. Scared, yes, but also *alive.*

It was almost the same feeling he derived from parachuting.

As an afterthought, he radioed Mackey and informed him they were sheltering up. Whether Mackey responded or not failed to register. Smoke closed in. The dreadful scorched breath of the fire monster sucked at the jumpers' shelters and at their lives.

45

FRENZIED RADIO TRANSMISSIONS FROM STORM King Mountain rippled the crisis outward to the command post in Glenwood Springs, to WSFCC at Walker Field and to all BLM and Forest Service posts within the district. Rick Blanton, smokejumper coordinator at Walker Field, could hardly get to his radio and desk for the number of off-duty jumpers, pilots and other firefighters crammed into his office at the Ops Center to listen to the action over the airwaves. BLM Fire Management Officer Don Lotvedt was in Hotchkiss near Paonia for a briefing on the dying Wake fire when someone burst through the door.

"They've deployed shelters at Storm King!"

That was how the word passed—from mouth and from radio to radio and telephone to telephone. *Shelters are deployed. Firefighters on Storm King Mountain have taken their final option.*

Fire Management Officer Pete Blume telephoned Mike Lowery and Paul Hefner at WSFCC. Hefner was already on his feet, too stunned to sit.

"Do you know what's happening?" Lowery asked Blume.

"From Glenwood Springs, it looks like the entire mountain has gone up. They've requested retardant to protect residences."

Hefner scanned his duty list for tanker pilots. Although tankers still bombarded the Wake fire, the crisis there had passed. A few of the pilots like Andy Wilson had even copped a day off. Those remaining went into an unhurried mode.

"Raise Tanker-23 and Tanker-131," Hefner ordered.

Mark Matthews in 23 and Tim Johnson in 131 had just refilled with Fugitive and were en route to Paonia. Hefner diverted them from the Wake fire and ordered them to set course for Glenwood Springs. Johnson flew the North Fork River to and over McClure Pass and then followed the valley to Glenwood Springs. Matthews cut directly across the Grand Mesa National Forest and picked up I-70 before it entered Glenwood Canyon west of Storm King Mountain.

Both pilots squinted through their windscreens in stunned wonder as they approached the fire. A thick plume of dark smoke billowed one thousand feet into the air. The mountain resembled an erupting volcano.

"Do they want loads on the houses," Tim Johnson asked Dispatch, "or do they want it on the fire?"

Dispatch was busy with radio traffic from a dozen different points. Finally, he came back with an answer: "Tankers-131 and -23, switch channels to the IC on the scene. I think they want retardant dropped right on top of them."

Matthews said he could do it all right, he could fly his heavy P-3 into the winds shearing and carooming off Storm King. But dumping a load of retardant—hell, dumping *ten* loads of retardant—on *that* fire would be about as effective as dashing a teacup of water into the bowels of hell.

46

BRAD HAUGH AND JUMPER KEVIN ERICKSON waited for Mackey and his contingent at the fallen tree two hundred feet below the top of the ridge. Erickson might have been down there with them except for Roger Roth. Roth had volunteered to lug the water cubitainer downslope while Erickson continued scouting the fireline. Haugh had snapped at Blanco over the radio when the alarm first sounded; he wouldn't personally run for safety until he had a visual on the crew farthest below.

And he wouldn't, but . . . *"Hurry!"* he breathed in silent plea.

Erickson pointed. "They're coming."

Haugh's next breath felt like it was the first he had taken since the blowup. He sucked in relief in a deep sigh. James Thrash appeared first along the cleared fireline that emerged out of the thick seven-foot-tall gambel brush. Yellow hard hats bobbed behind him. Mackey brought up the rear of the long file. With him walked Bonnie Jean Holtby. She staggered from exhaustion and lifted her strained young face to see how much farther they had to go. Mackey prodded her on.

Although airwaves crackled with exhortations to *"Get out! Get out!"* the firefighters were either so tired from the forced uphill march that they retained insufficient energy to run or they didn't believe the situation was as critical as it sounded. The thick oak that surrounded them buffered the fire wind and blocked their view of the towering flames breaking out of the steep drainage behind them. They still carried their equipment, including packs and shouldered chain saws.

What they didn't know, what even Erickson and Haugh couldn't see from their slightly better vantage point one hundred yards uphill, was that one edge of the blowup had already caught up with the fighters on their left flank. It kept pace with them, then leaped ahead in a pincer movement.

Haugh yelled, "Hey, kids. Let's pick up the pace, willya? Get the hell out of there, huh?"

Erickson turned his back to Haugh. "Can you get my camera out of my pack?" he asked. "Nobody's going to believe this."

The jumper concentrated on framing his viewfinder around the struggling file of worn-out firefighters. The wall of flame in the distance formed a dramatic background. He snapped one frame before Haugh grabbed him by the shoulders and bodily turned him toward a tremendous avalanche of flame lunging up from behind the nearest hogback.

"Oh, Jesus!" Nothing else expressed his awe and horror.

The avalanche traveled on its own winds with the speed of a tidal wave. It sounded like one hundred runaway locomotives all in a line. It had taken three minutes for the fire monster to marshal his fiery forces below for the final assault on the ridge. Once he got things going, however, he pounced out of his lair and lunged upslope to cover 1,190 feet in less than two minutes.

His size diminished Mackey's firefighters in comparison. Cast with their backs to the flames, the thirteen tiny forms in yellow appeared as inconsequential as pedestrians standing before a molten structure thirty stories tall and five blocks long.

A structure that was about to engulf them.

Erickson's pleading radio call to Mackey alarmed listeners all over the mountain and at the command post in Glenwood Springs and in Grand Junction. His voice, cracking in the middle, warned, pleaded, prayed, all at the same time. Its note of desperation caught Tony Petrelli's attention as he and the jumpers with him fled for their lives up the mountain nearby.

"Mackey? Mackey? It's spotted just below you. Get the hell out of there. Run!"

The bearded smoke jumper leading the procession had his head down as he labored hard on the climb. Thrash looked up, acknowledging the shouts ahead of him. He paused. Haugh and Erickson pointed and jumped around like they stood on a hot stovetop.

"Run! Run!"

Then Thrash felt it—the blast from the blowup. It knocked him forward several steps. He whirled in unison with those all along the file. They gazed deeply into hell. For only an instant. Then, as in one breath, they stampeded. The air filled with meteors.

It was everything they had now. All or nothing.

Mackey in the rear grabbed Holtby and shoved her ahead of him. She screamed. Kept screaming. He wouldn't leave her. Her hand grasped in his, he dragged her screaming and stumbling up the fireline.

"Shut up and run," he snapped. "You gotta give it everything, Bonnie."

Eric Hipke gave it everything. The thirty-two-year-old jumper's hair shone like barnished copper in the sheen of the fire. He grew up in the forests of Washington State and was now into his fifth season as a firefighter, but he had not once witnessed a wildfire the size of this one. He recognized instinctively that his only hope lay in running for the ridgeline, not in sheltering up among the thick gambel.

Something's happened, he thought. *The whole canyon just blew up. Both sides are burning. Everybody knows we gotta get out of here.*

There's no place to put up a shelter because of all the places that haven't burned yet. The only option is to hoof it.

He motored up the hill, sprinting, driven by survival instincts to a split-second decision that meant life or death. Everything had come down to basics.

James Thrash reached Erickson and Haugh first at the fallen tree. From there, the fireline led almost straight up to the top of the ridge. He saw other firefighters scrambling around near Helispot 1. So close. Yet, Thrash who had always wryly suggested "'taters" in the same breath as "fire shelter" asked above the howling winds, "Shall we deploy?"

"No!" Haugh shouted back. "Our only chance is to make it over the ridge."

No time remained for anything except running. Haugh and Erickson bolted together as ashes and blowing firebrands chewed through their clothing and goaded them to greater effort. Thrash hesitated. His hand darted for his belt. He whipped out his silver shelter.

"Shelter!" he yelled to the others below him.

"No! No shelters!" Erickson screamed. *"Run!"*

Big Scott Blecha, the hotshot with the heavy aftershave and the constant twinkle of humor in his eyes, also broke for the ridgeline. His heavier bulk was no match for the more wiry Eric Hipke. Hipke started out near the back of the file, but reservoirs of speed released by adrenaline pushed him past Blecha. He passed Roger Roth, a slow runner who was having greater difficulty outdistancing *this* blowup than the one a week ago. When he flew past Thrash at the fallen tree, Thrash was trying to get underneath his shelter while preventing its taking off like a kite.

"Run! Run! Run!" Hipke yelled at all of them.

He fumbled to retrieve his fire shelter. Not once did he think of deploying it, but it might reflect the intense sear of the heat that scorched his back. He had eyes for only one destination—the top of the ridge. He spotted it now, dimly ahead through the swirling smoke. Haugh and Erickson were just below it, scrambling for a safe zone.

He glanced back in time to see the rest of his group, all twelve of them, surrounded and engulfed in flame. A few of them, like Roth and Blecha, were running for it, but they were still twenty yards back. Some of the others were pulling out fire shelters.

He didn't look back again.

He was almost to the top of the ridge. The other two runners were just ahead of him.

A sudden blast of superheated air knocked his face hard

into the ground. Falling was the only thing that saved him. Brilliant firebands electrified the air above his head as the main explosion passed over him.

Somehow the blast missed Erickson and Haugh. They turned to shout encouragement.

"Get up and run! Get over the ridge!"

Hipke scrambled to his feet. He knew he was burned, but he didn't know how severely. Flames burst and bloomed around him. Brad Haugh topped the ridge and dived over the crest. Erickson piled on top of him. As they untangled themselves, they heard shouting and awful screaming from firefighters caught in the oak brush. They jumped up and covered another one hundred feet downhill into the east drainage before the panic passed and they stopped to look back for whoever else might have made it. Both were too stunned for speech. No one appeared behind them.

There were no more human sounds now. Just the dreadful cracking of bones, the roar of the fire winds, the popping of resin exploding in trees, the rumble of loosened boulders rolling downhill.

Gigantic flames fringed the entire ridge crest. They leaped and pantomimed. The mouth of a volcano opened beyond the ridge. The entire west drainage had gone up and now the flames started into the east drainage, albeit more slowly downhill.

Erickson couldn't make himself say what he thought. It was too terrible for words. He and Haugh merely stood looking at each other. Then they turned slowly and started walking down through the unburned PJ toward where the east drainage opened onto I-70.

They thought they were the only survivors.

They thought it so intensely that when the charred figure appeared out of the brush it was almost a physical shock. The apparition moved like a zombie with awful blackened hands thrust out in front of him. Charred strips of flesh hung from his hands and arms. His shirt had been cindered away. His pack had burned off, leaving marks where nylon straps branded raw imprints across his shoulders.

Erickson finally discovered his voice. He murmured disbelievingly, "Eric?"

Hipke's eyes stared straight ahead, unblinking.

"It caught them," he whispered. "The fire got them. It got them all."

47

JIM BYERS AND ERIC CHRISTIANSON OF MI-chelle Ryerson's BLM squad found themselves cut off from the ridgeline and safety as flames hooked up the ridge, drove the survivors of Mackey's gang over the top and engulfed Helispot 1. They had been working near what had been dubbed the "Big Rock" about two hundred yards downslope from the summit. When the alarm sounded, they simply dropped their tools and scrambled away. To hell with trying to save a Pulaski or a chain saw; you could always purchase new ones. Let the government take it out of their pay.

Helispot 1 was already covered with fire. Byers and Christianson retreated and ran ahead of the flames in the direction of Helispot 2 at the saddle. They heard other firefighters screaming and shouting for each other as they separated in the smoke and became disoriented. The sun glowed bloodred through the dark smoke, like the single mocking eye of an angry god. Storm-created winds shrieked fiercely through the dry trees, rattling them like so many dry bones tied together and left hanging in a hurricane.

The two fighters stumbled into a gang of hotshots and BLM firefighters led by Michelle Ryerson. The frightened firefighters were trying to find their way to the safe zone beyond Helispot 1.

"Run back down!" Christianson warned. "Run back down. We're cut off."

Huge black clouds picked up the cries of despair and soared them aloft.

"What are we gonna do?"

"We're dying. We're all going to die!"

"We are not gonna die!" hotshot Louie Navarro shouted as he brought up the rear to police stragglers. Christianson and Byers led the way.

The fire seemed to gasp for air. Then it surged like a tidal wave and slammed against the ridge. Trees exploded on either side as the little band of terrified fire warriors fled for their lives along a gauntlet of raging flames.

"We've got to deploy shelters," someone cried out.

Byers thought it a crazy notion. It was admitting defeat. Just lie down and get roasted in the ovens. The shelters were never meant to withstand the full temperature blast of a blowup. He urged the firefighters to keep running.

It was their only chance.

Kim Valentine stumbled along near the tail of the loose formation. Her eyes bulged with terror. Christianson saw that fatigue and fright had taken their toll. She was giving up, becoming hysterical, stumbling and flinging her arms and crying and plaintively wailing for a friend lost somewhere below in the smoke.

"Kathi? Kathi?" Valentine raved.

Kathi Beck, the most daring member of the hotshots and the team's Mother Teresa. Kathi was making her own race up the mountain with Don Mackey and his contingent.

"Kathi? Kathi?"

Kim was crying for her friend and, Christianson saw, going into shock. As the fire closed in on them she gave up. She collapsed in the forest, too spent to continue on her own. Brian Scholz and Louie Navarro refused to leave her behind. They risked their own lives to try to save hers. They jerked her to her feet.

"Run! Go!" Navarro barked, sticking his face up to hers like a Marine DI. "Get up! That way! That way!"

She was too exhausted even to resist. She stumbled through the trees while the hot wind showered her with sparks. The other firefighters dragged her along with them.

"Run—or *die!*" they screamed at her.

Flames kept pace and drove the firefighters past exhaustion and cramps and fear. Byers sprinted ahead to try to scout a way out. All he saw was hell in every direction. Just when he started to give up and admit they might have to go to their final option, he spotted an orange helmet in the smoke ahead and heard a shout of encouragement.

"This way! Hurry. Run. This is the way out."

Smokejumper Sabinio Archuleta acted as a traffic cop north of where the upper fireline tied into Helispot 1 on the ridgeline. He seemed almost fearless. His swarthy face remained ruggedly impassive as he waved the battered refugees down the more-gentle grade that led to Helispot 2 in the saddle. If they reached that part of the ridge, he hurriedly explained, they could cross over into the east drainage and safety.

As far as he could tell, the east drainage hadn't blown up yet.

He stopped Navarro as Navarro brought up the rear. "Is this all of them?" The searing wind brittled his words.

"Valentine?" Navarro called out.

"Kim's with us. We have her," came a reply.

"That's all we had with us," Navarro said.

Not very many. Archuleta waited behind another few seconds, just to make sure others weren't coming. Most of the smokejumpers had been working the lower firelines. The only other jumper whom Archuleta knew for certain had gotten out was Sarah Doehring. She came uphill scouting the fireline for burning material just before the blowup. Kevin Erickson had been with her earlier, but Archuleta hadn't seen him since.

Archuleta dared wait no longer. No one could survive that inferno below. He turned and ran. Butch Blanco's deep voice booming from the ridgeline guided him through the thick smoke.

Flames from spotting bombarded the saddle. The IC and hotshot superintendent Tom Shepard literally threw firefighters over the ridgeline into the east drainage as they arrived. Since the hotshots had choppered in and were unfamiliar with the terrain, Eric Christianson, Derek Brixey and Jim Byers hung back to guide them down the east drainage to I-70.

Yellow or orange helmets and combat suits flashed against the dull green PJ the fire had not yet reached. Firefighters bounded like deer downhill through the scrub. The promise of salvation at the end renewed their energy.

48

FATE STUCK OUT BONY FINGERS ONCE AGAIN TO tamper with helitack Rich Tyler's life. Tyler always thought he might be living on borrowed time after he missed the helicopter crash that should have ended his life nearly ten years ago. And maybe he had been.

Instead of following the other firefighters down the east drainage to safety, Tyler and helitack Bob Browning took off running in the other direction. They followed the top of the ridge leading through the jump spot in the saddle and on toward the mountain. Apparently, to them, the slope to the northeast appeared the best escape route. It looked relatively flat with natural fire breaks in the form of generous rock outcroppings ledged among the PJ.

"No!" Butch Blanco shouted after them. "The other way. Go down the drainage."

The helitacks continued running.

"This is the best way," Tyler slung back over his shoulder. "Follow us. Run the ridgeline."

Blanco had no choice but to let them go. Some of the hotshots attempted to follow them, but Blanco grabbed them and slung them into the drainage.

"That way," he said. *"That way."*

What the helitacks could not see, what they failed to

notice from the air, was that the game trail they picked up contoured past the jump spot and led into a rocky chute fifty feet deep. A blind draw with only one way in and one way out.

Firefighters always said you might cheat Fate once or twice, but you couldn't keep cheating him.

49

BRAD HAUGH AND KEVIN ERICKSON LED THE wounded Eric Hipke deeper into the east drainage after their harrowing escape over the ridgetop. Then, watching the fire cautiously, they paused briefly to tend his injuries, bandaging his arms and hands with their T-shirts and bandanas and then pouring canteens of water over them to ease the pain. They kept talking to him to ward off shock. Nonsense talk. Nothing talk. What about your family? Where did you go to school? Anything to take his mind off his pain and what had just happened.

"Should we deploy shelters?" Erickson asked Haugh. "It might spot below us."

Erickson had parachuted in. Haugh had hiked to the fire with his BLM and Forest Service crews and knew the lay of the land.

"I've been down the drainage before," Haugh explained. "It opens out onto the highway."

Normally, running down a gulley which could act as a chimney for flames was never a good idea. The forest might explode in another uphill charge if the wind shifted and spotted fire below. Yet, under the circumstances, the drainage offered the only escape route. For all any of the three of them knew, they were the only survivors from the Storm King fire. And they weren't out of it yet.

"Can you make it?" Erickson asked Hipke.

"Do I have a choice?"

"Yes. But you don't want to think of that other choice."

Fire traveled much more slowly downhill than uphill. The three weary and charred firefighters cast final anxious looks behind them and started out. It would take the fast-moving blaze another half-hour to consume the east drainage and start up Hellsgate Ridge toward West Glenwood Springs. They should be able to outrun it. If they hurried. But the fire would be chasing them all the way.

50

WSFCC DIVERTED AN AIRTACK, AN AIR COM-mand ship, from Paonia to Storm King to control and coordinate air support. Chopper pilot Dick Good almost gnawed off his own arm in frustration over his inability to find a channel to communicate with the inbound tanker bombers. He fussed over the airwaves until Dispatch finally came up with the correct frequency and solved the problem.

"What's the ETA on Airtack?" Good asked.

"Twenty minutes."

"Advise the tankers to look out for my chopper. I don't want to get swatted like a gnat."

Like all firefighters on the mountain that July Wednesday, Good displayed extraordinary courage. As soon as the mountain blew, he abandoned his water bucket at the Commons in Canyon Creek and pulled the little Bell Ranger back into the air. He nosed it down at top speed and buzzed back to the mountain.

"Hold on," he advised Steve Little, "this could get a little rough."

Hoping he might set down on the helispot to rescue firefighters, he found the entire ridge rolling with flame and smoke instead. Globlets of flame shot into the air like antiaircraft fire. Winds hurled rancid smoke across the sky and shook the little helicopter until even the rivets rattled. It would be pure and simple suicide to even attempt a landing in such a storm.

"A big fire," Good radioed the command center. That was an understatement. "I can't see anything."

He returned to the Commons and picked up a second crew member, Bruce Dissell, and a trauma kit. Thwarted in his rescue effort, he thought to spot survivors and at least drop them something for first aid if he couldn't evacuate them. He assumed from the constant frantic stutter of radio transmissions rising off the mountain that not everyone had escaped.

Little and Dissell leaned out into the wind against their safety tethers, peering down through fleeting breaks in the smoke as Good fought to control the helicopter. Several objects glinted brightly in the char. Good circled.

"We can see five or six shelters deployed below Helispot 1," he reported, "and another two downslope on a little spur ridge."

"Somebody's waving from one of the shelters," Little exclaimed.

There were no other signs of life on the ridge. Survivors fleeing ahead of the pursuing flames gathered on I-70 at the mouth of the east drainage. Colorado troopers and ambulances with emergency lights flashing worked their way through traffic stalled all the way back to Glenwood Springs.

No one wanted to give the thought substance by voicing it aloud, but it was readily apparent that anyone not in his shelter or off the mountain by now had probably perished. Butch Blanco and Tom Shepard tried to get a count as fighters straggled out of the bush. The count came up short.

It came up way short.

51

TIM JOHNSON IN TANKER-131 AND MARK MAT-
thews in Tanker-23, the heavy P-3 from Andy Wilson's
Minnesota outfit, took over the sky from Dick Good's
chopper. Good got out of the way and let them have it. The
only way to save the jumpers hootched up in their shelters
was to glop pink Fugitive right down their necks. Blanco
requested it.

The two tankers first made a reconnaissance flight over
the blowup. They flew in loose formation. They circled wide
out past the rising cone of Storm King Mountain. It showed
red from the fire. Then they cut back in low and upwind to
avoid the smoke that leaned with the wind toward the
mountain.

It required skilled flying. Downdrafts inside the giant
smoke rings could slam even the P-3 into the earth. Wind
shears cut the air into opposing masses.

"Okay, we see shelters," Matthews radioed. "We're circling around and then making a run to dump on them.
They're in the middle of the fire."

The fire had already made one run up the ridge off the
smokejumpers' left flank. It missed rolling directly over
them. The jumpers death-gripped the corners of their flimsy
shelters against the gale winds as burning faggots filled the
air and pelted their shelters like fiery hail. They shouted to
each other. They made frail jokes about roast pigs that no
one laughed at under the circumstances. Trying to keep up
morale.

One or two of them nurtured their terror in cold silence.

One or two of them prayed.

The tankers dropped their loads, a combined total of
around four thousand gallons, upon and around the shel-

ters. Risky as it was flying into the hurricane, Matthews and Johnson gave it no more of a second thought than Wilson and Dahl gave it when they flew underneath the fire-and-smoke curl at Paonia two days ago on the Fourth of July. They zoomed in low like combat pilots, flying by the seats of their pants. Bold. Almost reckless. Like smokejumpers, they considered themselves a special breed—and they were.

Besides, those trapped down there were *firefighters*.

"If need be," said Matthews, "I'd get out and *push* my tanker and its load up to them."

Slip blast from Johnson's low-flying tanker whipped at the flames. He dropped his load to the left flank of the silver tents, attempting to create a barrier between the trapped jumpers and the fire's main blowup. Matthews applied flaps to his lumbering red-and-white P-3 and shaved the top off Hellsgate Ridge to the northeast as he made his run behind Johnson.

Tony Petrelli on the ground peeped out from his shelter for a quick second as the big airplane roared overhead. It amazed him that the P-3 flew so low he saw Matthews's worn and anxious face grim behind his cockpit glass. The airplane released. Heavy pink fog filled the sky, displacing smoke. The Fugitive was like heavy, thick water. Like mucous. It plopped instead of spraying like the old slurry did that the eco-freaks hated.

But it seemed to cool the air nonetheless. It fell hard and heavy and wet on the shelters and rolled off. Quentin Rhoades felt like cheering. He lay in its wetness. He reveled in it. He rejoiced in its life-giving qualities.

Petrelli revived enough to check in on the radio for others who might remain on the mountain. After a try or two, a loud voice boomed from the small black box.

"I'm okay," said the voice.

"Longanecker? Is that you?"

"In person. I'm okay. How are you? I'm on the ridge below you—at the lunch spot."

"Are you sheltered?"

"It wasn't necessary here."

Surely the others on the mountain had survived if Longanecker made it okay *without* a shelter. Petrelli felt better. He and Longanecker joked with each other a minute to rev up their spirits. "Feel like an apple in a roast pig's mouth." That sort of thing.

"There's still fire all around," Longanecker said. "I can't get out of here yet."

"Neither can we," Petrelli replied. "We're staying sheltered. I think we're going to make it now."

From the Commons below in Canyon Creek, Ken Wabaunsee, George Steele and the other smokejumpers held in reserve overheard the first haunting voices aired from the mountaintop since after the blowup. They clumped around the radio.

"Petrelli, we're trying to account for everyone. . . ." Wabaunsee inquired.

"There are nine of us here on the ridge that I know of," Petrelli responded. "Six below Helispot 1—Petrelli, Thomas, Cooper, Feliciano, Shelton and Rhoades. Woods and Soto are farther down, but I can look out now and sometimes see their shelters. Longanecker is okay at the lunch spot. You heard him. We're okay so far, but we don't know what the fire's doing below us."

"Stay hootched up where you are," Wabaunsee advised. "It's still blowing."

The fire made two more runs at the jumpers, as though reluctant to give up. Wind snatched at their shelters; they dared not relax their holds on the corners. Glowing firebrands flew underneath them. Petrelli used his elbows to brush the embers away from his body. He lay in his own sweat and the moisture from the runoff Fugitive. The Fugitive kept the fire monster at bay.

In between runs, cowering jumpers caught their breath. They drew in great quantities of hope. They peeked out from underneath their silver covers and called out to each other. Although smoke still rolled up thick out of the drainage and ash and dust filled the wind, Keith Woods and Sonny Soto felt sufficiently emboldened to pick up their shelters and scramble uphill to repitch with the others. Soto said his cramps were going away.

What the jumpers needed most now was news about the others. Wabaunsee radioed that jumpers Kevin Erickson and Eric Hipke had escaped to the highway with a BLM firefighter named Haugh.

"They needed an ambulance to take them to the hospital," Wabaunsee reported.

"How bad are they?" Petrelli asked.

"Erickson took in a lot of smoke. Hipke is burned pretty bad. That's all we've heard so far."

"How about the others? Hold on . . . we're getting another run."

The fire monster seemed to have lost his edge. He huffed and puffed and pelted the shelters with hot debris, but it was clear his focus and ferocity had shifted elsewhere. Presently, Petrelli returned to the air.

"If we're 'taters," he joked, "we ain't done yet. The others . . . ?"

Wabaunsee told him supervisors were at the mouth of the east drainage at I-70 holding count on survivors. The fire had swept through the east drainage and was already up Hellsgate Ridge and heading full steam toward West Glenwood Springs on the east. On the west, flames now threatened the Canyon Creek Estates. Overhead talked about evacuating residents. It had become one hell of a big fire.

"Archuleta and Sarah Doehring also made it to the freeway," Wabaunsee said. "With your group up there, that makes thirteen jumpers accounted for."

"And three are missing? Who . . . ?"

He did some quick mental calculations, saying the names softly as they came to him: "Mackey . . . Roger Roth . . . and Thrash. Jim Thrash."

"Yes. Mackey, Roth, Thrash."

Petrelli passed the news to the others. There was no more joking.

"We keep trying to raise Mackey on the radio," Wabaunsee said.

"Maybe there's a dead spot between here and there. We can't hear transmissions from down on the freeway. Maybe they made it out another way. I'll give it a try from up here and see if he's on the air."

Deep inside, in the pit of his stomach, he knew it was futile.

"Mackey?"

No one answered.

"Mackey, are you out there? Don Mackey, can you read me?"

No reply.

"Don Mackey?"

Nothing.

"Roger Roth?"

Static.

"James Thrash?"

Static emitted from the radio, trapped with him underneath his thin metallic shield. He heard his heart thudding against the scorched earth, felt it pounding in his chest. He suddenly felt so alone and overpowered by the howling of the wind, the roaring of the unleashed fire monster, the assault of burning debris against his shelter.

"Mackey? Are you guys out there? *Is anybody else still on the mountain?*"

52

THE WAKE FIRE AT PAONIA DESTROYED THREE houses. If the fire at Storm King Mountain escaped into the settlements on either side of the mountain, someone noted unnecessarily, it would make the Wake fire look like a campfire by comparison.

Grand Junction Fire Control Officer Winslow Robertson assumed command of an interagency incident management group that moved into the command post already set up at the Middle School in Glenwood Springs. He beefed up the secondary command post in Canyon Creek where resident Bob Fritsch generously donated his two-car garage. Whereas the Storm King blaze had languished from Saturday to Tuesday as a low-priority fire, its rout of the forces attacking it and its break for freedom now created a sense of urgency that infected the entire western slopes of the Rockies. Stopping it became a community effort. Neighbors who might never have spoken to each other before pitched in shoulder to shoulder to do what they could.

Volunteers from Silt, New Castle, Glenwood Springs, Carbondale and Basalt responded to the alarm. At one point, fire engines stationed themselves at nearly every home along that stretch of Mitchell Creek from Highway 6 to 24 and from the Storm King Ranch to out past the Mitchell Creek Fish Hatchery. Glenwood Springs firefighters guarded the lower west end of Canyon Creek Estates and Ami's Acres RV Park. Greg Rippy commandeered his construction company's four-thousand-gallon water truck and motored up and down roads watering down foliage in the line of the fire's progress. His wife, Marilee, kept vigil in their Mitchell Creek home where a thin layer of ash sifted onto the furniture.

Other volunteers enlisted with the Salvation Army at the Middle School to help build and support "Fire City" which would be needed to feed and shelter some five hundred firefighters. Children delivered homemade cookies and sandwiches. Former firefighter Norm Gould set up a free espresso coffee stand at the Glenwood Springs command post; twelve-year-old Melani Britton showed up to run it. High-schoolers Tracy Morrick and Amy Hodgden operated a Red Cross evacuation center at the Middle School. Richard Drew provided food, water and cold drinks to hundreds of firefighters who rushed in to battle the wildfire.

"My wife, Vicky, doesn't even want to look at the grocery bill," he said. "I'm not going to look at the phone bill. I'm just going to pay it. We told the firefighters to call home direct and not fool with credit cards or collect calls."

Wal-Mart manager Tim Clark heard some firefighters weren't getting enough to eat.

"We emptied our counters," he said, "and sent out about six pickup trucks loaded with peanut butter, bread, juices, snacks and all the cola we had."

Tension settled like a clammy cloth over the Commons at the Canyon Creek Estates. Somber over the news that at least *some* fighters had not made it off the mountain, people scanned the char with binoculars in hopes of detecting signs of life. All they saw were the silver fire shelters glinting through the smoke.

Refugee fighters, their faces blackened by soot and despair, clung to the rail fence around the Commons while people yammered at them with questions. Their eyes never left the flaming ridge; they had escaped it only through some combination of luck, strength and Fate.

"It wasn't my time," Sarah Doehring said. "Fate didn't get a good hold on me."

"Where is Brian Rush?" someone wanted to know. "Have you seen Brian?"

"Has anyone seen Rob Johnson?"

A wife waited at the Commons from almost the moment she heard of the blowup. She anxiously inspected each vehicle that arrived carrying refugees. She burst into tears when she finally spotted her fire-blackened husband. She ran to him and gave him the firmest hug. He left a black palm print on the back of her shirt.

"I'm taking you home," she cried.

"I can't leave until I know about the others," he replied.

Rumors spread about injuries and the missing. At first, the number of those missing reached as high as twenty-five. Gradually, however, as more and more were found and accounted for, the number dwindled. Finally, word went around that at least eleven, maybe more, remained shrouded in smoke on the mountain, not counting Dale Longanecker at the lunch spot and the eight smokejumpers holed up in their shelters.

George Steele crushed a paper coffee cup in his clenched fist and hurled it away. Someone else booted a plastic jug.

Short heartfelt bursts of profanity marred what was otherwise a profound silence that held the Commons in its grasp.

One by one, firefighters whose names had not made The List for Storm King learned about friends and comrades missing in the fire. While their first thoughts were to be thankful that Fate had somehow omitted their own names from The List, and feeling guilty about being thankful, they nonetheless knew the sorrow of loss.

Tanker pilot Andy Wilson heard about the blowup on his car radio late that afternoon. He had left his ranch and was driving back to Walker Field to prepare for tomorrow's flying. When he reached the airfield, Earl Dahl took him aside. Tankers were bombing the fire, Dahl said, and search parties had organized to look for the missing as soon as the mountain cooled down.

"Rich hasn't been accounted for," Dahl said. He knew how close Tyler and Wilson had become.

Wilson gave a nervous laugh. There was no mirth to it. It was his way of denying reality.

"Rich won't go down that easy," he said, hoping he was right, blaming himself at the same time for not having been in the air where he should have been when his friend needed him. Maybe he could have done something—flown under a curl of smoke or something. You went to greater length to save a human than you did a house.

But knowing too that he couldn't have done any more than anyone else had done.

"Rich won't cower like a sheep and wait for the flames to get him," Wilson insisted. "He'll run for his life. He's got Patty and his little Andy. Andy's only one-year-old. He'll show up around Steamboat Springs tomorrow, still running."

Kent Hamilton simply wanted to hold his wife, April, and pretend his friend Roger Roth would show up anytime now with that familiar grin splitting his lean face. He felt he should have been up at the fire with Roth and the others, not tied down at his desk with a broken clavicle.

His first reaction, after shock and the desire to go do *something,* was to sit down by himself and try to remember everything he could about Roth. How he came to know Roth on the California hotshot crew, what Roth was like. He wanted to get a full picture of Roth, like Roth was standing directly in front of him, so he could hold onto it and always remember. What would they be talking about, laughing about?

He had a mental vision of Roth running up the mountain, running slow because Roth was not a fast runner.

"It's scary because it could have been any of us up there," Hamilton mused. "We all think the same way. We all come from somewhat the same fire background. All of us as jumpers share a common experience no one else can ever relate to."

Something reminded him of the best parachute jump he or Roth or any other jumper, for that matter, had ever made. You always remembered the cruddy jumps for different reasons, but then, every once in a while, along came a jump that was absolutely perfect and made up for all the others.

The fire was a small one burning in no more than two or three trees. The air lay so calm in the beautiful light of a mountain sunrise that smoke eddied skyward as straight as a pencil mark. When Hamilton's parachute opened, he found himself soaring above an incredibly blue lake. He soared in that utter quiet only eagles must know.

A lush meadow of short green grass opened to receive him at the end of the lake. The whole lovely morning seemed to be smiling. It made him reluctant to land. He could have gone on flying and flying forever, like Icarus before his wings melted.

He flared above the meadow and landed as daintily as a sparrow on a tiny twig. It was the absolutely perfect ending to the absolutely perfect jump. He thrust both fists into the air and jogged a little dance of jubilation. He couldn't help himself.

"Life is wonderful!" he decided then and there.

A jump like that, that perfect, was like a monument to all the smokejumpers he had ever known or would ever know, to those in the past and those today, to those like J.C. Curd, Brent Johnson, Tim Pettitt and the others who would continue to bump their names onto The List no matter what happened here today. They were smokejumpers, fighters of wildfire. They thumbed their noses at Fate, even as Fate made his selections. Tomorrow, the day after, this year or next or three years from now, perhaps Curd's name would come up on The List for a Storm King Mountain. Or maybe Hamilton's. The rotation of The List decided who it would be.

And they would go.

"It's not just firefighters whose names come up on a list," Hamilton said. *"Everyone's* name is on The List somewhere and sooner or later he gets bumped to the top of it."

53

EVACUATION OF AT-RISK RESIDENTIAL AREAS BE-gan even as firefighters and volunteers labored to build secondary firelines and establish fire security zones. Reporter Nan Johnson of the Glenwood *Post* listened to strategies for evacuation and battle over her radio scanner as she inched along in the immense traffic jam on I-70. Winslow Robertson sounded unruffled and in control as he called for additional air support and directed placement of reinforcements.

Smoke filled the streets of Glenwood Springs. Ashes rained down onto cars. Pedestrians headed for a jazz concert near the overpass bridge lingered on the streets. Enormous clouds of gray, brown and black smoke blotted out the westering sun. The sky assumed an eerie orange pall.

Nan Johnson made it through the traffic jam before she overheard emergency communications about shutting I-70 down completely and evacuating everyone in both Canyon

Creek on the west side of the mountain and West Glenwood Springs on the east. Even from her home seventeen miles away she saw the giant cloud of brown smoke undulating in the winds of the passing cold front. Her heart went out to the people living at the foot of the mountain in the path of the fast-moving flames. She had covered the Wake fire at Paonia over the holiday weekend and experienced with residents there the tragedies of lost homes and dreams burned to cinders.

Would this fire season never end?

Caravans of automobiles and trucks loaded with valuables fled Canyon Creek as gusting winds fanned flames downhill toward the houses. More than two hundred people evacuated to move in with friends and family in Glenwood Springs and other regional communities. Refugees left with tears in their eyes. They thought they would never see their homes again as fire crested on the ridge above Mitchell Creek.

Karen Haff was alone when Garfield County deputies drove up and shouted, "Get together what you want and *go.*"

She gathered up pets and pictures and jumped into her car.

"Smoke was just billowing up," she said. "It looked like it was right over our house. It wasn't, but it looked like it."

Nearby, the owner of the Mountain Mobile Home Park waited things out.

"I got pretty worried when I saw that big plume of smoke," he said. "We're just kind of waiting for someone to come along and tell us to move."

One of his residents was taking no such chances. Barbara Lavender darted back and forth from her car to her mobile home with one eye on the smoke and the other on valuables she loaded up to take with her.

"We're leaving behind everything that can be replaced by money," she said.

Richard Carney also evacuated his house at Mitchell Creek, saying, "I was up there all day so we saw it coming."

While many vacated, others dug in for a fight. Homeowners in the fire's broad path mounted their roofs with garden hoses or sprinklers in attempts to save their property. One man had to be treated for blisters on his hands after he single-handedly tried digging a fireline around his house.

Don Halkanson sent his kids to stay with friends while he packed photos, documents and other items, wetted down his property and then watched and waited to see what the fire would do.

"I'm going to wait until the last minute," said Ben Tipton as he sprayed his house with a garden hose. "I'll keep my motorcycle pointed downhill."

Ken Kuehlman said he had no intention of leaving his trailer in Robin Hood Trailer Park. "I have faith in the firefighters to do their job."

The desk clerk at The Inn in West Glenwood Springs refused reservations, explaining to callers that the motel might have to be evacuated before the evening was over.

"We're throwing everything we've got at the fire," said BLM spokeswoman Kathy Voth. "Yes, we're missing some firefighters on the mountain. We don't know how many yet."

54

THE FIRE MOVED ON AND OUT, DRAGGING GIgantic plumes of smoke with it and threatening the valleys. But nearly two hours passed before the eight smokejumpers trapped below Helispot 1 dared emerge from their shelters.

One by one they silently emerged. Stunned survivors of holocaust. They rose slowly to their feet, as out of the ashes of the fallen phoenix, and looked around. The wind had started to lay from the fast passage of the front, leaving the solemn aftermath of a storm. As far as the eye could see, all the way to the ring of bellowing smoke that surrounded them with the fire's spread over distant ridges and mountains, stretched a desolate moonscape of blackened boulders and earth punctuated by stark black exclamation points that had once been trees. From this world of desolation and ruin, of glowing embers and smoldering tree remains, hissed primordial steam reddened by a dying sun that made the earth look like it might explode all over again in flame.

It was a world that might exist after the nuclear destruction of civilization.

Frozen against this stark tableau stood the survivors, their faces as blackened as charred tree stumps, their clothing scorched and burn-spattered by flying embers. Quentin Rhoades had part of a fire shelter melted to his back. The jumpers blinked. Words failed them.

A boulder loosened by the heat crashed down the steep ridge and broke the spell. Tony Petrelli started. Slowly, as moving through a dreamscape, the jumpers drew close to each other. They touched shoulders or grasped hands.

They had survived. They had survived *this*.

Dale Longanecker found them like that, still marveling over how it was they were selected to live. He came hiking swiftly uphill through the wasteland. He stood with them and looked.

"Did you have to deploy?" Petrelli asked him.

"It was fine where I was. Have you seen Mackey and the others?"

It was not a question. It was a spoken hope.

Petrelli suggested they organize a sweep of the hillside to look for the other firefighters instead of immediately evacuating. Longanecker offered to climb uphill to the helispot and anchor the sweep. He walked away. Some of the jumpers noticed a folded poncho fly sticking out of the pouch that should have held his fire shelter. Had Longanecker replaced his shelter with a rain poncho? Was that the reason he hadn't gone to shelter at the lunch spot? He didn't even have one with him!

Lady Luck be a winner today.

A bad feeling swept through the jumpers as the search began.

"We got out of it okay," Rhoades noted optimistically. "Maybe they've sheltered up too."

Again, it was more hope than actual expectation. Hope that soon dashed itself against the side of the dead hill. Petrelli spotted blackened lumps scattered along the fireline. At first he thought them to be fallen burned logs, only they were shorter and thicker than any of the trees that grew in the gambel brush. Then the glint of a silver shelter caught his attention and he knew.

Dread welled inside his heart as he strode directly to the site. He summoned the others.

There were six in the first group. Six things not human now but which had once been human. Grotesque things. Charred lumps of soft coal to which were attached what had once been heads, now without features, and stubs of limbs still poised as though in terror or flight. Like the burned squirrel Harry Gisborne found after the Half Moon blowup. Temperatures of 2,000 degrees made sight identification impossible.

Everything that could be burned was gone. Littered in among the corpses were melted shovels, disintegrated fire shelters, ash, melted watches, a religious medal, pieces of chain saws and not much else. It would take the Garfield County coroner's office and eight specialists, including an anthropologist, fingerprint experts and photographers, five days to identify the remains and pinpoint their death sites on the mountain. Out of this effort emerged the true horror of the victims' last dying seconds in the wildfire.

Although smokejumpers had no way of identifying the corpses upon which they gazed with tears in their eyes, they eventually learned that Don Mackey lay last in the line. His body lay almost side by side with that of Bonnie Jean Holtby. Mackey must have been pulling her up the mountain even as the fire overtook them.

Slightly uphill of Mackey and Holtby was hotshot Rob

Johnson, whose younger brother, Tony, had been working the upper fireline and therefore escaped over the ridgeline into the east drainage.

Hotshot Levi Brinkley who had telephoned his mother yesterday about "going to heaven" in Colorado ended his first year on the squad by dying next to lovable small-town Jon Kelso. They must have held on to each other as they tried to drag each other up the mountain ahead of the flames.

Tamera Bickett who resembled actress Marilu Henner died near her friends Brinkley and Kelso and slightly uphill of them. She had fought fires since she graduated from high school in 1988.

This first group of bodies rested only 270 feet from the top of the ridge and what would have been safety on the other side. The flame front flashed directly over them, moving so fast it caught the firefighters literally in mid-stride.

Chopper pilot Dick Good circled the scene in 93R, preparing to land to pick up survivors. Medevac helicopters chandelled higher in calmer air. Petrelli's saddened voice leaked out of the air over Good's radio.

"We've found six," Petrelli said. Nothing more.

The dazed smokejumpers worked their way uphill. About twenty yards on up they found another group of corpses.

"Five more," Petrelli radioed.

This group had been caught 212 feet from the ridgetop. The last time Kevin Erickson saw jumper Roger Roth, just before flames swept all the way to the top, Roth was deploying his shelter. He almost succeeded.

Extreme heat delaminated the shelter layers and cracked and melted them. As Roth dropped to the ground, he released his backpack at his feet. Fuses in the pack flared from the heat, causing Roth to jerk his feet away from the pack and release the shelter bottom. Wind turbulence yanked the fire blanket off the prone jumper and further exposed him to killer flames. He died with his knees drawn up fetallike toward his chin.

Hotshots Terri Hagen, the "Go Girl" entomology student from Oregon State University, and Doug Dunbar, who intended this to be his final year before he finished his degree in business and entered the corporate world, lay uphill of jumper Roger Roth and slightly downhill of jumper James Thrash. Neither Hagen nor Dunbar deployed shelters. The fire caught them on the run.

James Thrash had joked about fire shelters in his *Playboy* interview. At the last second, however, he deployed his in what must have been a last act of heroism. He deployed his shelter and tried to pull Kathi Beck, the hotshots' Mother Teresa, underneath it with him. As he rolled to his right and lifted the edge of the blanket to let Kathi in, flames surged underneath and caught both firefighters. Not that the shelter would have saved them anyhow, not in that hell storm, but Thrash died at least attempting to save a fellow firefighter.

Petrelli and the survivors with him had seen all they could stand. *There but for the grace of God . . .* They climbed on up the hill toward Helispot 1 where Good would pick them up in the Ranger. They slogged past the iron head of a Pulaski, past the remnants of a fire shelter. The last victim had dropped 121 feet from the top.

Big Scott Blecha, the former U.S. Marine with the big sense of humor, almost made it. He took off when Kevin Erickson screamed, "Run!" He wasn't fast enough.

Of the thirteen firefighters in Don Mackey's group, only smokejumper Eric Hipke survived. He presently prepared for skin transplant surgery at Valley View Hospital in Glenwood Springs.

"Twelve bodies altogether," Petrelli radioed the chopper.

That left only two firefighters missing—the helitacks Rich Tyler and Bob Browning.

"Do you need medevac?" Good asked.

Petrelli lifted his head toward the hovering chopper. His reply came broken, strained.

"It's too late for that," he said.

55

DICK GOOD AIRLIFTED THE SURVIVING SMOKE-
jumpers off the ridge while the fire charged out in all
directions. A fire that picked up momentum continued its
rampage long after the conditions that gave it impetus
abated. The jumpers were charred and cheerless when
Good set them down at the Commons. Their comrades
greeted them with silent handshakes and embraces.

The pilot flew George Steele, Ken Wabaunsee, Wayne
Williams and other reinforcement jumpers back to the ridge
as a search party for the two missing helitacks. All Butch
Blanco and other survivors knew was that Tyler and Browning were last seen racing northeast across the ridge saddle in
the direction of the mountain.

At 9:00 P.M., Good landed his helicopter at the Commons. He cut off the engine and climbed stiffly from his
seat. He had flown constantly for more than twelve hours.
The county coroner wanted him to make one more trip to
deliver body bags.

"I've had enough," he said.

The red flaring of wildfire surrounded the ridge. The ridge
was a black pincushion of fire. Embers like glowering eyes
burned holes through the cloak of darkness.

"I'm not going back up tonight," Good said. "It's too
dangerous for everyone."

Winslow Robertson agreed. He called off both the search
and the fight until dawn.

"We're not taking any more chances getting anyone else
killed trying to fight up there at night," he said.

Many survivors from the mountain waited at the Commons most of the night for further word. So far the word
was grim; twelve known dead, two still missing and pre-
sumed dead.

* * *

The battle went on the defensive. Firefighters built line around occupied areas in Canyon Creek and West Glenwood Springs and assembled reserve troops for an all-out assault at first light. They held their positions and let the fire monster tantrum at will between the lines. Overnight, flames consumed nearly two thousand acres and maneuvered to within three hundred yards of West Glenwood.

Residents who chose to make a fight of it stayed up all night wetting down their houses and preparing to evacuate only as a last resource. Firefighters at Walker Field gathered in sober groups on the tarmac in front of Ops. They itched to join the fight at dawn. They spoke softly of comrades who had died on the mountain during the day, whose bodies still lay in the char where they fell.

BLM and the U.S. Forest Service quickly assembled an investigation team. Secretary of Agriculture Mike Espy said he would "get to the bottom of it." *Somebody* had to be at fault for what happened. Somebody's head would roll. "Acts of God" simply did not happen anymore in American society.

Andy Wilson pressed his forehead against the cool night metal of his tethered red-and-beige airplane. He had to face it. Even a marathon runner like Rich Tyler couldn't stay ahead of flames like those that swept up the Storm King ridge. No use looking for him at Steamboat Springs or anywhere else for that matter. His friend Rich lay up there in the char along with thirteen other wildland firefighters.

Press from across the nation thronged to Glenwood Springs. Talking TV heads, late editions and then the morning papers spread the news:

WILDFIRE KILLS 12

Glenwood Springs—Overcome by a ferocious wildfire that blew up at Canyon Creek, 12 federal firefighters wrapped in their silver fire tents perished Wednesday afternoon and two remained missing this morning on the steep hillsides of Hellsgate Ridge.

Gov. Roy Romer has called the tragedy the worst in Colorado firefighting history and among the worst ever. . . .

At dawn, 140 federal firefighters, several hundred volunteers, three tanker bombers, eight bulldozers building line and seven helicopters attacked the fire enemy. Wilson and Dahl helped extract payback against the killer. The fight became a kind of personal vendetta. Even though most active flames were extinguished by noon, the attack continued. The nation watched. The nation wanted that baby *out*.

The worst part for Wilson was looking down from the air at the body bags. He remembered seeing them as bright yellow against a field of black. All morning he flew over the body bags laid out and full on the ground awaiting transportation to the morgue. Flying over them and still not knowing the fate of his friend Rich Tyler and the other helitack Bob Browning. Search parties in yellow helmets spread themselves out in line across the tortured landscape. They no longer looked for survivors; they looked for the rest of the corpses.

Searchers brought out the bodies. Congressman Scott McInnis, a former cop and firefighter, became more than a casual observer when his helicopter landed on the patch of charcoal that had been Helispot 2. Twelve corpses lay cocooned in body bags. It required six people on each bag to carry it, the terrain was so steep. McInnis lent a hand.

"There was not a piece of green around," he said. "The only thing sticking out of the ground were black sticks."

Helicopters airlifted the bags to the Commons where the grim remains were stacked inside a plain wooden trailer drawn by a Colorado Bureau of Investigation van. They were transported in slow procession to the Farnam-Holt Funeral Home in Glenwood Springs.

Rusty-haired Eric Hipke, the young smokejumper who outran the blowup while the rest of his contingent perished, confronted the fact of his friends' deaths after undergoing surgery. He had jumped fires for four years. Although he stopped short of saying he was through with it, he admitted Wednesday's tragedy took the thrill out of it.

"I think I've pretty much pegged the old excitement meter," he said.

He choked up when he thought of fellow smokejumpers Mackey, Roth, Thrash and the nine hotshots and two helitacks lost on the mountain.

"It hasn't really sunk in yet. Even when I talk about it, I can't believe it happened to me. I've thought about that. I don't know . . . I don't know . . . Everybody was doing their best. It's such a horrible way to go. I just don't have any words to tell their families. . . ."

Andy Wilson learned about Rich Tyler that afternoon when searchers found his body within an arm's reach of Bob Browning's. They still wore their packs and flight helmets. Their fire-seared bodies lay partially covered in earth and debris in the blind chute below a rock outcropping a quarter-mile north of where the other victims had gone down. Apparently trapped in the chute, they tried to climb up the outcropping before smoke and flames overtook them. Tyler the marathon runner dashed farther than anyone else in attempting to escape the fire monster.

In spite of his youth, Wilson had faced death enough to construct a philosophy around it.

"The gratifying thing about it is they ran for it," he said. "They went for it balls to the wall. That makes me feel good, to see they got to fight for their lives."

His speculative gaze eased along the bright fuselage of his P2V bomber.

"When I go," he said, "that's the way I want to go—balls to the wall and surrounded by Mother Nature. To let Mother Nature take your life is an honor."

Afterword

THE FIRE ON STORM KING MOUNTAIN DE-voured 2,430 acres before firefighters finally stomped it into submission. The estimated total cost of the single fire was over $2 million. It took fourteen lives—ten men and four women firefighters.

Even while smoke still curled from the distant fire, three thousand mourners thronged to Two Rivers Park in Glen-wood Springs on the first Sunday after the tragedy to commemorate the dead heroes. Almost everyone wore purple ribbons. Purple ribbons sprouted on trees, cars, signs and on fourteen empty chairs placed down in front.

"Purple is the color of courage and heroism," explained Jeff Feater, who originated the idea, "such as the Purple Heart award given to soldiers injured in battle."

A formation of five helicopters streaked across the sky above the memorial celebration. Hundreds of federal, local and volunteer firefighters stood to pray.

"They may not have been able to save the world," eulogized the Reverend Jim Warn, "but they answered the call to save their particular part of it."

President Bill Clinton telephoned Governor Romer to ask that his condolences be passed along to the families of the victims. Vice President Al Gore came to Broomfield, Colorado, to plant a pinyon pine tree in memory of the slain firefighters. The tree was decorated with fourteen purple ribbons.

"We thank (all wildland firefighters) for their selfless dedication and courage to protecting homes and the people of the communities that are threatened by fire," Gore said. "We are especially moved by the fourteen men and women who we are dedicating this living memorial to today."

Residents of the high-desert town of Prineville, Oregon, first learned of the tragedy when NBC-TV interrupted its coverage of the murders of Nicole Brown Simpson and Ronald Goldman with a report that firefighters were missing on Storm King Mountain in Colorado. A young woman dining at Dad's Place jumped up in tears and dashed out of the restaurant.

Names of the dead finally reached the little town. Nine of them were Prineville Hotshots based out of Ochoco National Forest headquarters. Employees at the forest headquarters choked back tears as they lowered their flag to half-mast.

The eleven surviving members of the Prineville Hotshots, uniformed in their blue T-shirts and blue baseball caps, marched with their arms over each other's shoulders behind nine riderless horses in the annual Prineville rodeo parade on Saturday. Superintendent Tom Shepard and foreman Brian Scholz led the contingent through town to the high school football stadium. Tears streaked the face of Kim Valentine, the only woman of the five on the crew to have survived. Townspeople lined the sidewalk in solemn silence. Men held hats over their hearts. Women dabbed at their eyes.

Colorado Governor Romer stood on a flatbed truck with Oregon Governor Barbara Roberts and addressed the fifteen hundred mourners at the stadium. Flowers, purple bunting and nine American flags decorated the truck.

"As that slope (off Storm King Mountain) revegetates," Romer stated, his voice choking with emotion, "I think all of us will look upon it as a living memorial."

In the meantime, Colorado mourned its own dead—the helitacks Rich Tyler and Bob Browning. Andy Wilson stood with head bowed in ceremonies in Grand Junction. Kent Hamilton was almost alone in refusing to wear a purple ribbon, although his friend Roger Roth was among the dead.

"It's not something I like to think about a lot," he said. "I don't need to wear a purple ribbon to remember. Each person you just keep in your mind and you just think about the whole thing. It's scary, because it could have been any of us up there that day."

Smokejumper "Captain Jack" Seagraves, whose fifty-second birthday was coming up in a few days and who missed the call to fight fire at Storm King because of his new cellular telephone, worked the operations board at the McCall smokejumper base in Idaho on the day of the blowup. Word came in from Colorado accounting for the smokejumpers one by one—except for three of them: Don Mackey, James Thrash and Roger Roth.

"I'm almost embarrassed to say that I felt relief when we found there were only three because at one time we felt there could be a dozen," he said.

Fellow smokejumpers escorted the bodies of the fallen back to Idaho. En route on the airplane, the jumpers started trying to work out the tragedy in their minds.

"Like, we started joking about Thrash," said jumper Brad Sanders. "About how he enjoyed riling people up and baiting them into arguments."

"Don Mackey saved my life and the lives of seven other smokejumpers," Quentin Rhoades told everyone. "And he almost saved the lives of the rest of the crew. He perished when he didn't have to. He's a hero."

All the firefighter survivors were pulled off the line for the rest of the season. One woman silently hugged her smokejumper husband for three minutes when he deplaned at the Payette National Forest Smokejumper Base in Idaho. He patted him on the back and looked away. Nearby, a small child sat wiping his eyes in the shade of an equipment room.

Survivors sometimes told their stories late at night when they were among others like themselves who would understand. They told of how flames roared up the mountainside, belching smoke and ashes and hurling flaming tree branches, of winds so fierce they knocked firefighters off their feet and howled and gnawed at everything in their path, of how frightened they had been. Quentin Rhoades glanced away whenever the talk died off into personal thoughts.

"The next day," he said before clamming up, "was Don Mackey's daughter's birthday."

Back on the western slopes of the Rockies, those smokejumpers whose names had not made The List for Storm King bumped up to other lists. George Steele rarely spoke of the day he watched comrades deploy shelters in the smoke on the mountain, except maybe after he had had a couple of beers after-hours with Tim Pettitt or Rod Dow. Then he might say a few words about it through his jaw that had been broken and wired and never quite healed back to normal.

J. C. Curd made nine fire jumps in Colorado after Storm King. Red-haired, bushy-bearded Tim Pettitt, the "old man" at Walker Field, made eighteen jumps before cooler weather and rains in the mountains in late August finally brought the fire season to a close. Curd and Steele spotted for the Sinbad fire, one of Colorado's last wildfires of the season. Pettitt and Brent "Big Johnson" Johnson jumped it, going out that awesome door into the Colorado skies to once more meld earth, air and fire as Icarus had done.

Less than twenty jumpers remained in Colorado by the third week of August. Two tanker bombers lingered behind as standbys. All the hotshots pulled out. Firefighters demobilized from Walker Field to battle fires in other states. The remaining firefighters had a lot of downtime, talking time, thinking time, but little overtime. The List rotated slowly. Fate caught his breath and prepared to hibernate over the winter. He'd be back next year, bigger and meaner than ever.

By the end of August, wildfires in the West had consumed more than 2.5 million acres, making 1994 one of the most destructive fire years of the century. The fire monster also claimed seven more firefighter lives by then, including another Oregonian and a helicopter pilot and two fighters who crashed in the rugged mountains of New Mexico's Gila National Forest.

Although many of Colorado's picturesque forests had

been turned into blackened, desolate landscapes by the summer's fires, Professor Rich Laven who specialized in forest and fire ecology said he thought, "Overall, the fires will enrich the forests and the diversity of species will go up."

Crown fires helped lodgepole pine regenerate by bursting cones at the tops of trees and scattering seeds over the ground. Nutrients concentrated in the ash and made themselves more available to young plants. Soon, the burns would regenerate. Life was like that. Come spring, fireweed, daisies and other wildflowers would emerge on Storm King Mountain, soon followed by pine and aspen seedlings. The once-deadly ridge off the mountain called Storm King would become a fitting and lovely memorial to the three brave smokejumpers, nine hotshots and two helitacks who lost their lives on it that fateful July 6, 1994.

In Memoriam

Don Mackey, 34, Hamilton, Montana. Smokejumper.
Roger Roth, 30, McCall, Idaho. Smokejumper.
James Thrash, 44, McCall, Idaho. Smokejumper.
Richard Tyler, 33, Grand Junction, Colorado. Helitack.
Robert Browning, 27, Savannah, Georgia. Helitack.
Jon Kelso, 27, Prineville, Oregon. Hotshot.
Terri Hagen, 28, Prineville, Oregon. Hotshot.
Bonnie Jean Holtby, 21, Prineville, Oregon. Hotshot.
Rob Johnson, 26, Redmond, Oregon. Hotshot.
Doug Dunbar, 23, Redmond, Oregon. Hotshot.
Kathi Beck, 24, Eugene, Oregon. Hotshot.
Scott Blecha, 27, Claskanie, Oregon. Hotshot.
Levi Brinkley, 22, Burns, Oregon. Hotshot.
Tami Bickett, 25, Powell Butte, Oregon. Hotshot.